CONCRETE JUNGLE

CONCRETE JUNGLE

Published in the United States by
INSIGHT PUBLISHING COMPANY
707 West Main Street, Suite 5
Sevierville, TN 37862
800-987-7771
www.insightpublishing.com
Cover Design: Steve Wilson
Interior Design & Format: Chris Ott

ISBN- 978-1-60013-949-9

10 9 8 7 6 5 4 3 2 1

Disclaimer: This book is a compilation of ideas from numerous experts who have each contributed a chapter. As such, the views expressed in each chapter are of those who were interviewed and not necessarily of the interviewer or Insight Publishing.

Table of Contents

A MESSAGE FROM THE PUBLISHER

CHAPTER ONE

Rethink, Refresh And Reimagine..........1
Lori Miller

CHAPTER TWO
The Spirit Of An Achiever..........15
King Pinyin

CHAPTER THREE
Concrete Success Strategies..........35
Dr. Joe White

CHAPTER FOUR
Social Capital: How To Build And Maintain Professional Relationships..........47
Mark Leader

CHAPTER FIVE
Plan Today, Achieve Tomorrow:
Take Charge Of Your Career & Discover Success..........69
Amy Letke

CHAPTER SIX
Information Technology..........91
David Papp

CHAPTER SEVEN
Navigating the Relation-Net™: Surviving or Thriving..........107
Dr. Lorraine Edey

CHAPTER EIGHT
Inspired Time Management..........123
Annette Denk

CHAPTER NINE
5 Secrets to Self-Healing..........143
Dr. Chuck McCabe

CHAPTER TEN
The Forgotten Laws..........165
Bob Proctor

CHAPTER ELEVEN
Lost in Your Own Office: A Path to Productivity....181
Anne McGurty

CHAPTER TWELVE
How to Market While You Sleep: The 10 Keys to Leveraging the Internet, Selling More, and Working Less in Your Small Business....199
Clifford Jones

CHAPTER THIRTEEN
Empowerment and Hidden Strengths....213
Diana Robinson

CHAPTER FOURTEEN
Life Transformation....231
Dan Morand

CHAPTER FIFTEEN
Your Job Is Not Who You Are....247
Steve Rizzo

CHAPTER SIXTEEN
Lean Forward Marketing....263
Eric V. Holtzclaw

CHAPTER SEVENTEEN
The New Law of the Jungle....279
Teri McEachern and Shelley Wilson

CHAPTER EIGHTEEN
Leadership Secrets to Thrive in the Jungle....301
Ted Gorski

CHAPTER NINETEEN
Achieving While Maintaining Life Values....313
Reverend Timothy Jones

CHAPTER TWENTY
The Key to Success in the Concrete Jungle: Be Nice!....333
Joshua and Dana Beil

Message From The Publisher

I totally agree—the business world can truly be compared to a jungle. I've been out here for many years and there's always something new around the next bend or some unexpected surprise getting ready to fall on me from a tree! The rules change often and fast and it is wise to stay one step ahead.

The authors in this book want to help you—the reader—to avoid the obstacles and jungle predators. These authors strive to learn what's new and how to stay ahead of the game. One of the authors said that achievers think outside the box, they trust in their instincts, they are purpose-driven, they focus on their dominant goals and strengths, they have a non-negotiable attitude toward achieving their dreams, they are persistent, they constantly invest in themselves, they are good at leading and motivating the key people around them, and they form strategic alliances with people of a similar mind-set.

You want to be an achiever because achievers are successful. We at Insight Publishing hope this book will inspire you, help you, and give you the tools you need to conquer the concrete jungle. In the concrete jungle there are predators and prey *and you don't want to become either one!*

David E. Wright
President
ISN Works & Insight Publishing

Chapter One

Rethink, Refresh and Reimagine

An Interview With...

Lori Miller

David Wright (Wright)

Today I'm talking with Lori Miller. Known as the Queen of Customer Service, Lori helps companies increase employee morale and bottom-line results while improving customer satisfaction. Leaders in some of the world's largest companies rely on Lori to provide solutions to some of the toughest customer service and sales issues. For more than twenty years, clients have worked with her company, Tooty Inc., to evaluate, train and monitor, and mentor their customer service and sales teams. Her innate ability to assess employee skills and identify areas of improvement enable her to create custom scripts, Web-based or classroom training, and strategies that change employee behavior, reduced turnover, and boost customer satisfaction.

Lori, welcome to *Concrete Jungle.*

Lori Miller (Miller)

Good morning, David.

Wright

So you have been a small business owner and speaker for more than twenty years. This is an embarrassing question but when do you plan to retire?

Miller

Maybe my answer is equally embarrassing. I plan to retire when I'm dead!

Wright

Does that mean that you don't have an exit strategy?

Miller

The first time I heard about an exit strategy was approximately four years ago. Someone who had been a customer of mine asked if my business was for sale. That is a dream many business owners have—someday somebody would offer you millions for what you have! After I laughed and said it wasn't for sale, he asked what my exit strategy was. I had no idea what that meant and asked him to explain. He asked me what I would do after Tooty Inc. His question threw me back on my heels because I had never thought about life after Tooty. I have been so busy working that I really didn't have time to dream about such a thing.

Wright

So what is your exit strategy?

Miller

I love working; some may consider that a sickness but I consider it a blessing. Each day that I can speak, train, collaborate, tackle a problem, invent something, inspire change, it's exhilarating and I love it. However, the question regarding my exit strategy has caused me to pause a bit to rethink some things—to re-imagine what my future could be and the future of the company. I have had to reexamine my own skills, my giftedness, what is it I love to do. I know I enjoy not only creating things but I thrive on interacting with people in the classroom setting, or speaking in front of a group. Those are things I love and things I have a talent for.

I have reevaluated our employees' skills and talents and strategically started to delegate to the right people, tasks that were bogging me down. This re-tooling has reinvigorated everyone. It was great to see people step up and say they wanted to learn new things. In today's world, you must constantly learn new things to be relevant and of value. This applies to not only a company, but to workers. Sometimes we limit that to maybe the people who are the decision-makers and so on, but from every level people need to know how to step it up, enhance their skills, and maybe look at other things they could do.

Wright

What is your philosophy on a healthy work environment?

Miller

I think I'm like many business owners in that I want a team of people who like to work and do work hard. Who wouldn't want that?

On the other hand, life-work balance is hard. One thing I personally grieved over when my kids were small was having to choose between caring for them and going to work. Those were tough days. Many people also have to balance caring for a sick family member, possibly a parent or a spouse. I do not want an employee to have to choose between work and family, to me that is such a tragic thing, yet it's understandable that we have to balance those things. We provide the opportunity for employees to work from home and set their own schedules but they have to be able to demonstrate they can do that. Not everyone is organized, reliable, and responsible in that kind of environment. We do have a few goals and rules—don't ever miss a deadline, don't lie, and give your customers and your teammates your best effort; I think that's been a good mantra for us.

Communication is so important, too. We meet every month to discuss what we've read, what our goals are, what we have actually achieved, and the game plan for the month. We also discuss concerns, glitches, and challenges that people are running into. It has kept us together as a team. I can't say enough to leaders about spending time with your employees and showing that you care genuinely, not just about whether a task is done or they showed up that day, but where they are with their family life and where they are with their personal development as well.

Wright

So has all this love and camaraderie in the workplace ever backfired on you?

Miller

Absolutely! There was actually a time when my husband (also my business partner) and I got into this rut of putting our employees above ourselves and what was best for the company and its customers. We felt responsible for them, and I guess, looking at it now, I consider that to be a rookie mistake as a business owner. It came to a head after 9/11. The business climate after 9/11 was horrible, and the fear was different than the fear we have now with the financial meltdowns and things like that. People were afraid for their lives it seemed.

The vice president of one of our biggest customers called, which was unusual because he never called me. He cut to the chase and told me that because 9/11 had happened, they were going to have to cut back on the work that we did for them, and the cutback would be immediate. It would be about 90 percent of the work we did and it was not a gradual slow down, it was going to happen right away. He also intimated that the terms of our contract were not going to be honored. When a small business like mine loses a big client it's devastating. I thought I reacted quite appropriately under the circumstances—while he was on the line, I fainted. I was alone in my office, and when I came to I was slumped in my chair and the phone was swinging back and forth, a really good reaction I guess.

To this day I really don't know if he knew I had fainted or not. We have never talked about it. The result of the phone call was that I needed to terminate all but a few employees; it was gut-wrenching because I loved them all and knew how much it hurt. We decided to keep two people whom we felt really needed the job most—neither one had any other source of income in their household. We had conversations with each person to explain what happened and that we wouldn't have enough work for them, but trouble began to brew within a few days. One employee felt that the American way was to retain people based on seniority and the two people who were not terminated had less seniority than this other employee. The backstabbing began. While we understood it was a reaction to the scary situation, it was hurtful because we felt that we had done so much and it seemed to count for nothing.

One of my cautions to business owners, or even managers, would be you have to have a healthy, realistic view of your responsibility toward the people who work for you. Be prepared to address those who believe that seniority trumps other details that a decision-maker must consider when having to down-size.

WRIGHT

So have you recovered from 9/11 as a small business and if so, what would put you in the position to hire people and expand?

MILLER

We have recovered from 9/11 and have come out of it stronger. I think we're much more innovative and in a better position to provide our customers with training tools that actually make their employees more effective. Whenever tragedy or trouble comes, look at how you can not only reinvent yourself but come up with something that is new and effective. There is a lot of talk about small businesses being the ones that actually create new jobs in our political atmosphere right now, but giving an incentive to hire someone doesn't make sense to me.

I would love to hire more people but the bottom line is to do that, we have to have more work. We can't just give people jobs without having something for them to do. As a business that provides employee training and consulting to medium and large sized companies, we want those bigger companies to have an incentive to hire small business—to give those contracts to small business—because sometimes that is where we lose out; the big players like to stay with other big players

WRIGHT

So how do you find good employees and what are some of the mistakes you have made in the past?

MILLER

We hire primarily by having a candidate referred to us by someone we know. We found that to be most reliable; it gives us a better chance of hiring someone who has good work ethic. We also have used an organization that actually trains and finds placements for disabled and older workers and we found great success with them as well. In reality, it may sound surprising but we have only run one help wanted ad in our entire existence and thankfully we found an amazing person. I admit that we have made some mistakes along the way. One mistake that I have found to be most mind boggling is that I have hired twenty-somethings I assumed would be computer savvy, only to find out they don't even know where their C drive is. I have a hard time digesting that because people are using computers as children, so I never thought that it was really a test that we had to give an adult.

Also, I assumed that well-spoken people could also write using good grammar and punctuation and found that this is just not true. Having to go back and correct people on basic writing skills was something that I was finding to be very draining. We made blunders early on in how we interviewed people, too. I spent a lot of time talking about how great Tooty Inc. was and what we did and by the end, who wouldn't want to work here? I didn't have enough emphasis on what a candidate had to offer us by asking some of the details on their skills, like the computer skills or writing, what their experiences were and asking some probing questions about their character.

I think too that somewhere along the line I found myself wanting to give people with a bad past history a chance. I don't know if I thought I was Mother Teresa and I could actually help someone who was down on their luck have a fresh start, but in the end I have realized that I am not Mother Teresa.

Wright

Strange you should talk about interviewing; I read a book recently that said in each interview the interviewer talks 90 percent of the time and the interviewee talks 10, when it should be reversed. I know I have made that mistake many times.

So the cost of everything has gone up, how do you handle pricing with your customers?

Miller

This is a topic no one likes to talk about, including me, because pricing is very tough when the economy is unstable; even big companies are watching their pennies. Small businesses can't bank on more volume to give us more revenue, so increasing the amount of work we do for someone is not necessarily where our payback is going to be. We have to be ingenious in creating new services that address important and specific needs our customers have when it comes to increasing their own revenue or their productivity with their employees.

What allows us to increase revenue without passing on any price increases for basic service are new services we provide. In today's world, we have to work harder and deliver more than expected.

Wright

How do you motivate your employees if they have to work harder and deliver more than before?

Miller

That's a great question. When you're unable to increase wages at all, you have to look at things that have value not measured in terms of money. People spend a lot of time at work so we try to look at things that money can't buy. Here at Tooty Inc., we have a good respect for one another and I think that's a start. But it also means that if there are frustrations or challenges with work, it's met with a helping hand from the rest of the team—managers and coworkers alike. This has value to people. We also have an environment that allows workers to actually share mistakes they have made knowing it's going to be met with problem solving—an approach to correct and improve for the future versus a punishment or reprimand. I think that's been a very healthy thing for everyone.

We also realize there are problems at home that can affect a team. We are quick to send each other e-mails or cards of encouragement. There is freedom to ask for prayers if someone feels like he or she is dealing with something tough and want extra support in that way. My husband and I try to relate to each person based on his or her personality and what the employee values. That's an advantage of being a small business—we can have those personalized relationships with each person. Some thrive on words of encouragement and others are uplifted by events that allow us to socialize.

Wright

Since training is your area of expertise, what training do you provide your own employees?

Miller

When people first start working for us, I explain to them that it takes a good six months of training before they actually feel confident and before we'll actually let them run on their own. It's fun to watch their faces when I say this because every person I have said that to gives me a look that says, "Well, maybe others need that much time but I'll have it mastered in a month." I like to see they have that kind of eagerness. I also explain that at some point, because they're learning a lot of different technology and information, there will come a time when all the sudden they feel like they've forgotten everything completely and now they don't know a thing. I don't want them to freak out at that point. I know when they have reached that point in training; it's good for me to take the time to test them on what they do know and reassure them of what they have actually learned so far. It gives them confidence and helps us determine where they need more help.

Being able to tell people what to expect, up front, eases frustration. Learning takes time and mistakes will be made along the way. We audit our teams' work on a regular basis, too. We have weekly audits, giving immediate feedback; it keeps everyone fresh and on their toes. If someone raises a question that affects the work being done, we send out instruction to everyone within minutes.

We also want to help people grow beyond their job and we have what we call our Tooty Reading Program. Each month everyone is given a book to read, it could be inspirational, it could be regarding a new technology, or a "how-to" business book for example. Each person is then asked to give a basic report on what he or she has learned personally from the book and what the person thinks Tooty could use. If there was an idea, a technique, something that Tooty could actually use to improve itself, the person shares that. When we get together for our monthly meetings we talk about what we have read, what inspired us, and what we might be able to put into play for Tooty Inc. I really like to think that at the end of the day, our staff is probably one of the best read companies worldwide considering most people never read another book after they graduate from high school.

Wright

So how do you keep up with technology?

Miller

Technology is amazing but it's also overwhelming; it's just a full-time job to keep up with it. I do have to say I learn a lot about new technology from an association I belong to, National Speaker's Association. It helps to have a group you can go to—a professional association or networking group—that can educate you on cutting edge technology.

It is the twenty- and thirty-something people in my life who are also the first ones to actually show me what's new and how it works. I'm not alone when I say that I buy a technology only to find out it's been revamped and replaced a few months later. We see commercials that show our frustration with that. As a business we have to be smart about what has value and what is practical. As a small business owner, I can change technology in my business fairly quickly but I have to be more concerned about using technologies that are compatible with what my customers have. If we get something and they're not up to the same latest technology, a rift in how we work together can develop. My focus with technology is that it must allow us to provide better service to our customers and help employees to be more efficient.

Wright

What is one technology you cannot live without?

Miller

I admit I can't live without my phone, and I never thought I would say that. I don't really like talking on the phone; maybe that's odd, but I don't use it to make calls as much as I use it for texting, reading my e-mail, and using the GPS when I'm on the road. Technology like that helps you to be better.

Wright

Speaking of texting, what effect do you think technology is having on people's communication skills today?

Miller

Texting is a blessing and a curse. I can remember a while back that I said I was never going to text. It seems like once you start, it becomes an addiction, I think. I want to emphasize the importance of already having good speaking and writing skills before you text. For those of us who already have good communication skills we're comfortable talking to others and have good writing skills, texting is quick and helpful. You can just give a piece of information and get a quick answer back. Sometimes I find it's even fun, but let's face it, texting removes the human connection that can sometimes be messy and time consuming. You can see now in society that technology enables people to avoid getting involved with emotions and relationships.

I believe that employers everywhere are worried about the younger generation entering the workplace, though. You can go to any retail store and the young man at the register never looks you in the eye. If a thank you is said it's without meaning because he is looking at the register and not at you as the customer. It also seems that the buttons we push are hypnotic or something; we're so focused on that keyboard. There are hundreds of acronyms now used in texting and many people have them memorized. That's mindboggling to me. However, try asking an adult when to use "you're" or "your" in a sentence, for example. You shouldn't be surprised when the response is "dkdc"—don't know don't care!

I think training and proper etiquette should be mandatory for grade school, high school, and college because we have now reached a point where people have stopped interacting. They don't know how to introduce themselves, they don't know how to have a conversation, how to comfortably have a debate, handle a difficult situation, or even how to properly end a conversation.

Wright

What a great conversation this has been. I really have enjoyed talking to you, Lori. There are some interesting things I have taken notes on here that I'm going to implement into my own company; this has been fascinating for me.

Miller

Well great, and we didn't even send a text!

Wright

That's right. My little fingers are too fat anyway; I can't reach all those little keys.

Miller

Well you know, David, you can start talking into your phone now and it will do that for you.

Wright

I really appreciate your taking all this time to answer these questions for me. You've given some good information that other businesspeople and employees need to hear. I'm so glad you are in this book.

Miller

This has been fun for me as well, David. Having conversations is the highlight of my day, so I appreciate your time also. By the way, my exit strategy is still a work in progress!

Wright

Today I have been talking with Lori Miller, a business owner, training expert, author, and business consultant. Lori speaks with business leaders, entrepreneurs, sales and customer service teams, and women's groups, sharing her journey as a successful entrepreneur and leader. She inspires her audiences as she candidly shares the obstacles she has faced and the triumphs. She gives commonsense ideas that help managers, sales, and customer service professionals to be more effective.

She is currently the President and Founder of Tooty Inc., a creative company devoted to evaluation, training, monitoring, and mentoring customer service and sales teams. She is also a board member of the National Speaker's Association—Illinois Chapter. She is the author of numerous customer service articles and is contributing author in the book *Mastering the Art of Success,* which was published in 2011.

Lori, thank you so much for being with us today on *Concrete Jungle.*

Miller

Thanks, David, and have a great rest of your day, too.

About the Author

Known as "the queen of customer service," Lori Miller helps companies *increase employee morale and bottom line results* while improving customer satisfaction. Leaders of some of the world's largest companies rely on Lori to provide solutions to some of the toughest customer service and sales issues.

For more than twenty years, clients have worked with Lori's company, Tooty Inc., to evaluate, train, monitor, and mentor their customer service and sales teams. Lori's innate ability to assess employee skills and identify areas of improvement enable her to create custom scripts, training, and strategies that *change employee behavior, reduce turnover and boost customer satisfaction.*

Lori's customer service expertise has helped transform an entire industry. Lori's extensive work with the waste hauling industry, which included specialized training and customized "secret shopper" programs, was an integral part of industry-wide change—no small accomplishment considering customer service and company image weren't on the industry's radar when she began.

Lori also speaks with business leaders, entrepreneurs, women's groups, and students, sharing her journey of starting Tooty Inc. and creating Telepicting. Lori inspires audiences and makes them laugh as she shares the trials and tribulations of being an entrepreneur in today's world while offering commonsense ideas that are easy to implement.

Lori is currently the president and founder of Tooty Inc., a creative company devoted to evaluation, training, monitoring, and mentoring customer service and sales teams. Lori is also a board member of the National Speakers Association-Illinois Chapter. Lori is an author of numerous customer service articles and a contributing author in the book *Mastering the Art of Success,* published in 2011.

Lori Miller

Tooty Inc.
P.O. Box 696
Orland Park, Il 60462
708-478-5772
lori_miller@tootyinc.com
www.tootyinc.com
YouTube channel tootytraining

Chapter Two
The Spirit of an Achiever

An Interview With...
King Pinyin

David Wright (Wright)

Today I am talking with King Pinyin. King is an entrepreneur, an author, John C. Maxwell Certified Coach, speaker, trainer, and woman of profound faith, who has mentored and inspired many to reach their peak in life through her seminars, coaching sessions, mastermind groups, workshops, and speaking engagements. She began her career in the IT field but her passion for public speaking led her to entrepreneurship and to the direct sales industry where she is a top leader in her company, and an advisory council board member. Furthermore, she was instrumental in the company's international expansion efforts to Africa as Vice President of Sales and into Canada. Her mission is to teach and encourage thousands across the globe to break free from disempowering beliefs and to explore the unlimited potential that lies within the human soul.

King has co-authored with celebrity authors Les Brown, Jack Canfield, and Mark Victor Hansen in *Mastering the Art of Success.* She has also co-authored with Brain Tracy and Dr. John D. Gray in *Words of Wisdom.* As a successful entrepreneur, King has been featured in *Your Business at Home* magazine as a home-based business superstar and mentored many individuals to a six-figure income. She has also been featured in *Success from Home* magazine as a successful entrepreneur and a top money earner in the direct sales industry. Having come to America from a third-world country and now at the peak of success, King is a living testament to the fact that your past or present does not have to dictate your future. She has appeared on *Wisdom Keys* television show with Dr. Mike Murdock and on ABC affiliate *At Home Las Vegas Morning Blend* television show.

King Pinyin, welcome to *Concrete Jungle: Survival Secrets for the Real World.*

King Pinyin (Pinyin)

Thank you very much. How are you, David?

Wright

I'm doing just fine this morning.

So tell us a little bit about yourself.

Pinyin

Thank you so much for taking the time to speak with me. I am very excited about this project because I know that everyone who reads the book will be ready to take the bull by the horns and reach for success. My name is Emeldine King Njoya-Pinyin. I am the first of six kids from the amazing continent of Africa.

I migrated to America many years ago seeking greener pastures. I currently reside in Maryland with my family. I'm married to a very wonderful, caring, supportive, and loving man, Babila Sunny Pinyin, and together we have an adorable ten-year-old son, Denzel.

I am an entrepreneur, a John C. Maxwell Certified Coach, speaker trainer, and success coach, and I am passionate about helping people realize their full potential in life. I am currently a leader, an advocate for, and a beneficiary of, the direct sales industry. I have been blessed with a business of my own, through a direct sales company. Our company markets for several well-recognized, name brand, essential service companies in North America and Canada. We represent companies that provide services in the energy, wireless, VOIP, text marketing, merchant account processing, Internet, and satellite television markets. This INC500, fastest-growing company retired my husband and me from corporate America in record time. We have since had the privilege of assisting several ordinary individuals to reach their full potential in the business and beyond, despite the current economic situation going on in the world. I would love to bless any reader who wants to discuss achieving and living his or her dreams with the same opportunity that set me financially free in just four months! Please visit my website after reading this chapter to see if we are a good fit for each other: www.sunnyandking.com/partner.

I'm also very purpose-driven; I recognize that my time on Earth is very brief. Hence I am doing everything I can to walk in my divine purpose. I know that there is more to life than just waking up to the alarm clock, going to work, following a daily routine, and retiring to bed at night. I am an avid seeker of knowledge and the real meaning to life.

I love to read, dance, travel the world, shop, and spend time with my family.

WRIGHT

Is it true that the world is a concrete jungle?

PINYIN

Yes it is! It's easy to think of a jungle as comprised of dirt ground, trees, shrubs, bugs, bushes, and animals only—a place where at the crack of dawn the animals wake up ready to prey upon each other! I have heard people say that in the jungle, the gazelle wakes up every morning knowing that it must run faster than the fastest lion or it will be killed; and the lion knows that it must outrun the slowest gazelle or starve to death! So it is with the world we live in today. It does not matter whether you are a lion or a gazelle; when the sun comes up, you'd better be running! Just like in the jungle, life is mostly about survival of the fittest. Our parents protect and provide for us from the time we are born until a certain age, usually eighteen years old in most countries. We are expected to take care of ourselves from then onward.

I like to think of the world as a concrete jungle because concrete is the first thing you step on when you leave the safe confines of your home to take on the whole wide world! And instead of trees, shrubs, bugs, bushes, and animals, our jungle is made up of people, buildings, cars, jobs, obstacles and opportunities, failures and successes, winning and losing, good times and bad times, sickness and health, and so on. In order to survive, you must make up your mind to put your best foot forward once you step unto the concrete daily. It takes the spirit of an achiever to succeed in our concrete jungle!

WRIGHT

You have enjoyed significant success in life so far. Congratulations on all your achievements! What is the secret behind your accomplishments?

PINYIN

Thanks, David. First and foremost it's been by the grace and blessings of God. As you already know, I am a firm believer that we are all created in the image of the most high God and as such we can be, do, and have whatever we set our minds to.

I learned earlier on in life that to be successful one must think positively about success and successful people. You must consistently hold in your mind the image of what success represents to you. It is very easy to slip into the trap of thinking that hard work alone will make you an achiever. But nothing could be further from the truth. I started out with nothing but radical faith and a very strong desire to be successful in life. Then I aligned myself with other successful people whom I admired and respected because of what they had accomplished in their areas of expertise. It is indeed true that in "a multitude of counselors, there is safety."

What I have learned and will continue to learn from these coaches and mentors is priceless! No amount of hard work can replace it. Even though I have thrown the word "faith" around casually, it is critical to realize that "faith without works is dead." It is not enough to say you want to achieve success in any endeavor if your actions and daily activities do not reflect a strong desire to succeed.

The evidence of a genuine desire to be successful is the ability to exercise self-discipline during the execution phase. For the majority of people, it is easier to start working on their dreams than it is to finish. The tendency to become impatient and distracted is a common cause of failure. The best way I know of to overcome this pattern of quitting before it is pay day is to always have a plan and to guard your passion and enthusiasm.

Nothing is as important to achieving success like the ability to chart your own course and to remain true to it. That is why we are advised to guard our hearts, for out of it are the issues of life. If you have failed at any endeavor before, the loss of enthusiasm was at the heart of it, because it is impossible to remain focused on anything that no longer captivates your heart. In order for you to remain true to yourself and your dreams, you must work with determination and commitment.

I had a major breakthrough moment when I realized that nothing can stop a mind that is made up! Sounds simple, but it is profound. I was at a crossroad between a high-paying job and pursuing entrepreneurship a few years ago. I have always wanted to experience life on my own terms financially and otherwise. So I started my own home-based business in 2005.

However, I got little or no support from my closest friends and family. My family in particular saw no sense in what I was doing, but most importantly, they did not understand why I was doing it. As far as they were concerned, I had a good job, with good benefits, and a good life! Hence they were very negative toward me and the idea of becoming financially free through direct sales. I naively thought that they would all come around once we started making some decent money through our business. I was so wrong! When I finally chose entrepreneurship over my "good job," my family was alarmed! They thought that I had lost sight of why I came to America in the first place. But my mind was made up! I knew that failure could not overtake me because my determination to succeed was very strong.

I always jokingly say that your determination to succeed should be so strong that the universe is almost scared of what might happen if she refused to give in to you, not because of your tantrums or wishful thinking, but because of your consistent commitment to your plan of action. "Let us therefore not grow weary of doing good, for in due season we will reap if we faint not." Achievers understand that controlling their thoughts and activities today will determine their success tomorrow.

I have been blessed with a very supportive husband, family, and friends around me all the time. They are the wind beneath my wings.

Wright

How does someone develop the spirit of achieving against all odds?

Pinyin

A few very important points come to my mind regarding how to become an achiever.

Know who and whose you are. There is potential for greatness in everyone. We are the only creatures on Earth who are created in the image of the Creator. We have been given dominion over the fishes in the sea, the birds of the air, and all of God's creation. We are asked to be co-creators with the God of this universe. Developing the spirit of an achiever begins with wrapping your mind around this truth. Achieving incredible success will become inevitable once you become aware of the kingdom within you. Just know that there can be no permanent obstacles in your path unless you choose to make them so.

Know what you want. Developing a definite aim and purpose for your life is a non-negotiable matter if you want to be successful. Achieving success of any kind begins with this simple step. Every achiever starts out knowing who they are and exactly what they want to accomplish in life.

Bishop T. D. Jakes had no doubt in his mind that he was a child of the most high God and that he wanted to spread the good news of the Gospel worldwide. Michael Jackson knew that he wanted to be an entertainer. In an interview with Oprah Winfrey just after winning the 2012 NBA championship, Chris Bosh said that he knew he was going to win the championship from the day he was born! Mother Teresa of Calcutta knew that she wanted to help the poor. Albert Einstein knew that he wanted to be a physicist. Jesus Christ knew that he was the Messiah. Do you know what your life's purpose is? If you have not already discovered your definite purpose in life, I want to encourage you to take a few days off and give these questions some serious thought:

- Who are you?
- Why are you here on Earth?
- Where are you going?
- What do you want?
- Why do you want it?

Setting the right goals and expectations is a must for every achiever. Once you discover what your mission in life is, the next logical step is to come up with a game plan. You must have heard it said before that if you fail to plan, then you plan to fail! Failure comes as a result of the lack of proper planning. Our time on this concrete jungle is very brief. I am yet to meet any human being who has lived for one hundred and fifty years! Yet this planet has been around for billions of years! In order for you to make your time spent on this side of eternity count for something, you must take time to plan your life!

The plans of the diligent lead surely to abundance, but everyone who is hasty comes only to poverty. “Abundance” is a word that is very familiar to all achievers. They believe in a life of abundance. As a matter of fact, we have been mandated to not only live life, but to live it more abundantly! Proper planning must precede a life of abundance. Ironically, many people struggle with setting the right goals and expectations.

I struggled immensely with goal setting in my earlier days. The general tendency is to become overwhelmed with the expected end result so much so that our minds go into panic or anxiety mode. When this happens, we become confused and fail to take action. The best way to eat an elephant is to eat it one bite at a time. The best way to accomplish any big goal is to break it down into smaller goals and then execute the big goal one small goal at a time. For which of you, desiring to build a tower, does not first sit down and count the cost, whether he has enough to complete it? In order for you to become an achiever, you must learn how to set the following goals:

Short-term goals: These are your daily, weekly, and monthly goals. What you do daily, you become eventually. The secret of what your future will look like is hidden in what you do daily. Therefore your daily, weekly, and monthly agenda should be based upon what your ultimate big goal or purpose in life is.

Mid-term goals: These are the goals you want to achieve within the next three to five years. They are a build up from your short-term goals. Get into the habit of assigning specific tasks to every day, week, month, and year. The bigger your goals, the longer the length of your mid-term goals will be.

For example, let’s take the case of two students who graduate from high school at the same time. It will take a longer time to achieve the goal of becoming a medical doctor for one student than it will for the other student to achieve the goal of becoming a registered nurse. Hence the mid-term goals review for a medical student will be set somewhere around the fifth-year mark, whereas the mid-term goal evaluation for the nursing student will be somewhere around the third year.

Long-term goals: These are the goals you want to achieve in your lifetime. They are the sum total of your short- and mid-term goals. It takes discipline, persistence, and focus to achieve these goals. It is also very important to constantly review your goals and to take corrective measures as you go along. If you do a great job of setting and managing your short- and mid-term goals, achieving your lifetime dream will be inevitable.

Guard your passion and dreams. In order for you to develop a winning attitude, you must embrace the fact that you are the master of your fate and the captain of your soul. Permit me to share one of my favorite poems by William Ernest Henley. I believe that his words capture the importance of guarding your dreams and keeping hope alive.

Invictus

Out of the night that covers me,
Black as the Pit from pole to pole,
I thank whatever gods may be
For my unconquerable soul.
In the fell clutch of circumstance
I have not winced nor cried aloud.
Under the bludgeoning of chance
My head is bloody, but unbowed.
Beyond this place of wrath and tears
Looms but the Horror of the shade,
And yet the menace of the years
Finds, and shall find, me unafraid.
It matters not how strait the gate,
How charged with punishments the scroll.
I am the master of my fate: I am the captain of my soul.
—William Ernest Henley

Invest in yourself. I can write a whole book about the importance of investing in the temple called *you.* This is one area where the achievers greatly distinguish themselves from the crowd. If you want to become an achiever, you must sow into, nurture, and develop your mind, body, and soul. Your mind is your most prized possession. That is why your parents and guardians invested so much in you by paying your way through high school in preparation for your adult life.

Unfortunately, not everybody realizes that they must continue investing in themselves past that point. Achievers, however, continue to invest in themselves. Personal development should be a top priority on your to do list. Instead of taking out a loan to buy a car, or a credit card to go shopping and vacationing, achievers use it to invest in themselves. They invest the money in a good college education, a professional or personal development course, a seminar, workshop, or conference, books, coaching, and mentoring. The point is this: whoever sows sparingly will also reap sparingly, and whoever sows bountifully will also reap bountifully (2 Corinthians 9:6).

Surround yourself with other achievers. Iron sharpens iron and success leaves clues. If you want to become a doctor, get into that circle. If you want to become a lawyer, find some lawyers and hang around them. If you want to become a teacher, get with some teachers. If you want to become an entrepreneur, then get into that circle. Your environment and who you hang around with most of the time matters! Do not be deceived: bad company ruins good morals (1 Corinthians 15:33).

Bounce back from failure or defeat quickly. Get out of the pity party zone and into the no whining zone quickly! Every achiever has failed woefully at something on his or her way to the top. You are not going to be the exception. Make up your mind now to pick up yourself quickly after every misfortune. Most importantly, learn from past failures and never make the same mistake twice.

Trust that God will perfect that which concerns you. He knows what He is doing. He knows why He created you. Be patient and just trust in Him.

WRIGHT

Those were excellent points, King. Are there some characteristics shared by achievers? If so, will you share some of them with our readers?

PINYIN

Absolutely! There are several characteristics shared by achievers:

They think outside the box. The ability to go against the grain in order to get what they want is a trademark of achievers. Conventional thinking is not in their DNA, for the most part. Achievers like Thomas Edison, Orville and Wilbur Wright, Henry Ford, Bill Gates, Steve Jobs, Larry Ellison, Sergey Brin, Larry Page, and Mark Zuckerburg are classic examples of this characteristic.

They trust and rely on their instincts or higher self for direction. I cannot over-emphasize the importance of shutting out all the outside voices in your ears right now! Achievers do not give in to third voices. They are in tune with the only voice that really matters; their voice. However, unlike the vast majority of people, they are wise enough to seek expert or professional advice when the need arises.

They are purpose-driven. Achievers are very aware of the choices they make in life. With purpose comes clarity and clarity makes choices obvious. When you know what you want from life, making the right choices becomes easier. Go back and review your answers to these questions:

- Who are you?
- Why are you here on Earth?
- Where are you going?
- What do you want?
- Why do you want it?

They focus on their dominant goals and strengths. The biggest misconception among the masses is that we need to spend more time working on our weaknesses as opposed to our strengths. Achievers, however, focus 100 percent of their time and effort toward perfecting their areas of strength. Every human being is naturally gifted from birth.

All you need to do is find out what areas you are gifted in and focus on developing those to the highest possible level.

They have a non-negotiable attitude toward achieving their dreams. These individuals refuse to give up on their dreams even when it seems that they have exhausted every possibility. They have no plan B, C, or D like everybody else.

They are persistent. Achievers refuse to give up hope! They are relentless in the pursuit of their dreams. They are always willing to try that one last option to give it one last push before giving up. They know that it's usually that one last desperate push that results in greatness!

They constantly invest in themselves. Achievers spare nothing when it comes to investing in something that will advance their skills. What most people consider as cost, achievers consider as an investment, if it will advance their skills and bring them closer to their lifetime goals. Continuing education and personal development are a must for these individuals. They have learned to grow through life.

They are good at leading and motivating the key people around them. This is a hallmark of achievers. No one can accomplish anything spectacular by themselves. The Achiever's ability to inspire and lead people to buy into his or her vision and remain focused until completion is a characteristic shared by all achievers.

They form strategic alliances with people of a similar mind-set. This could be in the form of partnerships or mastermind study groups. Perhaps you might have heard that many business deals are done on the golf courses around the world. Well, that's because achievers like to hang around other achievers for the purpose of networking and sharing business ideas and strategies. I encourage you to find a few friends with whom you share a similar vision about the future and form a strategic alliance with them. They do not have to be in a similar profession or industry as you are. All that matters is that they want more out of life.

WRIGHT

Are there any sacrifices and costs involved in the journey of life?

PINYIN

Absolutely! Life is a series of tradeoffs. There is no such thing as something for nothing in life. I grew up hearing older folks say that life is not a bed of roses. I think that life *is* a bed of roses, but in order for you to pluck the roses you will have to deal with the thorns! The alternative is sacrificing the bed of roses for fear of the thorns. Something has to give for anything that you gain in life. History is full of people who had to make huge sacrifices for their accomplishments in academics, sports, government, the arts, business, religion, and beyond. Nothing good comes easy! I encourage you to read the biographies of your favorite heroes. You will be amazed at how much they had to give up to go up!

WRIGHT

As a life and business coach, is there any system or strategy that you can share with our readers about how to be successful in life?

PINYIN

I sure would love to offer our readers a mini coaching session. I came across a worksheet many years ago that I have tweaked to suit my purpose. I have successfully used it in guiding my life and business decisions for many years now. I use it often with my coaching clients to help them gain clarity and to develop a successful strategy in life and business. I also use the results they obtain from going through this exercise to make recommendations about what they need to do next in order to achieve success and balance.

I strongly suggest that you go through each question below with absolute honesty. No one will see or know what your result is. You must answer every question in order to benefit from this exercise. I have italicized the key words in the worksheet for additional reflection on your part.

Instructions

Circle a number according to how much you agree or disagree with the statements below. With 1 = No, 2 = Somewhat, 3 = Undecided, 4 = Agree Somewhat, 5 = Agree Completely.

1. I have clearly identified my life's *priorities*.

1 2 3 4 5

2. I use these life priorities to set my direction and guide my decision making.

1 2 3 4 5

3. I have a clearly articulated purpose that provides focus and direction for my life and/or business.

1 2 3 4 5

4. My *purpose* is in line with my life priorities and is an accurate description of who I am and what I am about.

1 2 3 4 5

5. I have a very clear *vision* of where I will be in three to five years and have put it in writing.

1 2 3 4 5

6. My vision is an energizing force that provides powerful incentives for everybody around me.

1 2 3 4 5

7. I know what my *core values* are and why I have them.

1 2 3 4 5

8. These core values drive the decision making in my life and/or business.

1 2 3 4 5

9. I understand the *core skills* that are required for me to succeed and I am constantly working to develop and improve them.

1 2 3 4 5

10. I know how to leverage core skills into new areas of opportunity in of my life and business.

1 2 3 4 5

11. I am clear about where I wish to build my career/business and I have an effective system in place for generating and attracting new leads in my chosen career path or business.

1 2 3 4 5

12. I have an excellent *knowledge* of my career path/business and I'm constantly on the lookout for opportunities and threats that will affect my career/business so I can evaluate them and take appropriate action.

1 2 3 4 5

13. I have a *system* that allows me to establish significant success in the areas in my life and business where I wish to excel and create effective duplication.

1 2 3 4 5

14. I am able to develop the support systems necessary to service the needs of my life and business.

1 2 3 4 5

15. I am familiar with the groups and individuals who are affected by the way I carry myself and/or run my business and am able to get consistent buy-in to my strategies from all these parties.

1 2 3 4 5

16. I am constantly working to develop true win-win *relationships* with everybody affected by my life and/or business.

1 2 3 4 5

17. I have clearly identified the *resources* required for me to grow in life and/or to run my business to achieve success.

1 2 3 4 5

18. I have ensured that these key resources support the focus of my life and/or business and that I have a regular supply of them.

1 2 3 4 5

Knowing Your Numbers:
Get your total score by adding up your numbers.
Divide the total by 90.
Multiply the answer by 100 to get your overall percentage.

Your total score will give you an idea of the amount of clarity in your life and/or business. The closer your score is to 100 percent, the clearer your life and/or business purpose is and vice versa.

1. 0 to 25 percent = Very Poor. Need a lot of coaching / mentoring / teaching to establish purpose, vision, and direction.
2. 25 percent to 50 percent = Poor. Need constant coaching/mentoring/Teaching to clarify purpose, vision, and direction.
50 percent – 75 percent = Average. Need help with coaching / mentoring / teaching to strengthen believe in purpose, vision, and direction.

3. 75 percent to 95 percent = Good. Need coaching / mentoring / teaching to effectively execute purpose, vision, and goals.
4. 95 percent and above = Excellent. These individuals know who they are, what they want, and why they want it.

If you need additional help with coaching and mentoring, please feel free to contact my office at info@kingpinyin.com. I will be honored to work with you if we are a good fit for each other.

WRIGHT

What has been your greatest revelation about the concrete jungle called life?

PINYIN

- There is a higher power in operation in the universe.
- We are all connected.
- The universe is abundant in nature. Think thoughts of abundance.
- There are laws that govern the universe. Find them, embrace them, and use them.
- The law of attraction is in operation in our lives daily. We are what we think! The subconscious mind is the secret gift to mankind. I call it secret because we all have it, but the vast majority of us are clueless about what to do with it or that it is even there in the first place.

WRIGHT

Do you have any final thoughts, suggestions, and next steps for our readers?

PINYIN

I encourage you to never give up on your dreams and aspirations. Believe in yourself and reach for the stars! I am seeking purpose-driven individuals who are looking to start their own home-based business to join my growing network of entrepreneurs. If this sounds like you and you want to become a part of a rapidly growing INC500 company that has been featured on CNN, NBC, the *Wall Street Journal,* and *Direct*

Selling News, please visit my website, www.sunnyandking.com/partner, and let's get started! I look forward to working with you if we are a good fit for each other.

WRIGHT

Any future plans for you, King Pinyin?

PINYIN

I am super excited about the future! I see myself doing seminars all around the world, teaching my message of anything is possible if you just believe, and showing ordinary people how to become overcomers by reinventing themselves. You can't get stuck in the same mind-set that has gotten you to where you are during the last couple of years. You've got to be able to reinvent yourself.

I see myself going all around the country and all around the world hosting Reinvent Yourself Conferences for entrepreneurs and Winning in Life Women's Conferences to empower women with the tools and the mind-set necessary to experience a breakthrough in life. I see many more book projects in the nearest future and I see myself on television, hosting a show for entrepreneurs, equipping, encouraging and empowering ordinary individuals, and sharing my journey. I believe that the sky is the limit and that anything is possible for me because I am a child of the most high God. Whatever I set my mind to will be accomplished, regardless of how much sacrifice and effort I have to put into it. Life is a Concrete Jungle, remember? Please visit my event Web site, www.kingpinyinconferences.com, for updates on conferences, workshops, seminars, and mastermind study groups. I look forward to seeing you at one of my events.

WRIGHT

Well, this has been an incredible conversation. I can feel the passion and enthusiasm in your voice. When you love what you do, it flows out of you naturally and nothing seems difficult.

I do appreciate all the time you've spent here with me to talk about this important topic. I have learned a lot and I have taken notes. Our readers are going to get a lot from this chapter.

PINYIN

Thank you very much for the opportunity. I have enjoyed spending time with you once more. I look forward to collaborating with you again in the near future, God willing.

WRIGHT

Today I have been talking with King Pinyin. King is an entrepreneur, a John C. Maxwell Certified Coach, speaker, trainer, and a woman of profound faith. Her mission is to teach by equipping, encouraging, and empowering thousands across the globe about how to break free from disempowering beliefs and explore the unlimited potential that lies within the human soul.

King Pinyin, thank you so much for being with us today on *Concrete Jungle: Survival Secrets for the Real World.*

PINYIN

You are welcome, David. It's always an absolute pleasure working with you and your team!

God bless you and our readers.

About the Author

Emeldine King Pinyin is the CEO and Founder of Agnitio Consulting LLC, a peak performance company focusing on helping businesses, organizations, schools, churches, women's organizations, and ordinary people reach their peak in life through keynote speeches, seminars, workshops, mastermind groups, and personal and group coaching sessions. King is a John C Maxwell Certified Coach, speaker, and trainer.

As one of the nation's dynamic conference speakers, King travels more than forty weeks a year, delivering keynote speeches, seminars, and workshops to a diverse group of audiences. Passionate, purposeful, motivational, humorous, and down-to-earth, King touches the lives of her audiences in a very special way, and inspires them to reach their peak in life.

Her purpose is transparent and her message is inspirational and transforming:

"We are spiritual beings on a physical experience on Earth. So we can Be, Do, and Have anything we want."

Her annual Reinvent Yourself Conference held in Maryland, and her Dreams 2 Reality one-day seminar, held in select cities worldwide, is a must-attend for anyone seeking a breakthrough in life. Her Winning in Life Women's Conference will uplift and refresh the soul of every woman who attends. Mark your calendars for her next big conference! You'll be so glad you invested in you!

Agnitio Consulting LLC
Abingdon, MD 21009
800-941-9541
Fax: 888-637-6293
info@kingpinyin.com
www.kingpinyinconferences.com
www.kingpinyin.com

Chapter Three
Concrete Success Strategies

An Interview With...

Dr. Joe White

DAVID WRIGHT (WRIGHT)

Today I'm talking with Dr. Joe White, author, speaker, and entrepreneur. Early on his entrepreneurial spirit allowed him to join the ranks of those entrepreneurs who can boast that they have never worked a nine-to-five job throughout their entire adult life.

Dr. White has always owned and operated his own business. His professional experience is quite varied and for many years he has sharpened his skills in various capacities. He has served as CEO of several companies and in 2001 he started Global Net Financial Inc., a Real Estate investment company. In 2005, Joe took to the road selling his Real Estate course, *How to Make $5,000 to $10,000 a Month Wholesaling Real Estate*. The book teaches the success strategies of Global Net Financial as they relate to buying and selling properties.

During the 2005 lecture tour, he was asked to be the keynote speaker at the 2005 graduation of Breakthrough Bible College in Temple Hills, Maryland. The college bestowed Joe White with an Honorary Doctorate of Human Letters.

Dr. White, welcome to *Concrete Jungle.*

DR. JOE WHITE (WHITE)

Thank you.

WRIGHT

These are turbulent times where we face record unemployment. Dr. White, would you share some concrete strategies to not only survive but prosper in this unstable economy?

WHITE

When I was growing up, I was taught to get good grades so that I could get into a good college, which would, in turn, get me a good job. I snubbed my nose at tradition and decided college wasn't for me. In the short-term this didn't seem like a good idea; I would later learn that the people who survive and prosper in hard times like these have a mental toughness and business savvy that no school in the world teaches.

I spent countless hours reading and studying the same books that business masters read and study. The first book was Napoleon Hill's *Think and Grow Rich.* This is where I learned how to use the ingredients of desire, faith, and definiteness of purpose. These are the key ingredients that will allow you to prosper regardless of the economy. I'm not suggesting that anyone skip college, but whatever you choose to do, read what you see leaders reading.

WRIGHT

What would you recommend to someone who is looking to make a change in his or her financial life start?

WHITE

Look around you! There are so many opportunities everywhere. I once read the quote, "Money is a reward for solving a problem." I recommend finding a problem you can solve and money is sure to follow. When IBM needed software, there was Bill Gates. When people wanted a different type of retail store, there was Sam Walton. Every service we use or product we purchase is an answer to a problem.

Now here is the twist: only solve a problem that you can allow yourself to be passionate about. I have started businesses that I hated waking up to go to, even though they made me lots of money. Money is a by-product that can be reached several different ways and you're more likely to succeed if you enjoy what you're doing. Once you have found the problem that you believe you were meant to solve, start at once to turn the solution you came up with into a full- or part-time business.

WRIGHT

So what are some of the key differences between business owners and those who work a job?

WHITE

It's just like a great movie director would do—he takes a script and puts it on film for the world to see. An entrepreneur takes his vision and makes it a reality and with it he creates three forms of currency.

Currency one is Money. But unlike a job, when a business owner wants more money, he turns up the intensity in key areas. This way he or she is in control of the revenue.

Currency two is Time. With the average job, you trade your time for money. As a business owner you apply systems to free your time, leaving you free to spend it with family.

Currency three is Equity. Unlike working a job, creating a business provides a mechanism for early retirement, as it can be sold or passed on as inheritance.

True freedom becomes self-evident when you take ownership of your life. A business owner can delegate or select, promote or demote, hire or fire, and has multiple options at his or her disposal. The job holder, on the other hand, is at a fixed disadvantage with limited available options. In other words, work or go home!

WRIGHT

With times being as tough as they are now, what would you share with people to keep their spirits up as they build their business?

WHITE

Most people don't know how to grow through small victories—they only count the home runs and label base hits as failures. In 2002 after closing my mortgage company, at my mother's suggestion I took a boarder into my home in order to help cover expenses. Little did I know the effect he would have on my life. His name was Marty, a twenty-three-year-old who was confined to a wheelchair because of Muscular Dystrophy. But his condition never affected his attitude—he was always happy and grateful to be alive.

The first day he rolled into my home, he parked his chair in front of my large screen television and said, "I'm going to like watching basketball on this." Marty loved Michael Jordan and it wasn't hard to see this! He covered his room with posters and owned almost every Michael Jordan souvenir made. Marty had been told by doctors that he probably wouldn't live past twenty-five. You would never have known it because he lived life in such a way that it let me know how insignificant my issues were.

Well, when Michael Jordan came out of retirement to play for the Washington Wizards, Marty set a goal to see his idol play live. We went online and saw that the Wizards had an exposition game in the next city, so we quickly purchased tickets. This was the chance he had been waiting for.

So there I was, pushing Marty into the arena while he was wearing his Michael Jordan hat, jersey, cologne, and, I didn't check but I'm pretty sure that he was wearing Hanes underwear. They called Michael Jordan's name and he came out in a business suit; he sat on the bench the entire game. I was outraged and disappointed but what I saw as a failure, Marty counted as a victory. I looked over at Marty and he was smiling from ear to ear. He counted seeing Jordan there at the arena as a win. I believe this was the reason Marty outlived the doctor's predictions by five years. It was all about attitude. Because he counted every day that he lived past twenty-five to be a small victory, each and every day for him was a win!

WRIGHT

Being with Marty sounds like a life-changing experience!

Will you describe business systems and how they are created?

WHITE

Enter any McDonald's in the world and order one of their Big Macs and it will taste and look the same. McDonald's Corporation is the best in the world at creating systems. Systems allow you to get the same results each time you perform a task by repeating the critical success factors. It is important for every business to find their Critical Success Factors, as these are likely the key ingredients to receive your desired result each time.

WRIGHT

What are some ways to avoid stumbling blocks as you strive to excel in the arena of business?

WHITE

Resist the urge to be comfortable. It's so easy to coast when you should be pushing. Surround yourself with people who consistently train and perform at high levels. Association with champions will raise your level of performance and your results will yield much better fruit. Complacency has tripped up many "would be" great entrepreneurs. Avoid this by setting short, clear milestones, so you can experience successes often. This allows you to build momentum and confidence. Success breeds success.

WRIGHT

Dr. White, as an expert in the arena of business and an entrepreneur who has never held a nine-to-five job, how do you help others who desire to start their own business.

WHITE

I'm extremely passionate about helping individuals reach peak performance. I conduct workshops and coaching sessions across the country, helping individuals and entrepreneurs identify their critical success factors and use them to find a daily routine that produces major change in their personal lives. This turbo-charges their business outcomes. Some of the key elements I have been able to help leaders and entrepreneurs with are:

Peak Performance Sectors
Finding their unique PTR (Performance to Training Ratio)
Constructing Daily Routines that increase productivity
How to develop systems that increase their bottom line
How to develop a Why that will keep them motivated
Mastering the art of Goal Momentum
Establishing performance programming

WRIGHT

Will you explain some of these strategies to us so that we can clearly understand what they are?

WHITE

Always remember that your Performance Training Ratio (PTR) dictates your ROI (Return on Investment). Serena Williams said she spends five hours a day practicing tennis and puts in an average one hundred hours per match. This is her Performance Training Ratio. A buddy of mine puts it in a simpler phrase: what you put in determines what you get out. The time and effort you put in to training directly effects your performance. Boxers like Floyd Mayweather train for six months for a thirty-minute boxing match. How much training must one do to be prepared for opportunity?

I went to at least one seminar a quarter for ten years spending more than a thousand dollars on my business education. I routinely attend community college classes and have read at least two books a month for almost a decade—just to be ready when an opportunity arises. Serena's ROI has been the winning of countless Wimbledon Titles; Floyd's ROI is to be ranked among the best fighters in history.

Another important strategy is "Goal Momentum." Most books will tell you that setting goals is important and not to be scared to set big goals. I think big goals are great but in order to achieve large goals you need what I call Goal Momentum.

We have all seen the movies where someone takes a little tiny snowball, pushes it down the hill and once it reaches the bottom it is huge! Well that's the result of momentum. Take your goals and break them down into smaller weekly or monthly goals. These are what I like to call "Success Bites." For example, if you have a goal to lose fifty pounds in six months, discover what three things that you know you could achieve during the first month. Some examples include: walk three miles a day, five days a week, don't eat after 7 pm, and attempt to lose ten pounds the first month. By achieving small successes, you start to gain momentum, which makes the overall goal more likely to be achieved.

Peak performance Sectors are the time blocks during the day that are the best physical times for you to perform certain activities. For example, if time block one is the point where my energy is the highest and the best time for me to work out and tackle my major task, then this is when I'll do it. Block one for me is from 7:00 am to 1:00 pm, Block 2 for me is from 1:00 pm to 5:00 pm and is the best time for me to have meetings, return calls, and read e-mails. Five pm to 10:00 pm is the time when my energy starts lowering, which is a good time for me to read or spend time with family. It is essential that you learn the peak performance schedule for your body.

Performance Programming is the ability to apply the key pieces of your routine in an almost unconscious manner. Tasks that you repeat for sixty-six days become programmed in your subconscious and once programmed, they happen on autopilot.

WRIGHT

You also spoke of developing a way to keep people motivated. Share with us the how and why.

WHITE

It was a cold day in January. I cranked my car and began to let it warm up as I planned my day. Sitting in the car, I noticed that the lights on the inside of my car were dim, but I didn't pay it much attention and pulled off and went to work. Nine hours later, I walked out of work to crank my car and it would not start. This car had served me well and I had just gotten a tune-up a week before. I had successfully taken the car on a one-hundred-mile road trip a few days earlier.

I called my mechanic, he jump-started the car and it started right up. I asked, "So, is it okay for me to drive it home now?"

"You can make it home in this car but once you get there it's not going to start again."

I asked why, and he said, "My friend, you need an alternator." I asked what that is and what it does do. The short answer was that it keeps the battery charged with electricity so that the car can continue to function.

My point is, your why is like your alternator. Your why has to be your core motivation for achieving any goal or objective and if your why isn't strong enough, your engine won't start. Your why will help you overcome adversities, disappointments, and setbacks. Your why can't be money alone because your why is tied to the emotion or feeling you associate with what the achievement will bring. I set a goal to send my kids to college. My why is the feeling of relief that I have done my part in helping to create a promising future for each of them.

In order to change your financial situation, you must first change your thinking. This is difficult but not impossible. It's difficult because most people are change-resistant. Thus most people simply refrain—they do not really change. The best change is internal, never external—first within, then without!

WRIGHT

So as you think back on your business life and on your entire life—both personal and business—who are those people who helped to put you where you are today and contributed to your success as an entrepreneur?

WHITE

Napoleon Hill, of course, is one of my favorite authors of all time; I read *Think and Grow Rich* at least five times a year. Dale Carnegie, author of *How to Win Friends and Influence People*, Dr. John Raye and Dr. Joe Dudley. I was inspired by each of their stories. In *Walking By Faith,* Dr. Joe Dudley provides an outlook on business and life in general like no other author I have read. Both he and Dr. John Raye have been two very strong role models for me. I love watching Ihsaan York's *The Inspired Life Series*. The late, great David Allen's book, *Succeeding On Your Own Terms,* had a great effect on me. I also follow the greats such as Anthony Robbins, Zig Ziglar, Brian Tracy, Bob Proctor, Bernard Dohrmann, and Les Brown.

WRIGHT

What a good conversation, Dr. White. I really enjoyed talking with you today. Your story is inspiring. In this kind of economy, if we ever needed entrepreneurial spirit, we need it now and that's exactly what you're doing. I appreciate all the time you've taken today to speak with me! It's been absolutely delightful.

WHITE

Thank you, I have enjoyed chatting with you.

WRIGHT

Dr. White is an active member of his community where he serves on numerous boards and commissions and holds several leadership roles. He speaks to groups around the country on how to be a successful entrepreneur and what strategies work best in a down economy.

Dr. White, thank you so much for being with us today on *Concrete Jungle.*

About the Author

Dr. Joe White is a nationally known author, speaker, and business leader. Early on, his entrepreneurial spirit allowed him to join the ranks of those entrepreneurs who can boast that they have never worked a nine-to-five job throughout their adult life; Dr. White has always owned and operated his own business.

His professional experience is quite varied and for many years Dr. White has sharpened his skills in several capacities. Dr. White has served as CEO of several companies and in 2001 he started Global Net Financial Inc., a Real Estate investment company. In 2005, Joe took to the road selling his Real Estate course, *How to Make 5,000 to 10,000 a Month Wholesaling Real Estate.* The book teaches the success strategies of Global Net Financial on buying and selling properties. During the 2005 lecture tour, Joe White was asked to be the key note speaker at the 2005 graduation of the Breakthrough Bible College in Washington D.C. (Temple Hills, Maryland). The college bestowed Joe White with an honorary Doctorate of Humane Letters.

As the Real Estate boom started to come to an end, Dr. White liquefied his business interests and partnered with his mother and sister to form My Sister's Place, Inc., a community support agency for the mentally handicapped. This company is now a staple in the community and Dr. White remains a board member and volunteer.

In 2006, Dr. White purchased a failed transportation company and turned it into Truliant Mobile Transport, which, during a three-year period, became the Triad's number one accessible transportation company. In 2010 he founded NEPAT, Inc. (Non-Emergency Professional Accessible Transportation), which is gearing up to become the largest Non-Emergency Transportation franchisor in the United States.

Dr. Joe White is an active member of his community where he serves on numerous boards and commissions and holds several leadership roles. Dr. White speaks to groups across the country on how to be a successful entrepreneur and what strategies work best in a down economy.

Dr. Joe White

www.joewhiteonline
www.wcpcommunications.com

Chapter Four

Social Capital:

How to Build and Maintain Professional Relationships

An Interview With...

Mark Leader

David Wright (Wright)

Today I'm talking with Mark Leader. As North America's number one Real Estate sales trainer and speaker, Mark has helped tens of thousands of salespeople raise their production and increase revenues by hundreds of millions of dollars. At age nine, Mark worked in his family's clothing store. His parents' guidance and tutelage provided him with a strong ethical and spiritual foundation. The self-confidence he gained during his early years set in motion his journey to becoming one of the most dynamic, humorous, and sought-after professional speakers and motivators in the industry. As a sales professional, Mark listed more than a thousand properties and averaged ninety-three transactions for eight consecutive years without the help of an assistant or a team. Earning virtually every production award available, Mark set records that remain unbroken today.

Never one to rest on his laurels, he orchestrated the transition from salesperson to office owner with his characteristic company commitment to excellence. He quickly created one of the highest producing, highest retention sales organizations in Canada. The journey continued as Mark launched his speaking and training career. His platform success has led him to the creation of Leader's Choice. The company was designed, according to Mark, to increase agents' production immediately and change their mindset by dramatically improving self-esteem and creating balance between their professional and personal lives.

With humor, enthusiasm, and genuine concern for his students, Mark speaks from his success to equip agents with the tools they need to break out of mediocrity and discover extraordinary success. Wherever he trains, he leaves behind sales leaders who credit him with jumpstarting their skills, improving attitudes, and sending their sales commissions skyrocketing. Mark has written the book, *Distinguishing Marks of a Leader,* and has co-authored the book, *Blueprint for Success,* with Ken Blanchard and Stephen R. Covey, as well as the book, *Success is a State of Mind,* with Les Brown, Mark Victor Hansen, and Deepak Chopra.

Mark, welcome to *Concrete Jungle.*

MARK LEADER (LEADER)

Thank you, David.

WRIGHT

We're talking today about understanding social capital, the currency of the twenty-first century. Mark, what exactly is social capital?

LEADER

When I talk about social capital, I am referring to the value of relationships and interaction that a Real Estate agent has built in his or her community and sphere of influence. It has to do with the role of cooperation and confidence between people if you want to produce positive results. It was originally a social science term used in the early 1900s. A man named L. J. Hannifin was writing about local support for rural schools and people's personal investment in the community—good will, fellowship, mutual sympathy among citizens.

WRIGHT

You're referring to gaining confidence to produce results. Is the idea of social capital a twist on the golden rule? Does it mean just being nice to people so we can benefit from them?

LEADER

No, in fact that's what separates it from the way that so many people today use social networking. I'm sure we've all seen individuals who just make connections so they can sell people something. Building social capital is not manipulative and it goes beyond just being nice to people so that good results will follow. That's self-serving.

The way I apply it is a practical approach to how and where you spend your time—the activities you build your day around without always attaching a dollar sign to every interaction. Some of the things I mentioned earlier—good will, fellowship etc.—are things that are often lacking today in society. But the good news is that when someone embraces those values, they stand out immediately in a very appealing way. It's as if you walked into a room where everyone was shallow and self-serving, rather than trying to fit in, you could be the one person everyone remembers as genuine and comfortable to be around.

WRIGHT

So why do you refer to it as capital? Is there a way for people to measure what they have built up in their capital account?

LEADER

Capital is anything that improves productivity, so a forklift is physical capital and education and experience are human capital. Building social capital reflects an attitude that the agent has a vested interest in cultivating strong mutually supportive relationships. It's not about keeping a balance sheet where people owe you favors, or the view that someone should buy a house from you just because you belong to the same club, whether you are competent or not. It's about being known as a person who has answers and resources and can readily share them to benefit others.

In a sense, the principle in this account is you, and the multiplier on that investment is how you interact with others and how people respond to you that is the interest on your principle.

WRIGHT

How is building social capital different than social networking and expanding our list of contacts?

LEADER

Great question, David. Social capital looks beyond sheer numbers and improves the quality of our interactions. It takes a longer view than social networking while incorporating many of the same technologies, and therefore, it is the merging of high touch with high tech. I know people who have many friends on Face book but they have no idea who those people are. They couldn't tell you if those people have a family, rent or own their residence, or what they do for a living, They interact with a lot of people superficially but not in a way that there is interest, that is not social capital. Social networking tools help but they don't do the work for you, it takes personal interaction and outreach along with technology.

WRIGHT

You mentioned teaching Real Estate agents how to build, conserve, and spend their social capital wisely. How exactly does someone begin to build up their social capital?

LEADER

Well, there are ten principles for building social capital. As soon as you adopt these principles, you immediately begin to attract others to you in a way that increases your social capital. May I take a moment and share the ten with you, David?

WRIGHT

Absolutely.

LEADER

Great. Well, the first one is a belief that I value my clients more than money and put relationships ahead of financial gain. As you know, particularly in the sales business, salespeople can give the impression that they are friendly and cooperative, but really when, it's said and done, it's about them making more money versus what's best for the customer. We always have to make sure that we put the customer's interest first.

The second principle is, I have a burning desire in my heart to be of service to the greatest number of people. I have been in the Real Estate business twenty-six years and I can tell you that I've seen a lot of really good people come and go. I've seen a lot of really great people who are able to survive through many different marketplaces, and it's not necessarily the education that separates them. Why do 20 percent of the salespeople do 80 percent of the business? Generally speaking, the long-term salespeople in the Real Estate sales industry really do have a desire in their heart to help their customers attain their dream home in a way that is practical and affordable for them.

The third principle is that I accept no favors from anyone without providing favors in return. In other words what you don't want to do is go around constantly asking people to send you business, if you're not doing something in return for them. In fact David, one of the questions I get asked quite often is that in the ten years that I was in the Real Estate business, how I listed over a thousand homes for sale and averaged ninety-three closings a year for eight years consecutively and I did that without the help of a personal assistant. The first question they always ask me is how, and we're starting to talk a little bit about it now when we talk about building social capital. Along with that they always ask me what kind of gift I gave the clients on closing. They're very surprised to find out when the deal was closed I never gave a closing gift. I always thought that I gave them the best gift that I could possibly give them and that was personal customer service. Now it didn't mean that on the person's birthday I didn't stop by and give them something. It didn't mean at Christmas they wouldn't get a poinsettia or at Halloween a pumpkin in order to maintain the relationship. But I always felt that the best gift I could give to someone was the ultimate customer service experience. When I did that, my referrals absolutely blossomed beyond what I even thought was possible.

The fourth principle is never enter into disagreements with clients about trivial matters. This is one of the things I had to learn and I have to relearn on a regular basis, David. Because I am high energy, hardworking (and I mean *hardworking),* I love to work, I love what I do, and I love to help others become successful in their lives. But sometimes in today's world with two kids and a wife and all the responsibilities that come along with that, with a training and traveling schedule that generally puts me in at least one hundred to one hundred and twenty cities a year, depending on the economy, I can become tired and impatient. I've learned to ask myself, "Will this situation affect me a year from now?" Truthfully, 99 percent of the time it's not going to.

So you have to learn to pick your battles and we have to understand that the other side is under pressure as well. So to argue or to get in disputes over trivial matters is counterproductive and not a good idea if you want to build a business based on your relationships.

The fifth principle is that I never flatter a customer for the purpose of gaining something. There is nothing wrong with giving a compliment when a compliment is sincere, but in today's world people quickly recognize fakery. It's the kiss of death to a budding relationship. If you go to someone's house and his or her garden is very nice, compliment the person because obviously he or she has worked very hard to create a lovely garden and deserve compliments. If you want to build a long-term relationship, honesty is your best policy.

The sixth principle is never compliment friends and associates unless it's genuine. The people you work with every day, are looking for the real deal; they're not looking for you to schmooze them or stroke their ego, just to gain their trust or confidence. Insincerity does not build social capital.

The seventh principle is, I sell my service and expertise at a fair price but never give it away for free. Now there is nothing wrong with helping someone out, we all sooner or later in life need a hand up, but to constantly be offering your services at a deep discounted rate or a free rate, eventually what happens is the public perceives that service to be worth exactly what you're charging.

I've been in the motivational speaking arena for sixteen years, and in that time I've done approximately sixteen hundred presentations. I've had the good fortune to work with some of the greatest entrepreneurs on this planet today. I count myself honored to be personal friends with many of them.

Harold Crye of Crye-Leike Realtors, RISMedia puts his organization at number five in transaction rank in the country for 2011. Howard Hannah Real Estate is a great family-run operation. Then there is The Keyes Company in Miami, Florida and Ebby Halliday Realtors over in Dallas, Texas, Ms. Ebby was named "The First Lady of Real Estate." She is a hundred years old and still works forty hours a week. All are honorable people and it's a pleasure to work with them. On completion of a Leader's Choice program I offer to come back and do something special for them. That's my way of saying thank you and showing my appreciation. But as far as going in and doing it for free, you will get the same results as what you've charged.

Number eight, I live what I teach and teach what I live. In so doing, I demonstrate that my philosophies work. Now the one thing I can tell you is that no man is perfect. When I say I live what I teach, I try every day to live what I teach; some days I do better than others. Every night when I put my head on the pillow, I thank the Lord for giving me an opportunity to work toward those values. Many people in the teaching, training, speaking, and writing field say one thing and then do another. We hear celebrated people give a speech on how we should live our lives and then two days later they're on the news because they are not living by those same values and have lost their standing within the community.

The values I share are about building relationships. When we talk about building relationships, there is a human element in there. Every day we have to strive to be the best person we can. It doesn't mean that we won't fall down but when we do, if we have done a good job living the best we can to this philosophy, the North American people generally will forgive you pretty quickly and allow you to keep going on your journey. What we have to do is constantly focus on living these philosophies and doing the best we possibly can with them.

Number nine, I constantly focus on speaking optimism and joy wherever and whenever I can. Now, I have to tell you something, David, being in the training and speaking business and specializing in the sales and Real Estate sales business, as you know over the last few years between maybe 2007 and 2011 we have had some very challenging times.

The housing market is very confusing. You go to California and they have foreclosure problems, but then you go to Alberta and Manitoba, Canada, and they have had a booming market with homes increasing in value. You go to Phoenix, Arizona, and they're having challenges. Then you go to Toronto, Canada, and home sales are doing really well. The Real Estate market in North America is going through some trying times, possibly world wide.

But I tell you this, American people are hard-working and resilient and that is no more apparent than in the Real Estate industry. The common thread running through the industry is the entrepreneur spirit that is embraced by everyone involved in the profession. These are people who may be knocked down but they're never knocked out. They may flounder for a time and then they hone their skills, reorganize, and regroup; when the storm passes they are still in the game.

It's important to focus on what we like about our chosen profession rather than what we don't like. We have an opportunity to make a six-figure income that some people can only dream of and be able to work within in ideal conditions. Think of the miners who recently spent two or three months in the mine in Chile. Most of those people got up that morning thinking they were going to work to help feed their family. They didn't think they were going to have to live two or three months underground. What about all the workers whose jobs have been outsourced?

I tell people in the Real Estate sales industry to take a hard look at the opportunity they have plus the environment they work in. Even on our worst days it's much better than so many people have it around the world. I always say that if you can't get excited about being in the Real Estate business, then you should turn on CNN and see what the rest of the world lives with.

Then, of course, the tenth principle is this: I am so thoroughly sold on my career that my enthusiasm becomes contagious and others become successful because of it. My claim to fame in the Real Estate training business is a program I wrote about twelve years ago called Leader's Choice. I've updated it four times in the past twelve years to stay current with the markets. I just recently did it again, adding all the principles of social networking and issues relating to the explosion of technology. You can send me into any marketplace in California, Florida, Ontario, British Columbia, or you could send me into Southfield, Michigan, and I guarantee you I will have the salespeople do more business than the average Realtor would do during the best of times. That's why I am so excited every day about the opportunities I have, and that spreads—optimism breeds optimism, success breeds success. You have to be excited about what you do every day in sales; if not, you're never going to make it.

WRIGHT

Those are ten good principles.

If someone is doing the right things to establish their social capital, what should they do or not do to conserve it?

LEADER

There are five behaviors that demonstrate you are genuine. The first one is to provide more service than is customary.

For the past ten to fifteen years there has been great controversy within the Real Estate industry regarding salespeople's commissions. The public is demanding that Real Estate commissions be reduced and Realtors are becoming obliging. I could line up a hundred people or I could line up five hundred people right now who use the philosophies I teach. They are getting a full market commission and quite often above market when they meet with the client.

There's an old adage, David: you get what you pay for. It's not in the public's best interest to pay a Realtor or salesperson less than the going rate and the truth is, they should actually pay a little more than the going rate. I use a silly analogy. For example, let's assume you are an electrician and the union sends you out every day on jobs. You have three jobs you can work today and they're the exact same job—running wire through a wall. One job will pay $25 an hour, one job will pay $35 an hour, and one job will pay you $55 an hour. If we're being honest with ourselves, and assuming that the conditions are all the same, you and I both know which job 100 percent of the electricians are going to accept. It's going to be the highest paying job for the day. It's similar in the Real Estate business. When the public understands that ultimately the lowest commission is not in their best interest and the salesperson who agrees to take a cut rate commission is actually doing it to make some quick money. He or she is hoping that by hammering up a sign on the property, it will sell, versus what's in the best interest of the home owner, and having the skills necessary to demonstrate to them why a full and fair commission is warranted.

So that being said, if you are charging $10 you give your customers a service as though they were paying $15. If you're charging $20, you give them a service as if it's $25. When you do that, I guarantee they will come back over and over and over again. I'll give you another analogy very quickly, David. There are two restaurants in town. In one the food is good and the service is phenomenal. They make you feel good from the moment you walk in to the moment you walk out. You go to another place, the food is fantastic but the maitre d' makes you feel unwelcome. Which one are we going to go back to more often than not?

WRIGHT

I'm going to go with the first one.

LEADER

Of course, that's what anyone would do.

Number two: engage in no transaction unless it knowingly benefits your client. Always put the best interest of your client ahead of your own. When a client entrusts the sale of his or her property to you, then you must honor that trust. Do that well and for certain your client will refer more business to you.

Number three: make no statements unless you believe it to be true. How often have we sat across from a salesperson who is telling us something, and we know in our heart the salesperson is exaggerating a little more than he or she should be? Good salespeople don't have to do that. Good salespeople would never do that, and good people would never do that to others. So we never, ever embellish or make any statement that is not 100 percent true. I always use a litmus test on that and my litmus test is this: if the person sitting there was my son or daughter, how would I want the salesperson to treat customers? If you are doing it according to that, then you are probably on track.

The fourth one is have a sincere desire to consistently offer superior service to your customers. In other words, promise less but deliver more. The odd thing about it is that in today's world with the "do not call," which we'll talk about in a couple of minutes, the salespeople are having to step up to the plate and they're asking people within their own sphere to send them referral business. I never had a problem with that. I never had to ask people to send me referrals because most people, when they have a great experience with a salesperson, are the first ones to refer them to others. They feel comfortable recommending your services to their family and friends.

Of course, the fifth one is treat your customers as if they feed, house, and clothe you, and sure enough they will.

This is a lesson I learned many years ago, David, working after school in my father's clothing store. It was a denim store north of Toronto back in the 1970s catering to young men and women. There was a local woman who came into our store on a regular basis. She had two sons and she was a regular customer who shopped for their school clothes. She was a generous mother and a good customer, so in return my father always gave her his undivided attention. She could be abrupt and demanding at times but she also had old-fashioned values and we knew that behind that abruptness was a woman with a big heart.

Anyhow this particular day she was in shopping. I was young and she was abrupt and one thing led to another and she left without buying anything. My father watching this asked me about it. I, of course, complained about her miserable mood. My dad just left it at that.

When we were closing the store for the day, I asked my father, "Dad, are we going to stop by and pick up a new hockey stick for me? I have a game tomorrow night."

As we're driving over in the car, he said, "Let me ask you something. Who is buying this hockey stick for you?"

"Well," I replied, "I thought you were, Dad.

He looked over at me and said, "Actually, the customer who came in today was buying it for you." he didn't say anything else. We picked up the stick and I didn't think any more about it. We pulled in the driveway and my dad said, "Let me ask you something, son. You want to get a dirt bike, right?" Who do you think is going to buy that for you?"

"Well, dad, I was going to save half the money while working in the store and you were going to give me half the money."

He said, "Well, actually, the customer who came in today was going to buy that dirt bike for you." He didn't say anything more.

We sat down to eat and my dad said, "Son, let me ask you something. Who do you think put this meal on the table for us today"? I said, "the Lord God and of course mom cooked it." He looked at me and said, "That's right but the truth of it is, the customer who helped as well."

"What do you mean, Dad?" I asked. "That's the third time now you've said that."

"Well, that customer left the store today without making a purchase and that affects the family income. It's the customer who feeds, houses, and clothes us and you have to always remember that, son. Treat the customer as if they feed house and clothe you and our business will do well, but when you treat them badly, your business will flounder and eventually fail."

That was a great lesson for me to learn and that's how I've lived my business career. Here I am a speaker in the Real Estate industry through the greatest meltdown since the 1930s and in the last four years I've averaged on hundred speaking engagements a year for some of the greatest companies in the world. *That's because I put their salespeople's interest and the company's interest ahead of my own.* Treat them as if they feed, house, and clothe you and they will.

WRIGHT

Will you give our readers an example of some things an agent would do differently before and after they adopt the social capital viewpoint?

LEADER

Oh absolutely, the first thing to remember is that social capital is built by a continuing interaction with clients. You should always convey that you are steadfast, grounded, and predictable. Consumers often feel there are too many unknowns and unexpected variables in Real Estate and that can be unsettling to them. You want to become the grounding influence that lets them breathe easy and have confidence that you know exactly what you are doing.

I'll give you just a little example of this, David. Often salespeople complain about the number of hours they work in a week with little accomplished. I learned early on that you have to run your business as a business and not a sideline. There is a time for you to be in the office and a time to leave the office. The impression you want to convey from your impeccable appearance to your hours of operation to how you interact with people is that you are the ultimate professional that the Real Estate industry has to offer. The client can put his or her trust and confidence in you. That alone is worth tens of thousands of dollars to your career.

So even when you are asking a client to step outside of his or her comfort zone, you want to present it as a customary step to take and is to his or her benefit. When you have adopted the principles of social capital and are truly acting in the best interest of your client, it's not that difficult of a case to make; in fact, clients will do it because you have suggested they do it.

WRIGHT

Do you make a distinction between spending social capital and investing in it for a return?

LEADER

Yes, I do. Generally speaking, when you spend your capital it's gone. You may have received something for it—a car, clothes, cosmetics—but these are generally items to use for your benefit. When you invest your social capital, the return on your investment is huge—thousands of times greater than if you had spent it. In my view, spending it would be entering into a relationship or a situation that is a win-lose—win for you, lose for the other party. Investing your social capital would be a win-win scenario. If you approach every business situation thinking, "How can I help or benefit the other person?" and at the same time achieve the greatest amount of value then this is a win-win.

For example, I've been advising salespeople for years to get involved in their community on a local level. It's to their advantage to participate in local charity events, become members of the PTA, Rotary club, Lions Club, etc. Membership in these organizations is declining because many people believe they do not have time for them or their lives are so busy they have nothing to give back. There is an old adage that we reap what we sow. When it's said and done, the more people you help, the more help will be given to you.

If salespeople want to expand the relationships they have, and they want their business to flourish, a very effective way is to become a person who is not only known but seen in the community on a regular basis. So when your marketing pieces land on their doorstep or you call or drop by, the relationship already has a foundation to build on. They see you as an upstanding person in the community who helps others. What better way to sell yourself without selling yourself. Plus, the self-satisfaction derived from being a benefit to others is immeasurable.

Several years ago, a politician came up with laws in the United States and Canada to restrict salespeople from soliciting business over the telephone. This did not stop companies that were not held to our laws from outside North America from using the telephone to solicit business at unprofessional hours. That being said, it hurt more small businesses and more small businesspeople in this country than stopping any home intrusion. Let's face it, someone from a developing nation does not care about the Do Not Call Laws, but if you have a predetermined relationship with someone, you are then allowed to reach out and contact that person.

Now, let's look at it this way: if you were a member of the Rotary Club, would you get upset if another member of the Rotary Club called you on the telephone? Probably not. You may not even sit at the same table at the Rotary Club but you see each other on a regular basis. This is what it's all about today—it's about giving back to the community and being out in the community.

Let's assume, for example, that you are a Lion's Club member. There could be two hundred, three hundred, four hundred, or five hundred people in the Lion's Club in your town, and because you are at those Lion's Club meetings on a regular basis, you are participating in the community. That is up to five hundred potential families you could help with their housing needs. You reap what you sow—what you give to the community, the community will give back to you tenfold.

WRIGHT

So how does a person spend his or her social capital, and does it deplete a person's supply?

LEADER

No, you deplete your supply when you put your interest ahead of the client. For example, if someone asks you not to contact him or her during the dinner hour and you continue to do so, your social capital with that person will probably be depleted. If you publicly embarrass someone or enter into a business deal for your benefit and broadside someone who trusted you, then that social capital is gone and will most likely never be replaced. There is a reason why doing someone an injustice or ending a relationship in a bad way is referred to as burning your bridges. Why? Because that bridge will most likely never be able to be crossed again. That person may forgive you, but believe me, the person you have wronged will never forget.

WRIGHT

You say that the social capital approach helps agents create more balance and fun in their lives. How is that?

LEADER

Well, a salesperson using traditional selling approaches derived from the premise of survival of the fittest, dog-eat-dog is being aggressively competitive. Traditional selling approaches are all about closing the deal. You have to do this but closing the deal at all costs is not building a business, and it certainly is counterproductive to the laws of the universe, which by the way we are all governed by whether we want to be or not. But when you regard each sales transaction equitably and understand it's not about hustling the deal and more about the clients involved, then you are building a business—a business that will sustain you in good economies and bad. You can eliminate the roller coaster ride many salespeople are on for the duration of their careers.

You see, David, in spite of the economy there are three requirements of life that have to be fulfilled—food, clothing, and shelter. Regardless of what is happening in the economy, a percentage of the population, for different reasons, will require one of these services at any given time.

Now, in good times when the economy is flourishing, it may not matter, but in a downturn clients are more likely to turn to the person they trust—someone they have a good relationship with and is known for putting the customer's interest first. When you build a business that will sustain you, in good economies or bad, you're now living a life with more balance, and certainly more cash flow which allows you to have more fun.

WRIGHT

You said earlier that you can build social capital and you touched on a couple of ways. Once you build social capital, is there any way to maintain it?

LEADER

Yes there is. You can do this by employing a marketing system that thousands of salespeople across North America are using and it's working very effectively for them. The plan is what I call the 4/12/48/365 marketing approach and it's rather very simple. Everything I come up with, whether in my seminars or in my books, webinars, or the coaching that I do, I try to come up with acronyms or ways for people to remember things they should be doing on a regular basis.

Let me take you through what the 4/12/48/365 stands for. Take the number 4 and multiply it by 12 and that equals 48. You need to have 4 personal touches a year minimum with the people in your database—people you have relationships with who have produced social capital. It could be one drop-by visit and three phone calls. It could be one phone call and three drop-by visits. The way you maintain relationships and friendships is by reaching out and being part of their lives. I'm not suggesting that you have to break bread with them, but I am suggesting that there is something touching when a special day comes up. The special day could be a birthday or it could be an anniversary. People recognize thoughtfulness.

I personally don't feel comfortable dropping by and paying unannounced visits to people I have a professional relationship with versus people I have a personal relationship with. But I do feel comfortable placing a call and leaving a message because I have something for them. It could be a little pumpkin at Halloween or a poinsettia at Christmas, or an Easter lily but you need to make sure that you have four professional touches a year. I personally like the gift of a rose bush in the spring. It leaves an enduring and lasting reminder that you are a full-time salesperson in their community and you value the relationship that you have with them.

You want to have eight to twelve mail-outs a year in what we call snail mail. I know some readers are going to object to this and feel it's a waste of time and money, but truthfully not everyone checks e-mail on a regular basis. So you need to make sure that you are grabbing your contacts' attention in many different ways. So four personal touches a year and twelve direct mailers. Those direct mailers can be a combination of different things. Try teaming up with a local pizza parlor or a chicken outlet for a coupon mail-out and I guarantee the recipients will read your mailer. The choice is yours but they need to receive something from you once a month.

Forty-eight is not accurate of course, but close. There are fifty-two weeks in a year so I use the four times twelve equals forty-eight, for forty-eight Internet-based marketing pieces. Generally speaking, you want these to be informative, brief, and something to make them smile. Everyone loves a good joke or a touch of humor. People will open your e-mails if they're lighthearted and humorous. Then we have three hundred and sixty-five days of social networking.

Now the big gorilla in the room is Facebook. We could do a whole book on social networking but let's talk just about Facebook for a minute. One of the most common mistakes businesspeople make if they are going to use Facebook or social networking to build their business is their number of "friends." They will have 5000 friends and the truth is that it's better to have less friends and better relationships. So rather than going, what I call, wide and shallow with the friends on Facebook, I'd rather see you go narrow and deep. In other words, I've always believed that if a salesperson in the Real Estate industry could build five hundred professional relationships, that would be all they would need. Let me explain it this way: If your son or daughter had an accident and he or she needed medical attention, you would call the person you know and trust for medical advice and that would be your family doctor. Well, in Real Estate I have to connect with you in different ways but when you need the advice of a Realtor, I want you to immediately think of me. That is the professional relationship that I want to develop with you.

What I would do is have a professional page built within the Facebook family for this purpose. Who knows what the next goliath will be in the social networking world, but right now it's Facebook. I wouldn't befriend the swimsuit model from Australia as part of that group. I would focus on developing five hundred friendships within your immediate community and social network with them. But you have to remember that when you are building a professional community, and social networking with this group of five hundred, that your Facebook page is not about you, it's about them. It's about how you interact within the community and are helping the community to improve. It's not a place for you to brag about your successes. So again, even with social networking, when you put your customer or your relationship ahead of yourself and your own ego, your friends are going to send you business that you never thought possible.

There is one other point I'd like to make. Why do I stress five hundred professional relationships? There are a couple of reasons for that. First of all, five hundred is an easy number to manage. Secondly, there are generally two relationships in a household. That means you are really marketing to two hundred and fifty households, which would mean five hundred relationships. This makes your marketing more plausible. You are spending less but getting a higher return.

Also, when you build a personal relationship with a group of five hundred people, the odds are that 20 percent of those people will send you a hot lead each and every year. That means a possible one hundred hot leads. And a hot lead is certainly going to close at a higher level than a cold lead, so you're probably looking at a 50 percent close ratio versus a 15 or 20 percent ratio. The bottom line is that it's all about relationships and social capital.

WRIGHT

What a great conversation, Mark. I really learned a lot here today and I can just imagine what the people are experiencing when you do your Real Estate training.

LEADER

I've been fortunate throughout my career. I've had some wonderful mentors in my life—outstanding people who generously shared their knowledge and insight with me. These people paved the road ahead and made my journey a little easier.

Of course my mother and father have been my steadfast supporters and I've always welcomed their counsel. If I had one wish, it would be that every young man or young woman could have those two as role models. I've been truly blessed by the relationship I have with my parents.

Also, I have had twenty-six wonderful years with my spiky blonde-haired, blue-eyed wife, Denise. She's the bedrock of our home and family and her French Canadian heritage is evident in the warm and loving environment she has created for us and our two sons.

I've also been blessed with two wonderful boys. My oldest son, Lucas Stone, is growing up to be a fine young man. Jacob Nathan, who was our miracle baby, weighing in at one pound, thirteen ounces. They're both teenagers now; this is new and uncharted territory for them and for Denise and me as well. When I become too critical of their fashion statements, my mother reminds me of my funky teenage Afro and wide-leg jeans. I laughingly back away and give them their space. Although I do attribute my sons' good school grades and college aspirations to

Denise who, with a firm hand and a soft heart, keeps them focused on the important things. This frees me to concentrate on my career so I can provide them with the best home possible.

I have to speak of Bob Proctor who is a friend. He is a wonderful, giving man and I was blessed when our paths crossed. I began building a relationship with Bob fourteen years ago and he has helped me help thousands of people. I hope someday that I have the opportunity to mentor a young speaker or trainer in the same way Bob has mentored me.

And it's been an enormous pleasure to meet and work with so many culturally diversified students of Leader's Choice and so gratifying when they accomplish their goals and increase their income so they can make positive life changes.

Throughout my years in the Real Estate industry, it has been my good fortune to meet and develop a relationship with many outstanding people who have risen to the top of their game and accomplished so much. Harold Crye and Dick Leike, Mike Pappas, Mary Frances Burleson, Bob Peltier, and John Coile are a few who are leaders within the Real Estate industry. They are all wonderful people who have "earned their stripes" and are shining examples to what can be achieved through dedication and hard work.

I have been very blessed. I've always said that everything I share is because others have shared it with me. I enjoy learning something new every day, and truthfully I've been a good student. I try to read a new book on a regular basis and I pay attention to what others who have been down this road before me have to say. I learn from their experiences just the same as I learned talking with you today, David. I thank Insight Publishing for allowing me this great opportunity and all of the authors who are participating in this book. I feel very blessed that I get to put my name alongside theirs.

Wright

Today I have been talking with Mark Leader, founder and creator of Leader's Choice. As North America's number one Real Estate sales speaker and trainer, Mark has helped tens of thousands of salespeople increase production and increase revenues by hundreds of millions of dollars with humor, enthusiasm, and genuine concern for his students, as we have found out here today. He speaks from his successes to equip agents with the tools they need to break out of mediocrity and discover extraordinary success. Wherever he trains, I hear he leaves behind sales leaders who credit him with jumpstarting their careers, improving their attitudes and skills, and sending their sales commissions skyrocketing.

Mark, thank you so much for being with me today on *Concrete Jungle*.

LEADER

Thank you for having me, David. The pleasure's been all mine.

About the Author

As North America's number one Real Estate sales speaker/trainer, Mark Leader has helped tens of thousands of salespeople raise their production and increase revenues by hundreds of millions of dollars.

With humor, enthusiasm, and genuine concern for his students, Mark speaks from his successes to equip agents with the tools they need to break out of mediocrity and discover extraordinary success. Wherever he trains, he leaves behind sales leaders who credit him with improving attitudes and sending their sales commissions skyrocketing.

With his unprecedented track record of success in generating productivity and increasing the bottom line, Mark Leader is the first step in *Putting Money in Your Pocket*.

Mark Leader Courses
8 Whispering Pine Place
Barrie, ON
L4N 9R9
877-730-6941
www.leaderschoice.com

Chapter Five

Plan Today, Achieve Tomorrow:

Take Charge of Your Career & Discover Success

An Interview With...

Amy Letke

DAVID WRIGHT (WRIGHT)

Today I'm talking with Ms. Amy Letke, a successful human capital and leadership consultant who speaks to us from real world, real learned experiences, as a business owner, entrepreneur, founder of Integrity HR Incorporated, a human capital, consulting and outsourcing firm, and cofounder of HRReview LCC, a publishing firm for human capital and educational materials. Amy's real-world experiences are backed up with the operational know-how and the ability to run successful entities, as well as a completed master's degree in Business Administration and a pending doctorate in Organizational Development.

Welcome, Amy, to *Concrete Jungle.*

AMY LETKE (LETKE)

Great, thank you so much, David. It's great to be here.

WRIGHT

Amy, in this day and age it seems like oftentimes many unfortunate things happen to jobs, be it a result of the economy, a shift in job needs, or shifts someplace else, when we think about things that happen to people as a result of either losing a job or being down sized—what does career management have to do with this?

LETKE

Career management is a critical process for every working individual or for anyone who anticipates being in the workplace. Whether you're a college student trying to figure out your path, a mid-career professional reconsidering your career options, or someone who's questioning current and future plans, having a career management plan is key. In my business, I often see people who "just look" for getting a job. Because it's not on the top of their minds every day, the last thing they may think about is what they can do to keep that job, what comes after that present job, and what they are doing to achieve the next job in their career progression. Career management addresses the life cycle of a person's entire working career. It is a little understood fact that an individual has a lot more control over the successful outcome of career opportunities if he or she effectively plans out "what they want next" in a job and keep that in the forefront of career and life opportunities.

Planning and action are keys to successful career management.

WRIGHT

That's an interesting perspective. People plan out family activities and savings, so it does make sense that planning for a successful career should be top of the list. Now tell us exactly why is career management so important and who needs it?

LETKE

On any given day, we can pick up the newspaper and read about unemployment rates, learn about downsizings, and see all the resulting disappointments with perhaps our friends, family members, and those in our community.

It may even adversely affect us! Why is that? Unfortunately the news can be more than a little bit depressing to say the least, but as I mentioned earlier, career management is critical to overcoming challenges the external environment inevitably will create, and if not prepared, will affect even the most savvy employee's career.

Let me share a specific story with you about a woman named Mary. Mary is someone I have known for quite some time. Throughout her working career she was a legal assistant—from the 1990s to about 2000. She worked very successfully for a law firm until early 2001 when her position was "eliminated." Mary had some disappointments along the way, including a challenging divorce and a few health scares. After all that, she had become very disenchanted with her life overall. When she lost her job, she allowed the pain of her job loss, her personal relationship challenges, and even a poor attitude, rule her entire life. From 2001 to 2009 she wandered in and out of numerous legal jobs, supplementing work in temporary agencies as well, trying to find happiness in finding a job.

Regrettably, Mary lived in a small community and word eventually spread about her. She had lost control of her focus on how she contributed to her position. She was aloof and didn't care about her work. She wasn't concerned about being involved in the law practice. The result? She couldn't get hired. She let her "bad attitude" blame everyone else for her lack of success. She had even taken up some work habits that rendered her labeled as "not a good employee."

That was certainly not a good place for Mary to be with respect to career management. Now what was missing in her choices? Let's talk about what Mary could have done differently. She missed the boat on managing the situations that confronted her, and she lost nearly a decade of potential success wallowing in self-pity and self-destruction.

It wasn't until she made the decision that she was going to get out of the rut she was in that she could really make some progress. When she finally did make that commitment, she started not only to turn her career around but her life, too. The mind has such a powerful way of providing us with opportunities. When we choose to let it drive our success, positive opportunities and intentional actions that lead to better results are bound to be in our future.

When we choose to let it drive our success, positive opportunities and intentional actions that lead to better results are bound to be in our future. Now, with that said, career management isn't just dealing with the stuff that happens to you once somebody else has made an employment decision. Career management means managing every aspect of relationships within your career. How you treat people at work, particularly your boss and you peers, as well as the people who might work for you, and how you manage relationships with those individuals is absolutely critical. Look around at the people you work with now, or those you have worked with in the past. There are probably a handful of people about whom you can honestly say to yourself, "Gee whiz, that person may not be the best widget maker, he [or she] may not be the best accountant, he [or she] may not be the best writer, but he [or she] sure knows how to get along at all levels in our business."

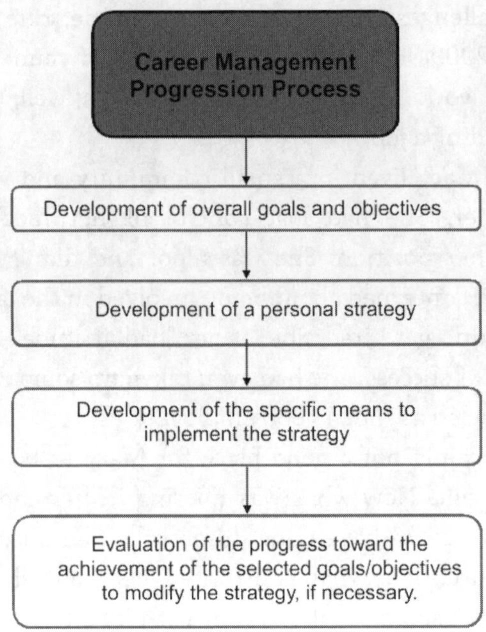

"Career Management is the combination of structured planning and the active management choice of one's own professional career."

The outcome of successful career management should include personal fulfillment, work/life balance, goal achievement, and financial security.

Why is it that some people have this magic about them that appears to protect them from the difficulties in the workplace? What makes them so special? If it is not exemplary work, it's the way they manage relationships they have with other people. That's what it is. Individuals who are successful in managing their careers have taken the time to understand what motivates others around them at work and probably at home, too. They know that one key to career management is to understand that the motivations and needs of others can provide exponential results for them when building and managing their careers.

WRIGHT

What are the major pitfalls people face when they fail to manage their career?

Letke

It's interesting that you ask that question. David. The major pitfalls I see include the following:

Pitfall #1: Forgetting that first impressions are lasting

When we meet people in the workplace, we have maybe thirty seconds to make an impression. I know from interviewing thousands of people, both on my own and with my clients, that my most savvy client can "fall in love" with a candidate in thirty seconds. That's amazing, isn't it? And the reason they "fall in love" is due to the fact that the candidate made such a positive impression during that very short period of time. Maybe it was eye contact or the way the person shook the boss's hand or the fact that he or she dressed appropriately for the interview. The fact is that savvy candidates come to job interviews prepared. They realized they had this one opportunity to create a lasting impression and recognized it. So, forgetting the power of the first impression is truly a lasting stumbling block for someone who is seeking that new job, change in career, or higher level opportunity.

Pitfall #2: Assuming You Won't Need to Work For It

A colleague of mine often says, "No good deed goes unpunished." While this saying usually addresses the frequency with which kindnesses backfire on those who offer it, my colleague often refers to this statement after he's thought his work resulted in going the extra mile, yet still didn't get the job done, or achieve expectations. Yes, there are no more "freebies" anymore. Expectations are higher, there's competition for the best positions, and we can't just expect that everything is going to be handed to us from our current or potential employer on a silver platter.

At one point in time, decisions about jobs, promotions, and opportunities were based on tenure, and even loyalty. This may have been more common in the 1970s–1990s, but recent college graduates need to realize they've got to "put their time in" before they're going to get a promotion. Starting out in an organization and expecting to be a manager without proven abilities, such as having requisite experience or a successful background in managing people, is probably not going to be likely. So we also have to manage our own expectations around the job, the business, and the organization while being more sensitive to what's happening around us.

Pitfall #3: Not Understanding Your Behaviors and Those of Others

We also have to understand that behavior strengths are critical. Do we really understand what the strengths are in our behavior? Now, there are a number of ways to understand behavior strengths. Sometimes our parents or family talk about what makes us strong in our behavior. Sometimes our behavior strengths can be positive and sometimes they may not be. What we really have to do is think about our strong points. Are we strong leaders? Maybe we're strong in terms of influencing other people, maybe we are a great team player, or maybe we're the person we know the rest of the organization can count on for getting the detail right and crunching the numbers. Whatever it is, really understand that and be able to sell that, because no matter what we think about in terms of achieving the position, we're going to have to sell ourselves to find that career and maintain the career that we want.

Now just as important as understanding our strengths is to understand where our weaknesses are. I prefer to call those "blind spots." Blind spots are those areas in our behavior that maybe we don't recognize because we like to play on our strengths so much.

An example of a blind spot might be that Joseph, who works in accounting, likes to go on and on about his family on Monday mornings. While the rest of the people around him are happy to hear about it, they're anxious to get to their work.

Joseph's blind spot is that when he is working with the people in his department he needs to limit some of that conversation because continuing to behave in that fashion could be "career limiting" for him. Whether it's something like talking too much or maybe not understanding the work culture and what's okay to talk about and what is not okay is a potential blind spot if we fail to recognize it.

Let me give you another example of this. There have been several times in my career history when I'm working with a client and we have a complete mismatch in terms of finding an appropriate candidate for a position. One organization I work with is a very well-established wealth management company. They have been around for many years; they are very professional and very well-educated.

Many "bluebloods" come to this organization because they are known for being successful with managing people's money.

One candidate came in and made a huge faux pas when she had her interview. What was the faux pas? There was more than one! The candidate had a limp handshake, she didn't look the president in the eye within the first thirty seconds of meeting, and then she also proceeded to use incorrect grammar while answering questions. Now for that particular organization, dealing with very high profile clients requires confidence, a solid demeanor, and command of the English language. Within the first thirty seconds, these errors caused the death of that interview, and there was no time for recovery. While that candidate was wonderfully qualified and she had excellent experience, she didn't meet the requirements for a good cultural fit.

How could this have been prevented?

- She should have paid attention to what was critical for that job and mentally prepared for that atmosphere.
- She should have practiced.
- She could have "done some homework" on expectations within the organization.
- She also needed to understand her behavioral demeanor would either win them over or leave them questioning.

Knowing what is expected of the business's culture, then determining if it acceptable to you is a critical first step. We all need to evaluate what level of sacrifice we are willing to make, if any, to meet the needs of that particular culture. Ultimately, understanding what works and what doesn't in terms of behavior at work will to help you be more even more successful in managing your career.

Pitfall #4: Not being astute about what you can or won't tolerate at work

Let me give you an example of not understanding the work culture. Sometimes people who go into a manufacturing job may go in not really understanding that the work can be rough and tough, and sometimes some tough language happens around there. So when working in that kind of environment, you have to recognize that you have to "toughen your skin up" a little bit and realize that you may hear some things that could be potentially "shocking." What level of communication are you going to be able to participate or not participate in? Successful employees understand where they are willing and not willing to draw a line at work. Sometimes it may be subtle shades of gray, but knowing what one can tolerate early on equates to good career awareness. Becoming more culturally astute with the organization where you work now or where you aspire to work is going to be important, and determining how you fit in that culture is equally as critical.

Another key area that can lend tremendous benefits in career management is the act of "spot checking." Spot checking is a means for finding out how your performance is measuring up, without asking for a formal performance review. Effective spot checking allows you to touch base informally with people you work with about where you are with performance. How often do you ask for feedback about your current performance with your peers, boss, or board of directors? Successful spot checking comes with critical turf, understanding that one of the number one tasks managers hate to do is give performance evaluations. They hate to do it because they only want to share favorable feedback. Sharing bad news is never popular is it? We have to constantly think about how we get feedback so that if we have some blind spots or problem areas, we can fix those before they become bigger issues and we lose track of managing our career. Find a way to spot check with people you work with about where you are. This includes more than your immediate supervisor. Maybe you can ask for feedback from some people you trust—people with whom you work closely. Ask, "How did I do on that report? Give me some feedback on the results of that quality assurance program I worked on. I am here on time every day and you can depend on me, but tell me, is there anything else I can do to be a better employee [manager, leader] for you?" Asking for feedback is a significant sign of workplace maturity that employers value.

Another pitfall is failing to fix problems and being unwilling to start over if necessary. All too often we can let pride get in the way of what we really set out to achieve. We've got to be willing to fix blind spots we have or, heaven forbid, we make a mistake that we need to promptly fix.

I've been working recently with an organization that struggles with the challenge of the blame game. Now you may have heard this, but if you haven't let me share what the blame game is. It is when one employee fails to take responsibility for his or her action and he or she constantly points the finger at someone else. Of course, when that finger gets pointed at someone else, the person is saying, "Ah-ha! That wasn't me, it was someone else!" and either that finger from the other individual gets pointed back at the original person or it gets pointed elsewhere. The blame game is never a successful answer; it's extremely unhealthy and it creates a very destructive work culture.

Being committed to fixing problems is the number one very responsible and professional way to deal with this. If you are in a culture where the blame game exists, it's not going to last for long without some kind of an employment consequence. Avoiding that pitfall is critical to helping people be successful. Then, people need to be willing to start over and fix things satisfactorily to move forward.

Pitfall #5: Not Being Current with Changing Skill Set Needs

Keeping up with the times in the workplace is also critical. If you are evaluating a new career opportunity and perhaps your technology skills are not where they need to be, you'll need to fix this deficiency quickly. Organizations want to hire new people who "can do it all," so someone who measures up only 70 to 80 percent may be out of the running. Learn what's required or what is going to be required to operate the technology associated with the role or the skill set that is necessary. It could be something industry specific, or something as complex as understanding social media, or the Internet. One thing is for certain, if it's new and up and coming, we have to constantly prepare ourselves to keep up with the times and take positive steps to constantly educate ourselves to be more "marketable" in our career.

Pitfall #6: Not Having a Plan B

We also have to realize that there are some pitfalls in not having a contingency plan if disaster should strike during our career. If a shutdown or downsizing happens at a manufacturing facility and you lose your job, what's next? Unemployment insurance is only going to last so long and it's back to coming up with a plan under desperate circumstances. My point is this: it's very important to develop a contingency plan, *while you're still working.*

Not sure what your plan should be? You're not alone. Many times I'll work with individuals who have lost their job, and have no Plan B. These folks haven't thought about two or three other career/job options. They may have lost their passion, and all they can think about is that last job they had.

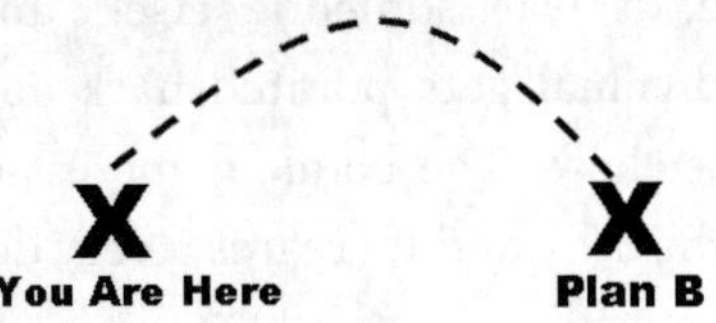

You need to have your own personal Plan B—three jobs that would be good next options, whether it's preparation for downsizing, or preparation for a promotion. Constantly working on your Personal Plan B gives you a plan. Maybe one of your jobs will require some additional skills. Now is the time to get those while you're still in your present role. And if you've lost the position you love, it's not too late; developing your Personal Plan B with measurable steps will help you keep focused on attaining the job or *career of your choice.*

There are also tradeoffs, and sacrifices may be necessary for effective career management. We have to realize that to achieve success those tradeoffs are going to be critical, and we have to decide if we do one thing we're going to have to sacrifice something else.

As an example, if I'm preparing for my next promotion, and my Personal Plan B indicates that learning Spanish will help me have a better chance of attaining that promotion, I will have trade-offs associated with taking classes, studying, and losing other personal time with friends and family. Having a written plan and understanding that there will be tradeoffs will help us avoid these major pitfalls we may face when we're managing our career.

WRIGHT

So Amy, you mention that there are some specific key steps to managing and understanding how to successfully manage careers. What are those steps?

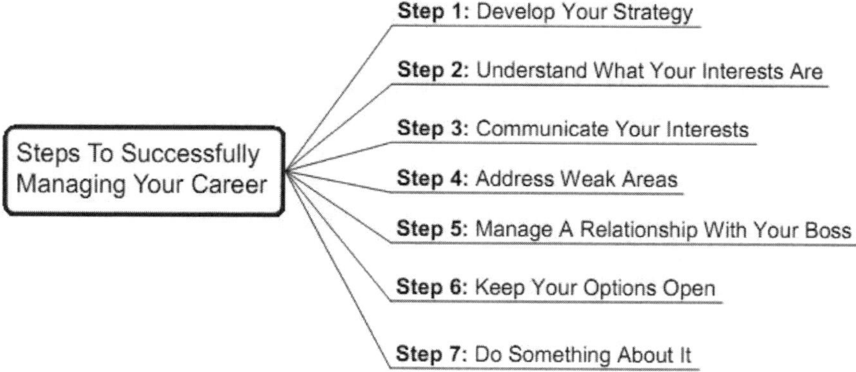

LETKE

There are seven key steps to help people effectively manage their career. Number one is to *develop your strategy* for your career and then be introspective. Perform some objective research on your actual strengths and weaknesses. For example, think about your behaviors, your technical skills, and your total person skills. Total person skills include how you tend to learn things, quickly or more methodically; mathematical skills; your written and verbal communication skills; and of course key behavioral attributes. It's important to evaluate your strengths and weaknesses. When is the last time you assessed your strengths in these areas? If you haven't assessed strengths and weaknesses in these areas, now is a good time to see what a prospective employer may see when you're asked to take an "assessment" of your skill sets. Know what they are and work on improving weaknesses and building strengths! If you aren't sure where to go or how to get a "total person" assessment, you can learn more at career centers at local colleges and even some human resources firms (such as integrityhr.com). These resources can help you evaluate your present total person skills so that you understand yourself from an employer's perspective. Smart employers are relying more on the objectivity of assessments in the selection and promotion process. Many times assessments may even be used to weed out candidates whose behaviors may not match the cultural standard or if the profile isn't a fit based on specific job requirements or skill set criteria.

The second element is to *understand what your interests are.* Oftentimes when I coach a professional who's at a career plateau, I'll ask what interests him or her. Sometimes I get very specific answers, and other times I don't. One thing is quite clear, people who have a good level of interests and hobbies tend to have an easier time planning next steps in a career process. Have you taken an inventory of your interests and your strengths and are those strengths or are they liabilities?

Constantly Assess & Develop Your Career Management Strategy

Let me give you some specifics about this process. When I interview prospective employees, I'll talk with them about what their interests are. Some examples include: working on cars, attending art fairs, or listening to music.

What's the advantage to understanding this? When you understand your own interests, you can use that to your favor when you are looking for that next career, promotion, or job. Ask yourself these questions: do my interests match with what this firm has to offer me? How can I take my current interests and expand them with what I already do well?

For example, if you have excellent administrative skills but your real interest is in something to do with sales, look for a firm that has a need for your present skill set but also has opportunities in customer service or sales. If you have an interest in management, consider working for a small company that allows an opportunity to learn office or other management functions. Whether you work in one of the degreed professions or work in an administrative capacity or enjoy working with your hands, temporary agencies can give you experience, the chance to check out new opportunities and build on your present skill set, and the time to see if there's a good fit before accepting an offer for that next move.

Number three is to *define your interests so that you can communicate them in the interview and promotion process.* Not sure what you're really interested in doing in that next job? You're not alone! Many college grads exit college without the first thought of a career, and without good career planning it can happen to just about anyone. To better understand your career interests, there's a tool that can help isolate career interests—the Strong Interest Inventory. Many universities provide this assessment to college students or in public forums to help people understand what their career interests are. So if you, a colleague, or friend think you need some help in defining your career interests, look at taking this assessment or another "interest inventory" to get you thinking about other possibilities

Number four is to *address weak areas*. If you've got some areas that are weaknesses, for example if writing isn't your strong suit, get out there and learn. Go to a community college, take a class, find a mentor—someone who can help lead you through the challenge you are facing. It's very important to understand what your weak areas are and if you aren't sure, be sure to ask those closest to you because they will probably be more than willing to share.

Number five is to *understand the importance of managing a relationship with your boss*. How you manage him or her could mean whether you have an advocate or not. This is probably one of the biggest flaws I see in the workplace today. People will get a job, they will go to work, and they'll have a great time with their peers. They'll go to lunch, they'll talk with them and find ways to build relationship; but oftentimes they forget about their boss. One thing you cannot forget is that managing the boss is absolutely critical.

Let me give you an example of this. One of the managers on the executive team in an organization I work with is much more effective managing the president of the company than the rest of the team. That one person is very effective because she makes sure to get productive time on the president's calendar. They know what to meet about, such as the department's performance or to get feedback. She also does something very impressive—she asks for a half hour once a week, or once every two weeks, "just to get some feedback to make sure that I'm on the right track." She has an agenda prepared in advance and shares it prior to the meeting. She gets that time, she gets the feedback, and she does something with it to make a difference. Over time she has become much more effective with the president. Now, the president looks at her more frequently than the rest of the team because the president sees the results of the pro-activity of this leader. This executive has learned the art of managing her boss.

It doesn't matter whether you report to the president of the company or not, you most likely have a manager or a supervisor. Scheduling time to get results and to manage a relationship with your boss is critical at any level in the organization. Remember, your boss can be your biggest advocate, so turn over a new leaf and start working this principle if you haven't already begun!

Number six of our seven key steps is to *keep your options open*. If you're not happy in your current role or you feel like you're in a dead-end job, now is the time to evaluate next step options. Maybe it's time to learn something new, get additional coaching, or find ways to become more valuable to your organization. The key to success in this step is to take action.

Only you have the power to make the change. Think back to my first example, Mary. Mary did not take any action to make change, therefore the employers made the changes for her. One of the seven key steps to take that action is so that you can make a positive difference in keeping your options open. Review your inventory of your interests, job opportunities, and possibly other organizations that would value what you bring to the business. This is absolutely critical to your success.

The final step everyone needs to understand to effectively manage their careers is to *be the person who knows how to solve problems and make positive suggestions*. It's not enough to say, "I don't know how to fix it so I'll just forget about it," take charge and find a way to make improvements in your work environment to get positive results. Did you know that statistics show less than 2 percent of people set goals for themselves? If you set goals for making a positive career change and you take steps to write them down, measure them, and you are committed to them, you will see success! Career management is just as much a mind-set process as it is taking action and getting results. So focus your mind on making a constructive difference at your present role or in making your next move the best one ever.

Wright

Amy, tell our readers why it would be important for someone to follow a process of career management as compared to taking other steps.

LETKE

"You're either Green and Growing, or Ripe and Dying."

—Ray Kroc, Founder of McDonald's Corp.

If we're going to be successful in managing our jobs and careers, we have to make it intentional. We have to be constantly learning, growing, and being intentional about what we do. If we're not, we're getting ripe and then eventually we're shriveling up and dying out in our careers. And that's not where we want to be!

Showing up every day and doing a job is not enough. We've got to actively engage and be part of the solution for the organization we're working for. In tough times companies are looking for people who are great problem-solvers, people—who are positive in their mindset and who say, "How can I help?" They follow through and they can be counted on to get the job done. Now there are plenty of people who prefer to be lazy, miss work, not care, not be engaged, and take their jobs for granted. So those who choose to be exceptional, even if they're not the best engineer or the best secretary or the best with math, can surround themselves with people who are great with those skills. Then, by understanding where their weak points actually exist, that exceptional person takes action to do something about and improve them. As a result, these people actually become much more valuable to their employer. Everyone has the opportunity to be exceptional; it all starts with the desire and commitment to it!

"Determine never to be idle . . .
It is wonderful how much may be done if we are always doing."

—Thomas Jefferson

Career management is a lot like being a lifetime student, except it's during your working career. You're either working to keep your job or you are working yourself out of one. So my questions are: "Where are you in this equation? Are you working to keep your job, to enhance what you have or are you not doing anything or not looking for someone else to help you in making future decisions?" If you are not constantly looking for ways to improve and being a positive contributor in the workplace, someone will make an employment decision for you. The choice is in your hands to be part of that solution or to let things happen to you.

We have to think about those seven keys. We all have choices about how we manage our careers. Being proactive and taking charge will inevitably yield significantly higher positive results. And remember, anything is possible!

WRIGHT

You mentioned unique ways for finding the career of a person's dreams. What specifically can people do to position themselves for this?

LETKE

There are specific keys for people to focus in finding the role of their dreams. This includes taking inventory of the things they like and things they don't like.

I was recently working with an individual who worked in management for a retail chain selling washers and dryers. He was very dissatisfied with his work and eventually was demoted from his management role.

I sat down with him and asked, "Tell me what you really enjoy doing."

His response was, "I really didn't like selling washers and dryers. I enjoyed managing the people, but if I had my choice, I would love to be in landscaping."

"Really?" I said. "Landscaping? Tell me more about that."

His face completely lit up and he told me about everything he enjoyed with respect to landscaping his home, his friend's yards, and all of the elements of joy it gave him. I could see that if he could find a way to bridge the gap from being a retail manager to becoming a landscaper he would be happy and incredibly successful. We talked more about it and he started working on his new career management plan—in landscaping! Taking inventory of what you like to do and what you don't like to do is critical to evaluating options that not only increase happiness, but ultimately make you successful with your career.

Career management also means you've got to decide what you want. Not doing anything or not having any kind of definition creates indecision. What happens with indecision? Stalling! Mary, from my first example, lasted nearly a decade of going nowhere because she was indecisive about making a career move.

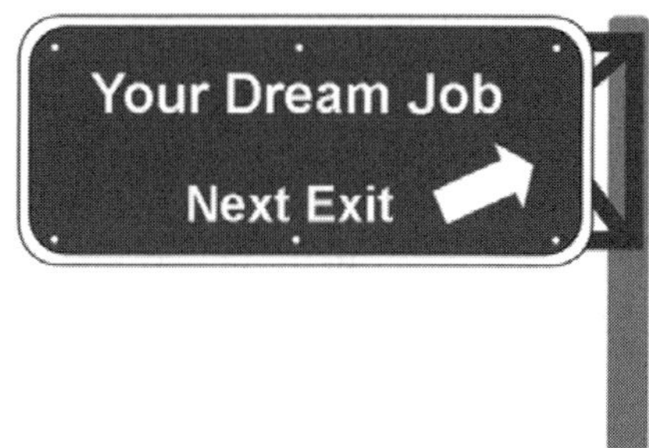

Take action—try new opportunities.

Sometimes, employers need to try new things too. In the summer of 2011, I hired a fresh-out-of-college graduate who had majored in Journalism and English. I hired her to come in and be our corporate intern to help us in writing articles, blogs, and materials about human resource management. She actually ended up coming on board as a full-time marketing and communications specialist because she did such a great job. Her dream job was to be an editor of a magazine and she had tremendous potential, but she was also willing to try new things. As an employer, it was well worth the risk to bring on an eager intern who was willing to try new things, put new ideas to work, and show results. Many employers will take that risk and see the benefits. If you're an employer and haven't taken that risk yet, give it a shot! Try hiring people with the right attitude, behaviors, and interests. You may need to do some skill training, but ultimately you might be surprised with the results.

Another unique way to effectively manage your career is through visualization. You must be able to "look past old values" and hang-ups, and actually see yourself performing the new job and living in the career. I fully believe in visualization in many aspects of life; how you see yourself oftentimes is how others see you. For example, if you go into a job interview and you think, "Oh wow, I'm not dressed appropriately!" Or, "My gosh, I spilled coffee on my suit, I can't do this today!" Or, "I'm not feeling great at this moment about myself." Now what's going to happen in that interview? The employer is going to sense what is going on with you that day, and it may not be a good vibe!

Proper execution of your career management strategy includes preparing mentally, creating an attractive image, getting your mind in the game, seeing yourself already in the job, positioning it, and preparing for how you're going to sell yourself to that future employer. Doing this is absolutely critical.

There are also some other unique ways to finding that career. You've got to spend some time with others who are in careers you want. Once you identify the career you want, start associating with people who have been successful in those areas. That makes sense, doesn't it? You could become a member of a trade association where you attend some meetings, or specific groups or business meetings. Find ways to be with people who are in those desired careers. Share with them, network with them. Develop a relationship with people who will help take you to that next level in your career.

Another avenue is to get some specific education or training in a new career. Find a mentor, a retiree, or someone you trust who's had solid career success—someone who can help be a mentor for what's next for your career. If you're seeking an executive or entrepreneurial opportunity, consider working with an association such as SCORE (www.score.org), which is comprised of retired executives who provide free coaching. Find someone who will be a good mentor to you and ask him or her to help.

Finally, it's important to be truthful in the process. Statistics show that resumes can be as inaccurate as 70 percent of the time, so don't take a chance on embellishing your resume to the point of it being untrue. If the truth came to light, it would destroy trust and it could also cost you the opportunity and your reputation.

WRIGHT

Well, Amy, you have worked with organizations and individuals to help them improve and plan for success with respect to succession planning, establishing career paths, and leadership development. What are the key components of your process that can help others achieve their career management goals?

LETKE

It's no secret that businesses are looking for goal-oriented people. Many organizations are very challenged to find people who can get the job done. This includes setting objectives and achieving those key goals. These same businesses are looking for positive, can-do, problem-solvers with winning mind-sets. These are all critical behaviors to businesses today and they make a huge difference in how someone is or is not selected for a job.

WRIGHT

What additional obstacles do you think an individual faces to helping him or her make long-term career management a success?

LETKE

Just because a person finds a great career doesn't mean it will last forever. The keys to successful career management are simple: you've got to manage your job, manage your boss, manage your peers and staff, care about those around you in a genuine manner, as well as the other things that I have discussed earlier.

WRIGHT

In summary, what key elements can our readers take away from this interview to help them achieve their goals in managing a successful, long-term, rewarding career?

LETKE

The key to career management is to recognize that it is not short-term. People must be intentional, even strategic, about managing their career. Just like anything else, whether it's getting your car maintained, covering your home with insurance, saving for retirement, having a great family life, or setting goals for your future. These are all important. Oftentimes I see people forget that managing a career is very critical to having a fulfilling and great life. Watch out for the pitfalls described in this chapter and work on developing the seven key steps to success.

Think about your answers to the following questions:

- What are you doing to manage relationships in a positive manner?

- What goals have you set to accomplish this? What contingency plans do you have to manage your career?
- Are you happy in your current employment situation and if not, what is your plan to fix it?

If you don't have these questions answered, then focus more on creating a written career management strategy and plan for yourself. If you have a family member who is struggling with career management, you can help that person, too. You can go to my Web site, amyletke.com, for additional information on career management and tools to help you get started to successfully manage your professional career.

WRIGHT

Today I have been talking with Amy Letke who believes you must continue to broaden your knowledge base and intentionally focus daily on managing your career, as well as keep up with the latest trends, strategies, and ideas to become a master of the "concrete jungle."

Amy, thank you.

LETKE

Thank you David! Here's to much success for our readers in achieving great results for personal satisfaction, thriving work, and successful long-term careers!

About the Author

Amy Newbanks Letke has more than twenty years' successful business experience as a successful human capital and leadership consultant who speaks to us from real-world, personally learned experiences. She has been a Fortune 500 executive, human capital strategist and consultant, business owner, and an entrepreneur. She has founded two companies, Integrity HR and HR Review LLC, a publishing firm for human capital and educational materials. Ms. Letke is a certified senior professional in human resources as well as a global professional. She is a successful business consultant and empowering international speaker on topics including developing superior leaders, success in goal-setting, successful job performance skills, recruitment and retention of top talent, and coaching for top performance. In addition to contributing to this book, she has also co-authored *ROADMAP to Success* in 2011 with well-known authors such as Deepak Chopra and Ken Blanchard.

Amy Newbanks Letke, SPHR, GPHR
Integrity HR, Inc./amyletke.com
2013 Frankfort Avenue
Louisville, KY 40206
877-753-0970
www.amyletke.com
www.integrityhr.com
info@amyletke.com

Chapter Six

Information Technology

An Interview With...

David Papp

DAVID WRIGHT (WRIGHT)

Today I'm talking to David Papp, author of *IT Survival Guide: Conquering Information Technology in your Organization*. He serves as a speaker and trainer on numerous technology topics. David is an international IT consultant with more than years' experience in IT systems. He earned his Computer Engineering Degree from the University of Alberta and holds many industry certifications. You can find him on the Web at, www.DavidPapp.com.

David, welcome to *Concrete Jungle: Survival Secrets for the Real World*.

DAVID PAPP (PAPP)

Thank you!

WRIGHT

So what does information technology mean for everyone?

PAPP

Information technology, IT, means different things to different people. For most business owners and leaders, IT equates to costs of operation. For an employee, IT refers to those frequent glitches that prevent tasks from getting done. I like to describe in easy-to-understand language exactly what information technology should mean and why it's important to organizations. In many respects I consider myself as a person who is capable of bridging that gap.

WRIGHT

So why is IT so important to the world?

PAPP

With the advent of the Internet, information became the most valuable commodity among businesses. Therefore, how information is managed, stored, communicated, distributed, and handled has become very important. If information technology systems are neglected, precious data could be lost and serious business setbacks could result. But if IT systems are thoughtfully considered, organizations can enjoy tremendous advantages ahead of the competition in both the short and long runs.

On the personal side, think about the growing data space demands we have at our own homes. Precious memories are now stored digitally. We have smart devices and cameras taking videos, which are commonly now all high definition (HD) resulting in very large data files. They are in different file formats. We have also larger and larger megapixel photos being taken by cameras and smart phones. We purchase digital copies of movies now instead of optical discs (DVDs). Our music is now all digital as well, no more discs (CDs). This results in huge amounts of data that now needs to be stored at your home. Most people haven't given any thought to how valuable this data is and what would happen if it was lost.

I have personally been contacted by many concerned people who have lost all of their irreplaceable pictures. Recently someone took many pictures at their daughter's wedding and left all of the pictures on the camera's memory card. They took that memory card into Walmart to get some prints made directly off the memory card. A few months later they went to access the card again from their computer and the card could not be read. They had not made any copies of all the electronic photo files—all was gone. We sent the card to a data recovery business and unfortunately nothing was recoverable. They were devastated!

Even if you did make a copy of all your data (home videos, movies, music, photos), where do you store them? What happens if there is a fire in your home? How much backup and archiving should you do? I feel if something is irreplaceable such as personal videos and photos, which are worthwhile memories, you should have an offsite copy. This could be as simple as having an additional copy made onto optical discs or portable external hard drives.

WRIGHT

So as a consultant, what do you think are the most common IT mistakes?

PAPP

In short, I would say the lack of planning. People don't ask themselves what would happen if they lost that data. They do not consider how valuable it is and if it can be replaced. Company executives don't often take the time to understand their company's IT systems. IT managers don't understand many of the tools and technologies available to them. They're all over the place. As a result, parts of the system are neglected and one by one, emergencies begin to develop. Before long, the organization's IT department is running from one fire to the next and they no longer have time to perform proper maintenance and planning. What I usually describe to most organizations is they're in firefighting mode and that's all they do. They're very reactive to issues as they arise. There is no proactive planning or maintenance occurring. In fact, there's no time for it.

This is where IT assessments or audits can be helpful. By having an outside consultant provide an overview of the current state of their IT system, high priority fixes and long-term strategies can get a company back on the right track.

WRIGHT

So when I come in in the morning if I want to find one of my clients or one of the thousands of prospects I've got, I have a system called ACT. Is that IT?

PAPP

Absolutely, and it's a very common one. So what's happened is you've put in a massive amount of hours into developing this custom database of information. This is your information and a huge investment. It is what you have created and without it you almost feel lost and can't operate your business. This is why we're saying that organizations and people who have irreplaceable digital files they consider valuable need to take proper precautions to ensure they're safeguarding the data. Are you backing it up properly and where are you placing it? For instance, are you keeping it all in the same location? What would happen if there was fire, flood or theft or some kind of natural disaster? Would you be completely lost or do you have a backup that is offsite?

The other problem we're running into is that many backups have a human component to them. It means you're relying on someone manually doing that backup for you. Very often we find that it doesn't happen on a regular basis as it should. Sometimes not at all! Other priorities come to mind and backups are quite low on the list.

The other issue we're running into is people don't test their backups. They have no idea if it is even there or of it works. Here is a scenario to think about: You've lost everything, the building burned down, and you have to reconstruct your ability to access your information in a new location. Most people do not even have the correct software or the right version of the software. They might have a backup of the data but they can't even access it. They don't even have a physical server to put it on. You must think through all the steps that are required to get your business up and running.

WRIGHT

I can answer yes to almost every question you asked and no to almost every question you asked. We did, in fact, lose all our information at one point. We then took those precautions you are now talking about. I couldn't agree with you more, having been on the bad side of that.

PAPP

Unfortunately it usually takes that negative experience in order to get someone to do something. In most situations it takes two bad experiences! They claim that most homeowners don't install an alarm system until they have broken into—twice!

WRIGHT

But you know what cost me the most money—the salaries of all the fifteen people who sat there for two weeks with nothing to do.

PAPP

Absolutely, that's a huge expense!

WRIGHT

As an owner or executive, why do I need to understand my company's IT if all is going well?

PAPP

If you don't understand your company's IT system, how do you know if things are going well? That's the question I would ask everyone. Unfortunately, the nature of information technology jargon is inherently complex; I often call it an alphabet soup. This alone can be very intimidating and by gaining a solid understanding, or even somewhat of an understanding of what your IT system can do for you, organizations and IT goals can be better aligned to achieve even greater success and greater efficiency. Productivity can be gained, resulting in greater profits. For the long run, proper maintenance and investments in your IT systems means less down time, less risk, and even less cost. Sometimes you don't even know what can really hurt you and in the information age, understanding your IT system could be a real asset.

WRIGHT

You were chosen for this book and your résumé is very interesting. Tell me more about yourself.

PAPP

For more than twenty years I've been consulting in information technology, as you stated. I own an IT firm and I have earned numerous industry certifications. I've also obtained a computer engineering degree. I love to speak and train people in technology-related topics. I host seminars and workshops. I find it very exciting as you indicated. I authored a book called the *IT Survival Guide: Conquering Information Technology in Organizations,* which is essentially a compilation of many of my observations and experiences during the past twenty-plus years.

After having been in the IT business for so many years, I began to notice patterns and trends. I feel like I'm an IT general contractor of sorts—I can see the forest from the trees. There aren't many people who can actually stand back and view IT as a whole.

IT is becoming such a very wide field that is has a huge number of sub-specializations that have been added. Many people are getting very proficient and very knowledgeable in certain areas but they have no understanding of how it relates or even affects the bigger picture. I'm finding that it helps to step back and observe how one area affects another. Frequently when you bring in a consultant, he or she can point something out and say, "Why is that light blinking red or amber? Is that normal?"

The reply is usually, "Oh! I didn't even notice that."

It turns out they've got a failed component in their IT system. Nobody either took the time to look things over or make any observations, or they became desensitized to it as they experience it day in and day out. They're in firefighting mode. Also, one easily becomes desensitized to one's own environment.

I would love people to be more open to the thought of engaging IT consultants and obtaining advice. It doesn't need to be expensive. Even only two hours can be very valuable. It is done regularly with other professions. Yet many organizations view IT as a big expense. They do not see IT as a critical component to their organization. It is part of the underlying foundation, and an enabler to help give the organization an edge.

Wright

You speak and write about IT assessments and audits. How helpful can they can be?

Papp

I feel many people have the "stuck-in-a-box" syndrome. They only experience the IT system of their own organization. Being an outside consultant, I have a huge number of benefits that I get to see inside many of these organizations' "boxes." I get to see what everyone is doing and how they're doing it. Everyone has different ideas and different ways they put everything together. I can share those observations—the good and the bad—with other organizations. This allows me to indicate if a combination doesn't work or if they have ever thought of implementing it another. Also, as an outside person, I can take a look at identifying things that you may not have noticed or perhaps have become desensitized to.

Personally this can be very valuable as well to have an outside opinion from someone knowledgeable in IT. Discuss with the person your current electronic needs (music, photos, videos), what you do, and suggestions for how to safeguard this data. For example, there are a number of online Internet-based backup providers. Several even provide free backup services up to certain amounts (e.g., www.mozy.com, www.idrive.com, and explore.live.com/skydrive).

WRIGHT

So where would someone even begin?

PAPP

As a business owner or executive there is a lot of value in bringing in someone for an outside opinion. The analogy would be other professions that are more mature, for example law, medicine, and accounting. It is expected that you go to a chartered accountant and get your books reviewed, or you go to a professional engineer to stamp a drawing of a bridge, or you go to a doctor and the doctor refers you to a specialist. It's the same thing with information technology.

I think that the IT field is very immature, it's very new. It's growing at an exponential rate and a lot of the best practices that other professions have are not in use. You should go out and get an expert opinion. It's not necessarily someone who is your uncle's neighbor whose son that is really good in computers. I'm talking about someone professional who does this as a living.

Knowing where to begin can be very overwhelming, but you can keep it simple by bringing in a consultant for what I call a discovery meeting. This should be a short two-hour meeting with no agenda, where some basic areas covered. It is a question-and-answer period where the consultant asks questions to paint the picture of what the organizations IT systems look like. Not everything will have an immediate answer. Certain areas may be focused more heavily based on the answer. The meetings are very organic. They usually help bring to surface unexpected areas of concern. The entire meeting might be sidetracked into a certain topic, but that's okay, it's just the first meeting.

As a result of that meeting, you're going to get some homework. I find that frequently in those discovery meetings it's very helpful to actually sketch out how the IT systems are related, what components are in play, and what your understandings are. It helps bring forth a lot of issues to surface, as many organizations don't have proper documentation. People are literally flying by the seat of their pants and they're in firefighting mode regarding their information technology. The documentation they have is several years old.

The discovery meeting will bring to surface a number of hot topics. Some might be immediate short-term issues and others that are longer-term. The discovery meeting also helps establish a new relationship between the organization and the consultant to see if there is a fit. When it comes to IT systems, you really need to trust the consultant, as you are divulging a lot of critical information about the way your organization is run. Many times it involves more access, user names, passwords, and knowledge than the owner or president of the company has. You really want to have a solid relationship in place with the consultant. These meetings helps determine if either want to move forward and in what capacity.

The other benefit from starting with an initial discovery meeting is due to most people not wanting to make a big investment. They don't have budget for this. They're worried this is going to cost a lot of money. You don't want someone coming to change everything. Having a two hour-meeting means paying a very minor consultation fee that many organizations use discretionary funds in order to initially pay. Then you can get a sense of feeling about whether or not you want to move forward.

WRIGHT

So can organizations conduct their own internal assessments?

PAPP

Unfortunately, there tends to be a gap between organizations, executives, and the IT staff. As I indicated before, consultants can help bridge that gap by helping everyone sit down to strategize together and understand each other.

One main problem I've run into with a lot of technology related personnel is their soft skills. Communication is always a critical component to success and this can be facilitated by a consultant who has an outside and objective view to help explain both sides. Having a snapshot view of where things are at and help create a baseline for comparison in the future. Even if you're not going to do anything based on that initial meeting, you've got something on record. This can be a baseline and if you decide to come back at some point in the future, you have something to measure against.

Identifying short-term and long-term needs, current vulnerabilities, and helping develop a strategic plan may require help. This is especially true if internal resources are concentrating on running the business and putting out fires. Having the important decision-makers present at the meeting is also very helpful, as you get a unified direction and it helps increase the productivity of the meeting.

Of course, the biggest challenge is the allocation of financial resources and a lot of IT departments find that to be quite the brick wall they run into. Having key decision-makers present helps greatly, as they gain understanding explained to them in a non-technical sense. One important document that can help put things into perspective is creating a disaster recovery plan.

WRIGHT

Explain to our readers what that is.

PAPP

The disaster recovery plan is probably the most important, as it helps address short-term crises that are acute and potentially catastrophic to an organization.

Response time, disaster detection, and resource allocation are just a few of the hot topics that need to be addressed as part of the disaster recovery plan, frequently referred to as the DRP. Unfortunately, most organizations don't have such a plan. The DRP helps identify unknown weaknesses in the IT system and also strongly helps documenting what's currently in place.

For example, I had a client, a company that had more than twelve thousand people on its payroll. The employees were all out in the field. This was at a time when it was difficult to hire people. It was of critical importance to never miss a pay run. If they missed one, people were sure to walk. Those were the types of workers they had in their employment.

We ensured that part of their disaster recovery plan was hosted at an alternate geographic site, somewhere away from their main location. Their entire accounting system was replicated offsite including physically having a printer with some checks.

In the event that something happened, it can be difficult to gain access to your own financial resources. Having all that in place is something you need to think about right down to whom you call, which manufacturers you call, what equipment you have and model numbers, and their serial numbers. You also need to know if they are on warranty, where you call for that, a list of 24/7 phone numbers?

This brings forth a lot of questions you might not have asked or that you might have taken for granted. They are brought to the surface and you must decide whether or not you want to deal with it. We call that risk analysis or risk management; you're deciding what the amount of risk is if data is lost and how much time you can be without it.

A few years ago, a person could be without e-mail for a week, it was no big deal. Now I have many clients who cannot live without it! If they're without e-mail for a day it's almost a disaster in itself. All communication is done that way and some organizations can attribute actual dollars lost due to missing a piece of equipment or someone's time. As your experience shows it is costly to shift workers from billable work to non-billable work because you had to reconstruct valuable data.

WRIGHT

When you mention e-mail, parts of the Internet are actually parts of your IT.

PAPP

Absolutely. The Internet is definitely part of your IT infrastructure and your disaster recovery plan. It's a key part of the overall IT system. It is your communication path to the outside world, such as for e-mail. Perhaps you need it to access outside services such as banking, databases, and payroll. Perhaps it is being used as part of your backup strategy for synchronizing files to an external location. A disaster recovery plan should take the Internet connection strongly into consideration.

WRIGHT

What else would you consider to be an urgent area to investigate?

PAPP

One of the first things I ask about when I conduct an assessment are the details behind the data backups and archiving. Many business executives and IT managers have a poor understanding of the difference between the two. Backups are constant copies of your IT system files. It should be a perpetual, ongoing backup and continually gets overwritten with the latest files. An archive is a snapshot of your data at a particular point in time.

For example, it's what your ACT database with all your contacts contained on December 31, 2011. That would be an archived copy that you perhaps run for yearend purposes. You might also need to know what your financial data looks like on particular dates. We call these archives.

The interesting thing with backups is that problems can manifest themselves without anyone noticing. Backups allow you instant file replacements in case you have an IT disaster. However, what happens if you have a problem in that data itself? Let's say you deleted an important contact from ACT database or something corrupted. You wouldn't realize this until you tried to access that particular data. Two months later you decide to look up some information regarding a particular client and it is no longer there or accessible. The information would be gone in your backups, as your backups keep overwriting themselves to make sure that you have the most current representation of all your data. An archive however, would have saved you in that instance because you could go back in time. You might remember having accessed that data three months ago and you could retrieve it from an archive made at that point.

Having everything stored onsite can be a huge problem as well. You should have some geographical redundancy. Not testing your backups can be a huge problem; it can be a fatal mistake.

I had one client, a law enforcement agency, where they had been working on a case file for more than three years. They had been religiously doing their backups every single day. However, they never tested it. There came a very unfortunate day when their main server died and when they tried to recover from their backups, everything had been corrupted! They weren't able to retrieve *any* of the information. They had to hire an entire room full of people for many months to reconstruct the information from all the files, get it back into the system, and all before a deadline had approached for court.

You absolutely have to decide how important your information is.

Organizations must decrease risk and assess what's being done and how it's being verified. You can't rely on a single process or single individual. You must rotate between two or more different processes and individuals to create a better failsafe. You should have a double-checking system in place where perhaps you alternate every week, which helps keep everyone honest.

WRIGHT

Is there anything else that our readers need to know?

PAPP

Nothing is 100 percent perfect. There is no such thing as a perfect environment or a perfect IT system. There is always room for improvement. Whether or not you want to do it, or if it's even economically feasible based on the risk analysis you have done, is up to you. It's important to have an open mind and to listen to other ideas and suggestions that are brought forth. I find that many people are very closed-minded about IT and they're happy with their environment. They don't want to share information and they don't want anyone pointing out that there might be a better way of doing something. Egos can get in the way. You really do need to admit when you don't know something. You should want help researching and being open to better solutions and other methods.

Here's a list of ten important questions I would probably ask my own IT department in order to avoid some kind of IT catastrophe:

Have recent IT system warning signals been ignored?
Do IT managers receive ongoing training?
Where are backups and archives stored?
Where are key resources and personnel located?
What happens if there is an IT disaster after hours?

What documentation system is in place and where is it stored?
Are power system backups in place?
How often are updates performed?
Are we losing clients due to IT malfunctions?
How often are outside IT assessments and audits arranged?

If these questions aren't asked, organizations will find themselves constantly addressing emergency after emergency. They'll be in firefighting mode. Instead of having invested time and other resources into core business strategies, they waste them on what seems to be perpetual IT problems. IT encompasses a very wide range of things out there. Not only does it include e-mail and the Internet, but think about your own phone system. Most phone systems in organizations now are running on their networks. They are no longer the traditional telephones connected to phone lines; but rather, they are integrated to run on your own data network.

I find technology is very fascinating. I love that it is constantly changing and there is always something new, and a better way of doing it. However, on that note, it means you need to keep up and you need to admit that there is just absolutely no way that you're going to know it all. In fact, the adage is true: the more you know, the more you realize how much you don't know. This is so true for IT.

WRIGHT

What a fascinating subject, and what an informative conversation. I've been taking notes here so that I can double-check our IT processes.

David, thank you for your time and for answering these vital questions. This chapter may help many of our readers to realize the importance of this topic.

PAPP

You're welcome. I definitely enjoy this; it's a topic I have made my career out of.

WRIGHT

Today I have been talking with David Papp. David is the author of *IT Survival Guide: Conquering Information Technology in Your Organization.*

He is an international IT consultant and he has more than twenty years of experience in IT systems. I think we have found out today that he has used those twenty years wisely.

David thank you so much for being with us today on *Concrete Jungle: Survival Secrets for the Real World.*

PAPP

You're welcome! I always enjoy discussing anything about technology.

ABOUT THE AUTHOR

David Papp, author of IT Survival Guide: Conquering Information Technology in your Organization, is a passionate, dynamic speaker and trainer on numerous technology topics. He serves to entertain and educate. David is an international IT consultant with more than twenty years' experience in IT systems. He earned his computer engineering degree from the University of Alberta and holds many industry certifications.

David Papp
Box 3642
Sherwood Park, AB T8H2T4
Canada
780-951-4869
David@DavidPapp.com
www.DavidPapp.com

CHAPTER SEVEN

Navigating the Relation-Net™:

Surviving or Thriving

An Interview With...

Dr. Lorraine Edey

DAVID WRIGHT (WRIGHT)

Today I'm talking with Dr. Lorraine Edey. Lorraine is a nationally recognized relationship coach and speaker. She is also co-author of *Wake Up Women: Be Healthy, Be Happy, Be Wealthy,* number seven on the Barnes and Nobles best seller list. She is a contributing author to *Life on Your Terms and Becoming a Wealthy Woman.* Dr. Edey is host of the *Married Again Radio Talk Show* that focuses on helping second and subsequent marriages thrive rather than end up in yet another divorce. Dr. Edey's innovative coaching methods have helped couples attain the next level of marriage mastery and enjoy a new love mind-set.

Dr. Edey, welcome to *Concrete Jungle.*

LORRAINE EDEY (EDEY)

Thank you, I'm really excited to be a part of this book. It resonates for me.

WRIGHT

Great, I'm so glad you chose to be a part of this project.

How did you begin speaking and why did you choose relationships as your main topic?

EDEY

I believe that we teach what we need to learn, and I chose relationships because they have been a challenge and a blessing in my life.

My own personal experiences as a child growing up in an alcoholic family, being taken away from my family of origin, and living in foster homes led me to see the value of relationships. My journeys through three marriages help me better understand myself and the true meaning and importance of relationships. My passion has been to help others heal and understand themselves through relationships, so I developed and trained with world renowned relationship experts, including Harvelle Hendrix, John Gray, and John Gottman.

I came to understand that we cannot survive without relationships. To show you how powerful relationships are, I want to share with you some examples of just how significant our relationships can be.

The article read: (sisters) Patricia and Joan Miller lived for nearly forty years in South Lake Tahoe, but after they shunned their neighbors, their shared life ended in a mysterious double death. Police found one sister in a bedroom and the other in a hallway during a routine welfare check on February 26 [2012]. They were seventy-three years old and the police did not suspect foul play; their home was clean and in order and it didn't appear that there was any dementia or any health issues. What police suspect is that one died first, and since they [had] lived together for so long, the other died as well. *(Huffington Post,* June 6, 2012, Cristina Silva)

I've heard repeatedly about couples who share their lives for years and when one dies the other one goes as well.

The New York Times featured an article about a couple who were married for seventy-two years. The article read: Gordon and Norma Leger married in 1939. They spent their whole lives hating to be apart and, following a car accident on October 12, the couple died in the hospital within seventy minutes of one another while holding hands in the Intensive Care Unit.

The last couple I want to mention was from Kingston, Washington. They died six hours apart. They were married for sixty-two years.

Of course we don't have to die to have close, intimate, loving relationships. A couple married earlier this year is an example: she was 100 years old and he was 85. I guess you are never too old!

According to the American Community Survey report, the overall national rates of marital events for men in 2009 were 19.1 marriages, 9.2 divorces. The overall national rates of marital events for women in 2009 were 17.6 marriages, 9.7 divorces. (*The statistics are based on marriage, divorce, and widowhood rates per one thousand men and women aged fifteen and older in the United States).*

These statistics show relationships matter to people, and my mission is to support those who want to master their relationships. This is the reason I began speaking, and what better topic than one I can learn the most from—relationships.

WRIGHT

So you say you grew up in the concrete jungle. How would you define concrete jungle?

EDEY

I grew up on the streets of New York City, better known as "the concrete jungle." The concrete jungle *is* New York City. By definition, a concrete jungle is a city with large modern buildings that are perceived as dangerous and unpleasant, where there is intense competition and struggle for survival. In New York, you either make it or you don't. It's a fast-paced, stressful, competitive environment and is called the "rat race" by many. People come to New York with big dreams and have made it, while others have come here and failed.

The hustle and bustle of New York City has long been hailed in songs like those by Frank Sinatra, Tony Bennett, and Jay-Z, to name a few. It is a city known to awaken its journeyers' deepest desires and longing to survive.

There is, however, another part of the concrete jungle that is also there but no one sees because of the brick and mortar. There are creatures that dwell within the concrete jungle that have built their homes and have become the very fabric of the city.

I use concrete jungle as a metaphor for my life—a life that has been challenged, I did not know one day to the next how I would survive, that is, having my basic human needs met. I've had a life filled with excitement, joy, fear, and danger, only to resonate with the song "I Will Survive." I have not only survived, I have learned through survival to thrive.

The concrete jungle is that place of surviving and thriving. I decided to write about relationships evolving or thriving, connecting to that relation-net™ where we helped each other to survive as well as thrive.

WRIGHT

So what do you mean by connecting to the relation-net?

EDEY

The relation-net is a phrase I coined to mean that which supports us in body, mind, and spirit, that allows us to navigate through life with a sense of safety and security, knowing that we are not alone.

My teacher and mentor, Hedy Schleifer, said, "Human beings need each other for the ultimate development of their potential."

Relation-net means those relationships that will develop throughout our lives that are significant and important to us. We can use those relationships—that net—as a safety net. The 'Net will help us to thrive and grow; however, we must pick our relationships intentionally in order to create the safety we desire. It is said that everything happens in seasons in our lives, so the relation-net is a mechanism for picking those individuals who are going to be vital to our growth and development. We have the relation-net for those dark times in our lives—times when we feel we are not going to make it or times when we are depressed. There are times when there might be a trauma in our lives—a family member dies, a friend dies, a child is sick, a husband is ill, or the loss of our livelihood. Having a relation-net, we know we have a safety net, we know we have someplace to go, and we know that we're not alone.

For example, imagine for a moment that you are walking on a tight-rope, step by step, slowly, and balanced. You focus on your balance and know that is the way you will reach your destination; however, you also know that you have a net, and that net is there to protect you and basically save your life if you were to fall. This is what the relation-net is about—having that safety-net of people in our lives so that when we are off-balance and fall, we have the protection and security that we will be all right. We will have a sense of being cared for and protected, that there is something or someone looking out for us.

The concept of the relation-net is that every relationship is a system. The system can include family, friends, husband, wife, lover, children, and community. It may be open and loving, or controlling and unloving. This system can begin early, sometimes within the first minutes or days of meeting an individual or it can take time to cultivate the system. No matter how it happens, it can be a part of our growth and experience.

Technology has developed a sophisticated relation-net. Mark Zuckerberg was a sophomore at Harvard University. He wanted to stay connected with his Harvard students, so he developed Facebook as a way to keep in touch by way of the Internet. It was also a way for students to get to know one another. Facebook became an overnight success, and the rest is history. It is now a supplicated relationship system connecting people all over the world.

People now connect through this system known as social networking, which includes LinkedIn, Twitter, Google, and a host of other systems. I would like to call them relationship networking because, after all, it began for the sole purpose of keeping people connected to one another, as well as developing relationships.

Here is an example of how this social networking system operates: I received an e-mail from an unknown individual, asking me if I was the Lorraine Edey who lived on 134th Street in Manhattan, New York. She was asking because her father, Louis, who was my first boyfriend, was looking for me. And so the relation-net, as I like to call it, brought us together after fifty years.

Do relationships matter? You betcha! Could this social networking thing cause problems for people? Yes, so proceed with caution. My situation turned out to be wonderful; however, not every situation does, so proceed with extreme care.

There are multitudes of ways we can keep our relation-net active. One net, that continues in spite of the social networking, is our community relationship. We now have groups such as “Meet-Up,” and a host of support groups such as Alcoholics Anonymous, Overeaters Anonymous, cancer survivors groups, and so many more. They are a type of family system or brother/sisterhood that can develop and support us as well as help us to thrive.

The relation-net is like a rhythm of relationships, with ebbs and flows of challenges, individuals who come and go, and ultimately our relationship to ourselves. And so the relation-net includes learning how to navigate through systems—relational systems—in which we can thrive and grow.

WRIGHT

So what is the difference between surviving and thriving in relationships?

EDEY

That's an excellent question. The *Merriam-Webster Dictionary* defines survival as: "to remain alive or in existence: live on and to continue to function." Thriving is defined as: "to grow vigorously, flourish and to gain in wealth or possessions."

Surviving and thriving are significantly different, even in the area of energy. When we are surviving, we are living our lives unconsciously—we are living a more primitive life.

Now imagine for a moment that you have a plant in your home, and you water that plant every week. It's there, and the plant looks nice, but you're not even aware of how that plant really is—you just keep it alive, you water it, and maybe if you remember, you feed your plant once or twice a year. Now imagine how much that plant adds to your home, to your environment—the oxygen, the energy, and nourishment. It brings beauty to your home, and when you look at it you see vibrant colors and you smile as you smell the fragrance. This is when you realize that this plant is alive, and because of this you feel alive. This is the difference between surviving and thriving in our relationships.

When surviving, we walk around unconscious in our relationships, just doing day-to-day tasks and routines like the movie *Groundhog Day*. We are living in quiet desperation. We function from our primitive brain (amygdala), which keeps us living in the past and in fear.

When we're thriving in our relationships, we're conscious and we're connected, aware of the connections we have with others and ourselves, and are willing participants in this journey called life.

WRIGHT

Do you think people are aware that they're surviving and not thriving?

EDEY

No, survival is a basic human need. It is a natural state and a more primitive way of functioning in the world. Businessballs.com states that, according to Maslow's Hierarchy of Needs, we must satisfy each need in turn, starting with the most obvious for self-survival—biological and physiological needs such as food and drink. Those are the things we need to survive. This is just the beginning, however, because once those basic needs are met we can begin to grow and develop into a more actualized individual. When we are self-actualized, that is when we are thriving.

WRIGHT

So how would you define a healthy relationship?

EDEY

A study conducted at Kansas University revealed that people with healthy relationships really do have more happiness and less stress. The definition of health is: "Soundness of body or mind; freedom from disease or ailment." The definition for relationship is: "The state of connected or related." Keeping in mind the word "healthy" has within it the word "heal," I see a healthy relationship as one that is healing to the soul—one where we connect with another in body, mind, and spirit; one in which we are able to grow and flourish. There are many qualities we can bring to a healthy relationship—respect, love, trust, understanding value and sharing.

In a healthy relationship we feel secure and happy when we're together, and we have a good sense of well-being that the relationship is wealthy. We're inspired by each other to fulfill our dreams. We are living a life of interdependency, which allows us to thrive as a couple as well as an individual.

WRIGHT

What do you think are the biggest obstacles people face in trying to have a healthy relationship?

EDEY

The top three obstacles people face in trying to have a healthy relationship are communication, finances, and sex. I have worked with couples for the past twenty-plus years, and the main complaint couples bring to the counseling session is, "We are not communicating." This is an umbrella for a multitude of challenges that individuals and couples face when they are attempting to cultivate healthy relationship.

Communication is the key component in developing a healthy relationship. That being said, it is important for us to learn to communicate effectively so that we listen, so that we can hear what the other person is truly saying to us. Developing the skill of listening is an effective key.

As an Imago Therapist, I have taught couples as well as individuals the "dialogue." This process was developed by Harvelle Hendrix, PhD, and Helen LaKelly Hunt, PhD, who coined the phrase *Imago,* which means "image," and is a process for working with individuals, couples, families, children, and co-workers who desire to enhance their relationships.

The process is as follows:

Listen: As the person speaks, agree to listen without interrupting until he or she pauses or until you ask him or her to pause.

Mirror: "What I heard you say is—" Repeat back everything your partner says without significantly adding to or taking away from it. Paraphrasing is fine, but be careful *not to send* while in the Receiver role. The magic of dialogue lies in allowing the Sender to be *completely* in charge of where the conversation goes. Once you ask a question or insert a comment or tone of voice not sent by the Sender, the dialogue is now about your agenda, not theirs.

Check it out: "Did I hear that?" Or, "Did, I get you?" Check to make sure you correctly mirrored all that the individual said. If the individual you are speaking with clarifies or corrects something, listen, then mirror again. Continue until the individual says you got it.

Ask for more: "Is there more?" If the individual adds more, mirror, check it out, and then ask, "Is there more?" again. Repeat until the person you are speaking to says there's no more.

Summarize: If a lot has been said, summarize. "If I got it all—" Check for completeness. "Did I get it all?" Mirror any additions the individual may have made.

Validate: "You (or what you've said,) make(s) sense to me because—" Validate the *content* of what the individual is saying. Remember, validation is not about agreement. Rather, it is about letting the other know that what he or she is saying makes sense from his or her point of view. ("I can see how when I didn't speak to you after I came home last night, you thought I was mad at you. That makes sense.")

If something the individual you are speaking with says doesn't make sense, ask him or her to help you understand by asking the person to say more about that. "Help me understand; would you say more about—"

Empathize: "I can imagine that you might be feeling—[angry, hurt, scared, frustrated]." To empathize means to imagine what another person is feeling about what he or she is saying or experiencing. Feelings can be distinguished from thoughts in that feelings can generally be described in one word: hurt, excited, hopeful, and so on.

(The "Dialogue" excerpt taken from *Getting the Love You Want,* by Harvelle Hendrix).

The money conversation is power-packed, and relationships suffer when one is unable to talk about money in a way that the individual is not blamed or shamed. Money is very often the main reason for disputes in relationships. People would rather discuss sex before they will reveal how much money they make.

Couples need to feel safe in their relationship in order to talk about sex, understanding that sex is not just about intercourse, it is about intimacy. The word *intimacy,* broken down, is "in to me see." When we are in a relationship and are having sex without allowing ourselves to be seen, or the other person to see us, we create a wall. Conversations about needs and wants related to sex are important; using the "dialogue" will help to create a sacred space for this to happen.

The key to a lasting relationship is making sure that you listen, set time aside for one another without any interference, look for the good in the other person, and let your mate or family member know daily how much you value him or her and how important that person is to you. This helps to resolve any obstacles and allows for the dialogue process to help you create the relationship of your dreams.

WRIGHT

You talk about the importance of relationships in our lives and how relationships were important to you in your life. Who are some of the individuals who influenced your life?

EDEY

I have been blessed with many positive influences in my life. As I reflect on your question, the one that comes to my mind immediately is my mother. I came to appreciate her later in life, for she was way ahead of her time. She worked in a factory for forty years and was the "shop steward" for one of the most powerful unions in America, the Teamster Union. She held that position for more than thirty-five years.

She was a role model for me in how to "swim with the sharks," be adventurous, and have a good work ethic.

The other powerful role model was Aunt Lil. I was five years old when my mother and father separated; my father was an alcoholic and my mother knew enough to get out of that situation. However, she had to find a job and work, so she found a place for my brother and me to live in the Catskill Mountains. The woman I later came to know as Aunt Lil, fostered children.

Aunt Lil was another woman who was ahead of her time. When I met her she was forty years old, had just married, and had her own business. She purchased fifty acres of land and developed a program for the children she fostered. Aunt Lil was a teacher and a very spiritual woman. She taught me everything I know about spirituality. She taught me how to cook, how to sew, and the basic foundations that I needed for life. Through Aunt Lil I learned how to create the relation-net. In her home there were always people who loved her and thrived in her teachings.

My paternal grandmother was an entrepreneur. She was another whose teachings led me to create the relation-net. Like Aunt Lil, my grandmother had people in her home. She helped people in the community financially and spiritually, and fed them if they were hungry. I recall people coming and going as she was busy selling her products and filling orders.

WRIGHT

So what helped you to thrive in your relationships?

EDEY

Thriving for me was a long process because there were dark times in my life. I had a substance abuse problem and I wound up hitting bottom. What helped me to survive this ordeal was the spiritual journey I embarked on and the people I began to meet helped me to increase my self-esteem and self-worth. I began thriving when I went back to school and pursued my education. I graduated from undergraduate, then graduate, then doctorate programs. It was a struggle. I was responsible for raising two adolescents with little or no help from their father. I was basically a single parent, working two and sometimes three jobs, and going to school. I was fortunate to have many individuals who were instrumental in helping me to thrive. It was as though each step had been put there for me as steppingstones. Each person was a steppingstone, and each helped me to move from surviving to thriving.

Individual therapy was another way I learned how to thrive. I had different role models—teachers I would read about. They include: Gandhi and teachers like Raymond Charles Barker, Eric Butterworth, and Tony Robbins. Even at that time, these individuals taught me that there is more, I am more, and I can be more.

WRIGHT

So what is the message you want people to hear so they can learn from your relationship journey?

EDEY

Having a relationship with yourself is so important, and to get to know yourself intimately is also important. Before having people in your life you know will build that relation-net for you, it's important that you get to know yourself.

Do things that help you to feel good about yourself. Then, if something terrible happens in your life, you won't feel fragmented—you won't fall apart.

Build your relation-net, one relationship at a time. Get to know many people and then pick individuals who resonate for you. Pick individuals you feel would be trustworthy—worthy of your trust.

Nurture your relation-net, take time to call people, to speak with them, to make sure that they know you care about them.

Family can be a part of that relation-net; however, some family members may not be the right pick. That doesn't mean that you don't love them, it just means you love them from a distance,

Remember you're a whole person, so take care of your body, mind, and spirit. You are here to thrive, to live your life to its fullest, "Dance like no one is watching, sing like everyone can hear you, and dream like there are no limits to what or who you can be."

WRIGHT

What are the steps or actions that our readers can take in order to have a healthy relationship and thrive?

EDEY

We can begin by picking our relationships consciously. Take time to talk and to listen. Be clear about your wants and needs. As I mentioned, I am a Certified Imago Therapist, and Imago is one of the therapies that can help to develop that bridge in relationships.

Use the "dialogue" script in this chapter. Practicing daily will help you perfect your communication skills.

One of the keys for a lasting relationship is spending quality time together. Plan to do this weekly.

Have a relationship plan. That means put something in place that really speaks to the things you are going to do to make your relationship better or to enhance your relationship. Follow the plan. It will show your partner that you are committed to the relationship and that you are serious about making changes that will deepen your connection.

Get the help and support you need to work through any relationship challenges you may be having. As a relationship coach and therapist, I am available to serve you or to make referrals.

WRIGHT

Well, what a great conversation. I really enjoyed the information you shared today and I've learned a lot as well.

EDEY

Well, thank you. I enjoy talking about relationships. They're so important to our existence. We cannot survive without relationships and we cannot thrive without loving people in our lives—that is what the relation-net is for.

WRIGHT

I appreciate you taking all this time with me to answer these questions today; it really has been enlightening.

EDEY

Thank you so much.

WRIGHT

Today I've been talking with Dr. Lorraine Edey. She has told us about relationship thriving rather than just surviving and connecting to the relation-net. Dr. Edey is a nationally recognized relationship coach and speaker who focuses on helping second and subsequent marriages thrive rather than end up in yet another divorce. Her innovative coaching methods have helped couples attain their next level of marriage mastery and enjoy a new love mind-set.

Dr. Edey, thank you so much for being with us today on *Concrete Jungle.*

EDEY

Thank you so much; it's been a joy.

About the Author

Dr. Lorraine Edey earned her Bachelor of Psychology degree at the College of New Rochelle in New York, and her Master of Social Work from New York University. She earned her Doctor of Philosophy degree from Westbrook University in Aztec, New Mexico.

Throughout her twenty-five-year career, she has continued her education through certification and enrichment programs that make her uniquely qualified to work with married again couples. She is a Certified Imago Therapist, focusing on communication in relationships to discover and resolve conflict. She is also certified as a Relationship Therapist and Relationship Coach, and a Prepare-Enrich Facilitator, having been certified to utilize the leading relationship inventory assessment tool for couples.

Her experience includes more than twenty years of couples and relationship therapy as a psychotherapist, training as a family therapist at Albert Einstein Hospital at The Minuchin Center for the Family, and conducting workshops and teleclasses on relationships for singles and couples.

An author and speaker, Lorraine has presented programs for the New York City Committee on Women and Alcoholism, the American College of Nurse-Midwives, the New York City Board of Education, Girl Scouts Council of Greater New York, Inc., Federal Emergency Management, Emory School of Business, and Bank of America, among others.

Her articles have appeared in *Connection Magazine, Orlando Life Magazine,* and *Natural Awakenings Magazine.* Lorraine co-authored the book, *Wake Up Women: Be Happy, Healthy and Wealthy,* which, at the time of this writing, has reached number seven on the Barnes & Noble best seller list.

She is the host of *Married Again Radio Talk Show,* a weekly radio program helping couples and singles who have been previously married to develop strategies for a new love mind-set and to create the relationships they have always dreamed of. Lorraine has co-hosted several radio and television programs providing advice on managing your money and relationships.

Lorraine Edey, LCSW, PhD, ACC

Second Time Around Love
PO Box 1779
Jasper, GA 30143
678-454-1272
loridey@aol.com
www.secondtimearoundlove.com
www.coachinginspirations.com

Chapter Eight
Inspired Time Management

An Interview With...

Annette Denk

David Wright (Wright)

Today I am talking with Annette Denk. Annette is a professional business coach, keynote speaker, Life Coach, and Founder of Profocus Coaching. She has more than thirty-four years of business experience and has been extremely successful.

Annette, welcome to *Concrete Jungle.*

Wright

I would like to talk today about time management.

What would you say is the biggest contributor to your success?

Annette Denk (Denk)

Time management is a big part of my success. I grew up in Europe, in a household that was super organized. I must admit, my parents—especially my mother—were a big influence. It was instilled in me at a young age that you first always do your homework and then you play. Being orderly, organized, and striving for perfectionism was really engrained into me.

In my eyes, there was not even a choice, I did not even believe in a choice. I had to work hard to deserve free time and be disciplined to do that, otherwise I would be considered a failure. I grew up knowing that when you give your word or commit to something, even to yourself, there was no going back. You had to do it, no matter what.

I came to Canada at age seventeen, not knowing English. I had to find work and work very hard to support a husband through seven years of professional school. I took evening classes and believed I could succeed in anything I put my heart into. I also wanted to prove I could make it in this new country. I found the first three years very hard, being away from home at a young age, and not having a support system. But it made me stronger. I believe that everybody has great potential and can achieve anything they want.

WRIGHT

What obstacles did you overcome and how does overcoming them relate to time management?

DENK

One of my bigger challenges was that I was sometimes too driven. Time management is not just about being organized, disciplined, and focused. I had all that, but I had no balance. I thought I had to be a superwoman to fit into this world. My day was packed; even wasting fifteen minutes was a misuse of my time. I understand that when clients deal with perfectionism, strictness, diligence, and fastidiousness, they then become slaves to themselves and are not happy. They need to look at time management in a different way. They need to learn how to achieve more in less time and have time for themselves. They need to work smarter, not harder.

With time, I learned all that. My upbringing and the instilled values helped me a lot. As a child, I would not have gotten away with being untidy and not having pride in my school work. Teachers' expectations were high, which raised my own expectations of myself. I learned at a young age that setting priorities, being organized, and working hard is a way of life.

Today, most children don't grow up in this kind of strict environment with these kinds of high standards and expectations. A lot of the time, things are given to children without their having to earn them. Having just a good enough attitude makes them unable to develop a drive of high expectations for themselves.

I had my first job at age fourteen. I worked behind a concession stand at a beach resort. Upper class kids are supposed to enjoy their summers with fun activities, but what do they really get out of that? Both my children had their first summer jobs at age fifteen and from then on every summer. Starting that young teaches how to manage time, and time off is much more valued.

For many years I have been a single mom, where only through great time management skills was I able to achieve what I needed to accomplish. Having the pressure of suddenly being the major breadwinner, paying bills for three, and being there emotionally and financially for my children was not easy.

Even though it was often very difficult, I see challenges as growth. If you can see adversity as learning and growing opportunities, you are already ahead of the game. Friends admired me and colleagues wondered how I became so successful in my business, most recently as a top producing Realtor—in the Top 2 percent in North America in my company. Mentoring and coaching became natural to me.

So, I had many obstacles in my life—more than I've mentioned—but moving to a new country, learning the language, becoming a single mom, starting all over again, and becoming highly successful were my major challenges.

WRIGHT

What helped you the most?

DENK

I would say integrity. True integrity is keeping your commitment to yourself, not just others. This is very important, not just for good time management, but for many other things in life. Self-esteem and confidence on the outside begins with integrity on the inside. When our daily actions are in concert with our core values and deepest beliefs, then you want to stay true to your beliefs and you have high standards and morals.

Again, that is part of a European upbringing. In my family, we could never be late for a dinner invitations, actually the opposite, we had to be three to five minutes early. Being late would show you are not organized, you don't control your time, and others would look down at you. So you made very sure that you were always on time, no matter what. Showing up late would show a weakness and would not be acceptable !

Discipline leads to integrity and freedom. Having that choice gives you personal power. Every choice we make will have consequences for good or bad. Our lives are based on our choices and we have that control.

Our lives deliver on the choices we make—good or bad. Learning how to say no is also a choice.

Planning your life, staying on track, growing, and being focused is achieved through structure and good habits. Who we become is always more valuable than what we get from it. We sometimes forget that.

When I was in my later years of elementary school, I had to learn how to plan out my week, I had to have a handwritten schedule showing all my classes, Monday through Friday. I had a written schedule of when I had my lunch hour, when I had after-school activities, when I had homework time, and when I had play time. I had to stick to that schedule and if something changed, I had to rewrite it. Time management lessons and integrity started at an early age. I remember that I did not want to rewrite my schedule often, so I stuck as much as I could to my original timetable. In those days we had no computers, so rewriting my schedule was done by hand.

WRIGHT

How do you define great time management and why is it so important?

DENK

I define time management as having the power to maximize your results with the least amount of energy and time. It also means being structured, organized, and highly successful in your business and personal life with a happy balance.

Time management is *really a misconception*. We can't really manage our time, we only can *manage ourselves*, and that is the biggest challenge we face. Most people think that time management is scheduling and being organized, but it is really how we handle and control ourselves. It is not just a nine-to-five job and trying to be better at work—it is how we are successful also in our personal life. Do we have balance and happiness? Do we have time for recreation such as sports and yoga? Do we have time for our kids and spouse, time for family times, holidays, meeting that deadline at work, and finding inner peace doing it all?

Most people float through the day dealing with day-to-day things as they come up instead of truly looking ahead at their day or week to see what they want to achieve, planning it properly, and accomplishing what they set out to do. Great time management is a constant evolving process where you learn about yourself, grow, and become a better person with it. In short, great time management makes your life better.

I gave a talk to a group of approximately fifty businesspeople, and when I asked who sticks to a daily schedule and has set goals, only a third of the room raised their hands. I was really surprised and it showed me how we need better time management habits.

Time management is not just planning your day—it is planning weeks and months ahead, having goals, and knowing how to get there. Once you have made the changes you need to make and they become part of you without thinking about it, you have evolved, improved, and know how to manage your time and life better. It will not happen by just reading these words in this chapter, but it will happen when you challenge yourself to change and improve.

For me, creating that balance was sometimes very hard. When you are in high stress situations in your business or personal life, you need to strive for balance to make life more fun. You need to look after yourself.

Often we forget to make time to recharge, to make us feel good, to take time out. Our world is so fast-paced, it is often a challenge to manage all of our endeavors. When the first fax machine came out, I remember thinking that sending letters would be so much faster and easier. Then the Internet came and we believed it would improve our lives tremendously. Well, in a way it has, but it has also taken us to expecting immediate or fast feedback from everybody. If you do not respond to e-mails within the same day, people think you are lazy or disorganized.

People expect a split-second response from you—instantly returned phone calls, and staying ahead of everybody else. So how do we deal with all that pressure pleasing the boss or clients, pleasing our friends and loved ones? Do we please ourselves? Or, if you are a person thinking mostly of yourself, where does that leave the rest? How do we win?

Clients in my coaching practice often come to me with feelings of being overwhelmed and not knowing how to deal with all the demands in their life. Or if they are self-employed, they want to know how to not work all the time. The business is running them, they are not running the business. They feel guilty if they take a day off, guilty if they don't get back to their clients right away, guilty if they miss their kids' soccer game, guilty if they can't make their deadline. They're stressed, stuck, and feeling snowed under.

WRIGHT

What is your advice for those who are overwhelmed?

DENK

Most people have habits that have them just spinning their wheels. They then find they can't get out from under those habits. They have been doing it the same way for years and don't know how to change things. They want to know how to move forward with a different, new approach.

When I evaluate clients, I look at all aspects of their lives, from their career, health, fun, and recreation, to their family/spouse situation, happiness with money, personal growth, and physical environment. What are they really looking for? Sometimes they know, sometimes they don't, but they know they want a more fulfilling life. They have trouble making it happen, they know they are not living and performing at their full potential, they lack clarity and focus, and they want to feel inspired, confident, and happy. They want to feel better physically, become closer to others, get on their path, eliminate stress, increase their quality of life, and be successful in their job.

True time management looks at all of these things. It is a personal process and it takes commitment to change. We have to step up and become our own leader. Leadership starts with leading ourselves first. Priorities and how we set them is very important and is all part of time management.

You might think that you manage your time well, but we all have days when we feel swamped by work or interruptions. Managing time is a skill that can be learned and, by regularly evaluating yourself, you can keep your life and work organized and in balance.

We think we control our own time at work, but most of our time is controlled by other people. Others interrupt us with telephone calls, e-mails, showing up late for a meeting, demanding customers or clients, deadlines, or friends/colleagues who intrude. When you think about all these interruptions, the amount of time that is really yours is very limited. This leads often to chaos and frustration.

I know how it can feel, and I know we often wish we could have thirty-five hours in our day, not just twenty-four hours. Wouldn't those extra hours be so helpful in achieving everything we want to accomplish? We would have time for those unanswered letters or e-mails, more time to visit friends, more time to read that book, more time to stay on top of things. But would our thirty-five-hour day really solve our problems? Wouldn't we be just as aggravated with everything as we are now with our regular day? Our work still would never be finished because we would just pack in more.

When we evaluate our time, our problem goes deeper than being short of time. It is the problem of priorities—knowing what is important. I heard once the saying, "Your greatest danger is letting the urgent things crowd out the most important things." That is so true.

We all experience times when there is tension between the urgent matters and the important matters. Urgent matters call for instant action; they make endless demands, and exert pressure every day. The important matters are often overlooked and fall short. The constant demands and distractions seem irresistible and more important and take up all our energy. We forget what we have pushed aside and we become dominated by everything else. Life becomes chaotic and stressful.

WRIGHT

So, how can we create calmness in our stressful life with all these commitments and demands?

DENK

We can create calmness by looking at ourselves, evaluating our daily habits, and by using time management techniques to make our life less stressful and more organized and orderly. Even unexpected interruptions can be dealt with in an effective way. It takes commitment to decide on your own goals and priorities and organize your time so that you can achieve what you want. You also need to know what problems you encounter so you can evaluate yourself and learn from them. It is a personal process that must fit you; additionally, you must have a strong commitment to change old habits.

When we do what we say we are going to do, we are honoring ourselves. Time management is a part of that. No one has control of our daily schedule. Something may come up, but we have more control than we realize if there is a plan in place. How exciting is that? Having a plan that will give us freedom, help us understand the importance of priorities and how to set them, how to overcome time-wasters, how to take advantage of our most productive time, how to analyze our time and plan for improvement, and how to create a *balanced life*.

WRIGHT

What are common time-wasters?

DENK

We all waste time. Some wasted time is a good thing because you need to "chill" once in a while—we all need to recharge, relax, reflect, and have fun. We all need days off and holidays. This is not wasting time, this is time well-deserved and needed.

When I look at the subject of "wasting time" with a client, I look at his or her daily and weekly schedule during a normal week. One of the questions I ask is, "What else would you have been doing that is of higher priority?" Other questions I ask are, "What is holding you back from achieving that? Which areas of your work or in your life are causing you most problems?" When those questions are answered, those are the areas we need to look at.

Time-wasting is usually self-inflicted or comes from an outside source. Examples of self-generated wasters would be: being disorganized, socializing too much, procrastination, trying to be too perfect and always playing it safe, missing chances. Some outside sources include: phone calls, e-mails, surfing the Internet, waiting, chatting with others, unnecessary meetings, waiting for a client, interruptions from friends.

You might think you control your own time, but once you actually write down how many people rule your time, you will be surprised. Write down a list of people you interact with often, at home, work, and in your free time, and write down how they spend and use your time. Seeing who controls your time is an interesting exercise that will bring you awareness of how to improve managing your time. You need to learn how to use your time wisely so you are able to achieve what you have planned to do with less stress and more focus in mind. You need to concentrate on what you want to accomplish with as few interruptions as possible. It will make you feel better and you will look back at your day, proud of how far you have come.

WRIGHT

So, how can we be more organized?

DENK

That is a question I am often asked. I look with my clients first to all aspects of their life and evaluate. One of the crucial things is that you need to be passionate about your goals. Once you are passionate about what you are doing, it is easy to motivate yourself. I improve the areas where my clients are weak and improve on their strengths. If their desk has files, folders, papers, and so on everywhere and they often become frustrated because they can't find things, they need to look seriously at their desk.

Being disorganized means wasting time because you're spending time looking for things and often can't find them. Have folders designated in priority order such as A, B, C. Do everything in folder A first and then B. With folder C holding the least important items, there is no rush to address them.

Do you have a system in place where things go after a certain project or sale has been completed? You should have a routine and a filing system. Evaluating your office and how to set it up more effectively is a vital step. Having a place for everything is really wonderful. You will know exactly where to find something and it will make you feel good arriving in the morning to an organized office.

I often coach clients on how to get systems in place. It is important to look at your office and systemize it so that everything is easily accessible. Take into account that it takes time to adjust to these changes, to adapt, implement, and to focus on being consistent in a newly organized work environment.

If you are a procrastinator, then always do the things you don't like doing first. You'll feel so much better and it will free up time for the other things faster. It will not hang over your head and preoccupy you. Doing tasks first that you normally don't like doing is a sure way to manage your time better. It is a liberating feeling and you will experience being more on top of things.

If you are a perfectionist and you spend extra time checking, rechecking, re-evaluating, and you can't make up your mind because it is still not perfect, that is a time-waster you need to overcome. Some things might need the perfectionist's touch, but if perfectionism is constant, you have to climb out of that rut. Many things don't require that level of quality. Striving for perfection will distract you from other, more important priorities. If you are a perfectionist, you might be spinning your wheels always trying to catch up but never quite getting there.

Realize that nothing is perfect—nothing will ever be perfect in this world. We can always improve things and try to make them better, but you'll have to be able to see what is more important for that day, for that week. I don't want you to think that I encourage sloppy work, not at all. But trying to be obsessively perfect with everything will cause your tasks to take too long to accomplish. Determine what is really important, and know how much time you can spend to achieve a quality outcome without going overboard.

Being a social butterfly can also be very non-productive. If you have your office door always open, people will know you are always available to chat. You love helping others and enjoy talking to everybody, learning, chatting, and being a part of your company or office environment. But when do you get your work done? People will often walk in, sit down, and tell you how their golf game went yesterday or how amazing their latest workout routine was. People with unsatisfied high social needs tend to waste not only their time but also the time of others. They love dropping in or picking up the phone to chat.

Learn how to respect the work time of others. Ask first if they have time to chat. If they are coming to you, learn to say that you need to finish what you're doing first and you will get back to them later. Learning to say no is a big part of that.

E-mails can be a big distraction as well. Red-flag the ones you need to attend to later. Don't answer every e-mail right away. Continue your work and schedule a time for answering e-mails. This way you are a lot more effective. You can have separate folders where you put your incoming e-mails in your Outlook or other e-mail account.

Surfing the Internet, browsing Facebook or other social media sites, and playing around with information that sounds interesting can be very tempting. It takes discipline and commitment to resist that. Schedule a time of the day for surfing the 'Net for information, news articles, interesting sites you like, stocks, or whatever you want to look up.

Time is often wasted in meetings because they were not structured properly. You talk in circles for hours and, at the end, nothing has been accomplished. We all have been in meetings like that. If you plan a meeting, plan what you want to accomplish and always keep that in mind. Explain your agenda and move right into the meeting. Keep a time limit on the meeting so it does not go on forever. Summarize where you are, assign responsibilities, establish follow-ups and dates, plan action tables, and adjourn when done. Congratulate everybody on contributing to a great meeting and getting a lot achieved.

Now that you are aware of the most common time-wasters, make your list of what your most common ones are. How much time do they consume? Where and when is your time being wasted? What is the cause? How can you reduce them? How much more time will you have to accomplish more important things?

When you have rid yourself of time-wasters and you finally have your time under control, you can become more stress-free and self-assured because you will achieve more.

WRIGHT

How do people assess themselves?

DENK

The best way to assess yourself is to look at your actual day. What are you doing now on a daily basis? Exactly how did you spend your day today?

What I recommend to my clients is that for four days they maintain a planner and write in hourly what they are doing. Don't plan anything at all—no goals or anything in mind—just record your daily schedule from the time you get up in the morning until you turn your lights off at night. Then look at what you've recorded and put behind every note a rating. Let's assume you are in sales:

CA = Client Activities. These are activities that have potential to bring in clients, prospects, and extra revenue. It includes sales conversations, follow-up with prospects, client-producing marketing activities, and so on.

PCA = Paid Client Activity. This includes working with clients or on client projects for which you get paid.

LI = Low Income per hour. This includes administrative tasks, errands, shopping, repetitive tasks, low priority e-mails.

ZI = Zero Income. This could include surfing the 'Net, calling friends to chat.

MT= Me Time. This is leisure time for you to spend on you.

You can adjust these and make up different categories, depending on your job. If your business is not client-oriented but involves production, managing, manufacturing, marketing, and so on, change the headings accordingly.

You can also use different colored highlighters to highlight different categories, count up the hours, and look at what your days really looked like. Be sure to include your workouts, leisure time, golfing, and so on.

If your CA (Client Activity) and PCS (Paid Client Activity) categories do not show much time spent on them, you are wasting too much time doing things that do not bring in money. You are wasting time on activities that will not move your business forward.

Once you have completed your Daily Time Log for four full days, analyze the log to evaluate where your time is actually spent. The goal is to identify time-wasters, reduce low value activities, and focus on high-value activities. Seriously look at your Time Logs with your ratings. It will often be a big eye-opener. Clients of mine who have done this are often very surprised when they see how much time they waste—coffee breaks getting Lattes, chatting with friends, surfing the 'Net, and other activities can add up to a lot of wasted time. Look at your daily logs and ask yourself:

How much time did I *focus* on activities that support my goals and priorities?

How much time did I *waste* on activities that *do not* support my goals and priorities?

WRIGHT

How do you suggest improving planning and goal-setting?

DENK

That's another good question. One of the hardest things to do is proper planning and goal-setting and then stick to it. We might be great at planning and goal-setting, but pack in too much and we will always get frustrated that we could not achieve what we really wanted. Overachieving, over-planning, or setting goals that are unrealistic are also problem areas when trying to achieve great time management.

So, how do we improve planning so that we can change our old habits, form better habits, stick to what we plan, and become wildly successful at our job or whatever we plan to do?

First of all, you have to be realistic and not afraid to push yourself at the same time. Is it better to play it safe and plan less so that you are not stressed, or is it better to push yourself and pack your day full of activities? The answer is to know yourself, know your speed, know how comfortable you are with yourself in planning your days, how successful you have been in the past, and know what to change and how to change it. Does it mean pushing yourself, or pulling back from certain tasks? Only you would know all the answers, everybody works differently and hopefully, with your self-assessment, you learned a lot about yourself.

Without a plan, we don't really know where we are going. If you want to do a road trip and have no destination in mind, what is there to look forward to? The destinations are the fun part of the trip. We set out to do something and feel good once we have it accomplished.

Planning tells you where you want to go and how to get there. Actually, that can be applied to all aspects in your life, from relationships to health issues to your workout schedule to your work schedule, your financial planning, and so on. With a plan in place you can evaluate afterward and learn how to improve.

Let's look at goals. You should plan your short-term and long-term goals. You can have daily, weekly, monthly, quarterly, and yearly goals. Your quarterly and yearly goals can include your vacations, saving up for a new car, moving to a new home, and so on.

It has been statistically proven that when people write down their goals and refer to them frequently, they are more likely to achieve them because they focus on them. What you focus on is what you create.

Write down what, how, and when you want to achieve your goals, then estimate how long each goal will take (e.g., three months, six months, a year, two years). This will help you be realistic and it will give you the idea of what is involved with each goal.

WRIGHT

How does one stay on track and change bad habits?

DENK

People find that they get all excited about their new time management schedules. They are excited planning their day and week and they want to learn how to manage their time better and be more effective, efficient, and organized. But what happens often is that after one month, they have slacked off and are back to their old ways. That is where a coach is beneficial because she or he will make you accountable for it and will stay on top of things with you until you have learned to get rid of your bad habits.

When things fall apart with clients shortly after we have made changes, I look to see where else this is showing up in their life and then we talk about the importance of having integrity with oneself.

WRIGHT

Why is integrity so important?

DENK

To understand why integrity is so important, first think about a time when you were not practicing integrity. Perhaps you broke a promise, you were less than truthful, or maybe you chose the easy way instead of the right way. How did it feel? If you are like most human beings, you likely experienced a host of unpleasant emotions including stress, guilt, regret, and remorse. Quite often, in an attempt to escape these suffocating emotions, our saboteur's voice overtakes us and we literally start beating ourselves up in our mind. This is one of the most destructive, counter-productive states human beings can live in!

Now, think about how you feel when you are empowering your integrity. Each day, your actions are in line with your core values and deepest beliefs—you are impeccable in keeping your word, honest in every way, and you are consistently taking the high road. How does this feel? When we live with integrity, we have peace, confidence, power, honor, and abundant self-worth. This is the single most productive and empowering state human beings can experience!

Your own true-to-yourself system is designed to help you create the habit of integrity so that you may experience the gifts that living with unyielding integrity has to offer. Among many benefits, the habit of integrity will help you eliminate procrastination, supercharge your personal and professional productivity, focus on priorities rather than urgencies, increase your self-esteem and confidence, dramatically improve relationships in every area of your life, and bring pure joy, peace, and serenity to your life daily.

Decide specifically what you want (or need) to be held accountable to on a daily, weekly, or monthly basis. It takes time to gradually create a new habit of consistent actions that are in line with your deepest values and beliefs.

These can also be part of your action and progress sheet. But you have to think carefully about what kind of a person you want to be. Visualize that person all the time and develop new habits to turn into a better "you."

You can have the help of a friend or spouse if you don't have a coach. Tell him or her what you want to achieve and that you need help being accountable to your progress.

Carefully assess when you have created a sustainable habit, then move on to a new habit.

WRIGHT

How does one stay motivated?

DENK

I would assume you love your job. It is always so much easier to be motivated if you love or are passionate about what you do. If you are excited, time management will be so much easier because you want to reach your goal. You will be your own best motivator if you are inspired and ambitious and if you wake up excited to start the day and you can't wait to get to the office because you love the work or project you are working on and you want to reach your goal faster.

We all have aspects of our job that we sometimes don't like. You can be dragging your feet because you don't like doing certain things. Maybe you're continuing to ignore those unorganized filing cabinets instead of taking some time out to reorganize them. Or you're avoiding that difficult conversation with a person who is always late, choosing instead to tolerate the tardiness. Perhaps you keep rearranging your priorities so that the tasks you hate always end up at the bottom of the list. The longer you delay doing something, the more stress and pressure you're likely to feel. After a while, you may even start to lose confidence in your ability to complete the task at all.

Many of us sometimes need help getting motivated. And it can be very frustrating when we know we have to do something, but we just can't get around to making a start. It is normal that in every job problems arise. We deal with difficult people or staff, we don't like tedious jobs like filing, completing reports, doing a sales call, getting that letter done, and so on. That is when self-motivation comes in.

I have used visualization with self-motivation. It is a great tool. When you want to achieve something very badly, close your eyes and imagine yourself "there." You see yourself clearly and visualize it; you truly believe it. This is a powerful and important technique for motivating yourself and building the self-confidence needed to achieve your goals.

Before you go into a difficult meeting, sit in your chair, close your eyes, take a few deep breaths, and visualize yourself in the meeting, how your voice sounds, how you talk, how calm you are, what an impact you are making, how you handle the difficulties and questions, and so on. Visualize every detail that is important to you, take that image into the meeting with you, and make it happen ! Visualization is a great tool.

Let's say you want to run a marathon. Cut out from a magazine a marathon runner; tape it somewhere in your office. Once a day, close your eyes and see yourself running in the marathon. Imagine how it feels and how proud you will be of your achievement. The picture is supposed to remind you to do that daily. Or you can write something on a piece of paper and tape it to your wall, or have it appear on your computer every day to remind yourself that you should close your eyes for five minutes and visualize your outcome.

It can be a sales achievement, a project deadline, or whatever you have a hard time doing. It will help you toward reaching your goal and help you on your journey to getting there. First clarify your goal and then visualize what will happen, or what you will have once you have achieved your goal. Visualize the journey toward achieving the goals. What will you have to do? What will you have to stop doing to achieve your goals? There may be important milestones or necessary sacrifices to achieving your goals. Ask yourself: What will I have? What will I be? What will I gain from achieving my goal? How can I celebrate my achievement? I have used this technique all the time myself, and still do. I also meditate in the morning and part of that is to visualize my day. If you have a great start to your day, it will be a great day!

Focus on your strengths and past achievements. Know you can do it! Seek out a coach, mentor, and/or other people who model the competencies and attributes you desire.

Once you realize how much you have already achieved and understand how much potential you have, you will stay motivated and have the confidence to set goals and achieve the things you want.

WRIGHT

How does one avoid procrastination?

DENK

The first step is to recognize that you're procrastinating.

Eckhart Tolle once said, "Awareness is the greatest agent to change."

Many people can't seem to see it, even though they do it all the time. They prefer doing first what they like to do and push all the tasks they don't like to do out of the way. They feel that eventually they will get around to doing them.

We all procrastinate to some degree, but if you are doing it all the time, you need to take a good look at yourself and your time management. Maybe you are afraid of being successful. Maybe you are sabotaging yourself. Maybe you don't believe in yourself. Maybe your family history and upbringing has predisposed you to being that kind of person. Maybe you play the victim role. Understanding your mind-set is important in understanding why you are procrastinating all the time. Awareness is the first step, and understanding why helps tremendously with changing a habit. Procrastination is another bad habit, and it takes time to change a habit. Some useful tools to help you:

First be aware that you are procrastinating and evaluate yourself daily. What could you have done but did not do and put off? Make your to-do list and focus on the important things you need to get done, even if you don't like doing them.

My personal upbringing was: do always what you do not want to do first, then move to the next thing you like doing. Doing what you like will be your reward. If you stick to your to-do list, you'll develop a good time management schedule. You'll always get the important, often not-so-pleasant tasks out of the way and you'll never have problems with procrastinating.

You can have a real reward for yourself when you get those undesirable tasks done, either at the end of the day or whenever you've completed them. Be proud of yourself and see how your procrastination habit is slowly changing. Acknowledge your potential and that you can change. It is never too late.

Wright

In conclusion, what brief pointers can you give about time management and finding that balance we strive for?

Denk

The most important items are:

Be excited about your goals. Identifying them and being determined is exciting. You will be motivated to get to the goal and time management will be so much easier. Have your own personal, daily routine and system that keeps you on track.

Keep good habits, kick bad ones: Time management and success is a series of continuous movements and adjustments. Be open and challenge yourself to change your habits and grow. Focus on the person you want to be.

Control your destiny by your thoughts. We make commitments with our heart and decisions with our brain. Give yourself positive affirmations and believe in yourself.

Be accountable to yourself and manage your inner self. This can sometimes be hard, but like anything else, you can learn. Be open to changing and improving yourself. Our greatest progress comes in times of challenge. The person you build is the most exciting challenge! Have integrity with yourself.

Think big and succeed big! Believe in yourself, deep down to your core.

Fear not that you might fail. Fear that you never discover your full potential.

Most of all, have fun with it all and enjoy creating *your* balanced, awesome, exuberant life !

About the Author

Annette Denk, ACC, CPCC, is a professional certified business, leadership, and life coach. Annette is also a member of the International Coaching Federation, a worldwide organization for coaches.

As a businesswoman, Annette *has been extremely successful in all of her business endeavors.* Coaching comes naturally to Annette. She is a passionate, enthusiastic, and creative person who enjoys helping people make positive changes in their personal and business lives.

In her thirty-four years of business experience, Annette has:

- Progressed to a management role with a large international corporation in the hospitality industry
- Worked as a senior department head in the fitness and health industry
- Managed and was involved in the set-up and design of several professional dental clinics
- Became a professional Realtor, beginning her career in West Vancouver and then moved to Okanagan, where she opened up an office for Sotheby's International Realty and managed the office while becoming one of their top agents
- Returned to Vancouver to become one of Prudential's Top Producers and Medallion Club Member, Top 2 percent in North America
- Started a successful project marketing company for medium to small Real Estate projects
- Served as President, Vice President, and Director of the BPAHA Board of Directors for six years, where she managed a large Board of fifteen and dealt with many issues on municipal and community levels.
- Organized and executed several large events as well as the municipal candidate election in West Vancouver for the mayor and council candidates

Annette Denk
West Vancouver BC Canada
annettedenk@shaw.ca
www.profocuscoaching.com

Chapter Nine
5 Secrets to Self-Healing

An Interview With...
Dr. Chuck McCabe

David Wright (Wright)

Today I'm talking with Dr. Chuck McCabe, Founder of REACH Wellness. He brings twenty-three years of practical experience in holistic healthcare and wellness-based programs to not only the individuals of his surrounding community but to companies and government offices as well. Dr. McCabe has designed a unique template for wellness that can even help people who have given up on the possibility that they can ever be well again. Through his own personal experiences and affiliations with numerous professional organizations, he strives to help people reach physical, mental, emotional, and spiritual wellness—true wellness.

Dr. McCabe, welcome to *Concrete Jungle.*

Dr. Chuck McCabe (McCabe)

Thank you for having me.

Wright

What influenced you to become a chiropractor and to treat people naturally?

McCabe

Out of necessity, chiropractic became part of my life when I was just a young boy. I was an athlete in high school playing football, basketball, and volleyball, and then continued my athletics in college as well. I had first visited a chiropractor at the age of fifteen. I had suffered an injury as a high school athlete, which left me with severe pain in my back. My mother had taken me to the doctor and I had been given medication, but nothing seemed to be working.

After lying around the house for days, and conventional medical treatment not helping me, my oldest brother John happened to walk into the house and see me. He knew something was wrong because I wasn't the type of kid to just lie around the house. I was usually always outside playing some sport or something. He asked our mother what was going on with me. She told him that I had hurt my back and I couldn't move without severe pain. He looked at me and said that he was going to take me to see someone that could help me.

He took me to see a chiropractor in our home town. I had never been to a chiropractor and didn't even know what chiropractic was. It took all the willpower I could muster to deal with the pain of moving and getting into his car and making it to the chiropractor's office. The smallest movement at the time would send me into severe spasm and pain, which is why I was lying around the house for days. I can still vividly remember what happened back then.

By the next day after my visit to the chiropractor, I was not only out of pain, but I was actually back to playing sports. It was quite amazing. With this doctor's help, I was not only pain-free, but I had found a career and a calling that I could truly align myself with and believed in. Now, granted I was only fifteen at the time, but I remember how much it touched me back then. This experience left a lasting impression on me, and made an enormous impact on how my future would play out. As I continued through school, I developed a burning desire to help others and learn about health and all its related areas.

Now, as a practicing chiropractor, I still get excited when attending continuing education seminars. There are always new breakthroughs in our field, and it's enlightening to learn what the latest have to offer. By immersing myself in the seminars I'm able to attend, I constantly stay informed of the latest research, as well as the newest treatment techniques available.

I hold various certifications in the profession. I'm a member of the International Chiropractic Pediatric Association. I'm certified in Neurologic Relief Center Technique, and my office is actually considered a Neurologic Relief Center office. I hold a diploma in Addictions and Compulsive Disorders. I'm a member of The Association of New Jersey Chiropractors, as well as maintaining other certifications. I remain up to date on the latest rehabilitative techniques, and also practice the very popular low force gentle techniques in our profession today. I have years of experience treating athletes, the elderly, infants and children, and expecting mothers. I've treated patients suffering with disk problems, neuropathy, scoliosis, degenerative problems, and even people who have already had spinal surgeries. As a chiropractor with many years of experience, I'm committed to promoting optimal health and the well-being of my patients.

I use a whole person approach. This approach to wellness means looking for underlying causes of any disturbance or disruption within the body that may or may not be causing symptoms. I Identify what these problems are, and apply any interventions and lifestyle adjustments needed in order to optimize normal functioning. Using this approach, I'm able to accelerate or maintain your journey to good health.

WRIGHT

I hear the words "Wellness" and "Wellness Programs" in the news, in companies, and in schools, but what exactly is wellness?

MCCABE

That's a good question, and I know exactly what you mean. Wellness is one of those terms that many people think of when they're free of disease, or they just simply don't have any ailment or symptoms at that time. Many people feel that if they're not having pain or discomfort at the time, they're well. In many instances, that is far from the truth. There are many people walking around today who are incredibly physically fit; some are even able to do marathons and triathlons. These individuals have the ability to endure great physical demands on their bodies. From the outside, they would appear to be the poster children of wellness.

I have treated many people like this in the past—people like professional sports athletes or ironmen or even iron women. However, no matter how physically fit they appear outwardly, when they discuss other areas of their life, they're sometimes far from well. I've consulted with many individuals who were in great physical condition, but have explained to me just how horrible they really feel emotionally—that other parts of their life are just not how they envisioned it would be, how inadequate they feel, and how overwhelmed they feel. Sometimes these people are sitting in front of me speaking of suicide. So obviously you can see that the absence of symptoms is not a good measurement of how well you really are.

On the other hand, I've had patients who feel emotionally strong and spiritually sound, yet they're one hundred and fifty to two hundred pounds overweight. They have expressed to me that they are happy with the person they are. They're happy with their appearance. They feel completely well and do not feel any disease or ailments. But if you think about the extra weight they're carrying, and the physical stress it's adding to their body every day, it's clear that they are not well. It's only a matter of time before that stress takes its toll and grave problems start to appear with their health. These are just a few of the ways that you can see that true wellness goes far beyond just appearing healthy through physical appearance or by the absence of symptoms.

Many "Wellness Programs" offered, often only address two components—diet or exercise. Schools, government offices, and corporations sometimes refer to these limited programs as their "Wellness Programs." So much more is required in order to reach a state of true wellness. Insurance companies and conventional medicine sometimes refer to diagnostic tests like blood pressure screening, mammograms, colonoscopies, etc., as preventative medicine, and they lump these procedures into what they refer to as their "Wellness Protocols" or their "Wellness Medicine." Think about what actually is being done here. Those diagnostic tests are not preventing anything, and they're certainly not teaching you how to live a healthier life by incorporating wiser lifestyle choices in order to reach a state of wellness. Don't get me wrong. Those tests are very important to detect disease processes and hopefully catch them at an early stage in case anything needs to be done. But that's exactly what they do. They detect disease, not prevent it. And certainly they have nothing to do with leading you to wellness.

Wellness is a state of being where you are physically, mentally, emotionally, and spiritually in harmony. Reaching this state requires much more than losing weight or checking your blood pressure or starting to exercise. There are five core components that need to be addressed in order to reach that state. In order to reach true wellness, all five of these components need to be addressed.

WRIGHT

What is REACH Wellness?

MCCABE

This is the path to true health and wellness. REACH Wellness is a unique program I designed for people to follow and feel the way they wish they could. During the last twenty-three years of being in practice, I've had many people ask me questions about what they could do to improve their health. These questions have ranged from how they can get out of physical pain to how they can help their emotional despair to how they can reach certain goals in their life to how they could lose weight, and so many others. I have treated thousands of patients over the years who have suffered from a multitude of conditions.

When looking back at all of these patients, I often found that many of their problems could have been improved or eliminated if they had incorporated certain changes in their lifestyle. But what were these changes that needed to be made? What could help these people gain health and vitality again? What could they do to be well? The answer to these questions is what spawned REACH Wellness. REACH is an acronym that stands for Relaxation, Exercise, Appetite, Chiropractic, and Hydration. Without these five core components being addressed, a person cannot reach true physical, mental, emotional, and spiritual wellness.

The REACH Wellness Program was designed to help people interested in living a healthy and active lifestyle, and reach their desired state of true health and wellness. It allows you to express your full potential and helps you reach the goals you strive for. The Program is designed to teach you how to reach your wellness goals. The REACH Wellness Program provides valuable information and instruction on how to achieve this physical, mental, emotional, and spiritual well-being. It does this by involving the body, the mind, and the spirit. It is a comprehensive approach that involves relaxation and meditation. It focuses on unique exercises that are so often overlooked and underrated. The appetite component encompasses your particular diet and any nutritional deficiencies. And it reveals the importance of chiropractic and hydration. The REACH Wellness Program demonstrates its ability to ultimately maximize your quality of life, your expression of life, and your longevity of life. The REACH Wellness Program provides the tools, encouragement, and guidance that you need to live this healthier happier life.

WRIGHT

What about serious illnesses and diseases? Can people who suffer from serious illness and disease be helped, and can they be helped by REACH Wellness?

MCCABE

If you give the body what it needs, it will give you back health. Many times people suffer from diseases and illness that conventional medicine has no cure for. Sometimes people don't respond positively to medical treatment. I'm sure you have heard of stories where someone has been told by their doctor, "There's nothing else we can do for you." Sometimes, taking a wellness approach is the only choice they have. But realize, it's not a choice without hope.

The body was created to be a self-healing, self-regulating organism. Think about the times when you've cut yourself. Your body heals without doing anything. When you're cold, your body shivers in order to generate heat through muscular contractions. When you're hot, your body perspires in order to lay moisture on your skin, so when the air flows across it, you will be cooled.

These are all ways that your body regulates and heals itself. That's how it was created. We need to take care of our body and provide it the things it needs. So you asked about serious illness or diseases. If the body has the ability to heal and regulate itself, it certainly appears that it could have that ability to fight against most anything as long as it's functioning at its full potential. The key is to provide the body with the ability to reach its full potential. Cells within the body are constantly dying. New ones are constantly forming. So the body has the ability to replenish and replace. If the body is functioning at its highest level, and you are providing the body with the nourishment it requires, it's only understandable that the body would be able provide protection against disease and illness. It does it every day naturally and constantly! The body doesn't grade the infection or disease as to whether it's serious or not. It just fights that infection or disease to the best of its ability, and that, of course, would be determined by how high functioning the immune system is working at the time. The key is to give the body what it needs so that it functions at its highest potential.

There have been many cases documented where a person was suffering from serious illness and disease and not responding to medicine or conventional medical care. Yet when treated naturally and given proper nutrition, the person bounced back and was no longer ill. There's a book I read years ago called *Patient Heal Thyself* by Jordan Rubin. In the book, Rubin describes himself as being riddled with Crohn's Disease and not responding to normal medical care. He later explained that his change to natural eating helped him regain his health. Remember, the body is created to be a self-healing, self-regulating organism. Let's give it the nourishment and the care it needs, and let it do what it does best—regulate and heal itself. This can easily be learned by following the REACH Wellness path.

WRIGHT

What about when a person is in pain and needs relief? Do you have any unique techniques to help people get relief from severe pain?

MCCABE

Whenever I think of people in severe pain or having severe problems, I automatically think of Neurologic Relief Center Technique. It's truly amazing. Remember, my goal as a wellness doctor, is to have you achieve a level of health and wellness in which you are not suffering from chronic pain and illness. However, knowing that many people are not at that level and sometimes suffering from severe chronic pain, I know that I must always have something that can provide them with quick relief.

As I mentioned before, I often attend continuing education seminars in order to take advantage of the latest techniques and advances available in our profession. There is so much more available today in chiropractic than there was years ago. So many more people can be helped. People still often need pain relief or symptom relief. I make that distinction between pain relief and symptom relief, because quite often the patient's symptoms may not be pain. I've had many patients with itching sensations or suffering from eczema. Sometimes patients come in because they need relief from seasonal allergies. I've had patients start treatment because of a lack of energy, fatigue, depression, or anxiety or all of these symptoms. I've treated many children with these types of problems as well. I've had patients undergo care because of infertility. I've had pregnant moms start care because they were carrying a baby in a breech presentation with the goal to naturally have the baby change position, or simply to reduce low back pain during pregnancy.

My point is, there are many times when the patient is seeking relief of his or her symptoms, but it may not be relief of actual pain. However, sometimes pain is the issue. It could be severe, chronic pain, like fibromyalgia, pain symptoms associated with multiple sclerosis, or even arthritic type pain. Again, when these types of symptoms are present, my first thought is Neurologic Relief Center Technique. My office is considered a Neurologic Relief Center office. There are only about three hundred offices throughout the country with doctors certified in this technique. This technique has provided relief to thousands of people suffering from symptoms associated with fibromyalgia, multiple sclerosis, rheumatoid arthritis, and a host of other very serious neurologic conditions.

Many times these symptoms can be brought on by what is known as meningeal compression. If so the Neurologic Relief Center Technique (NRCT) can often provide patients with tremendous relief. This relief can literally change their life. This is sometimes relief that they may not have felt in years and sometimes not for a decade or more. NRCT is focused toward relieving meningeal compression at the base of the brain, allowing the nervous system to function normally as it once did. It's an amazing technique. If anyone is interested in learning more about this technique, they can go to the Web site www.NRC.md and learn about how it can help them.

I personally stay in constant contact with doctors all over the country who practice NRCT; we often share our ideas and our experiences to better enable us to help our patients. NRCT is definitely a unique breakthrough technique that I feel has given me a great advantage in providing relief to many people who suffer with severe chronic pain or severe neurologic conditions.

WRIGHT

With all of your past experience in healthcare, what do you feel is the one most important thing a person can do to be healthy?

MCCABE

That was actually the thought going through my mind when I designed REACH Wellness. I was thinking about the most important things that needed to be done in order for someone to become healthy and maintain good health. I tried to remember, throughout the last twenty-three years, all of the different diseases and disorders I've seen walk through my doors. I thought of all the different problems that people faced and asked myself what I could've possibly done to help those patients. I tried to think of what information I could've shared with those patients that could have possibly saved them from the disease or disorder that they were currently suffering from. What health information or techniques could I have imparted into their lives that could have saved them from traveling down the path that led them into the condition that they were dealing with at that time? When I thought about that, I kept coming up with the five core components of REACH Wellness. That is the reason that I refer to them as the five core components. It was always a lack of one of those components, if not a lack of all of them, that I'm sure played a role in their ending up with the condition they were suffering from at the time.

When I'm asked, "What is the one most important thing that one should do to be healthy?" it's difficult for me not to say that you must include all five core components of REACH Wellness. But if I had to pick one that was the most important, I would have to say, having your spine adjusted regularly to reduce interference in the nervous system is the most important component. This is the most important thing that you can do to become healthier and maintain good health. Nervous system interference can cause all kinds of symptoms in the body. Once you understand the brain-body connection, you understand the importance of regularly seeing a chiropractor and having your spine adjusted.

WRIGHT

So, what's the Brain-Body Connection?

McCabe

Your nervous system runs every system in your body. Your brain and spinal cord make up the central nervous system. Remember, your body only does what your brain tells it to do. How does the brain communicate with the rest of your body? The brain sends information down the spinal cord and out all of the nerves to the different organs and tissues of the body. That's how the organs and the muscles and the blood vessels know what to do. The brain is telling them what to do through these nerve pathways and vice versa. This is how the organs and muscles and cells in the body tell the brain what problems they might be encountering. By sending information back up to the brain through these same pathways, the brain can be alerted about a disease process that might be starting to occur. The roots of all of these nerves are located at the spine. All of these nerves enter and exit the spinal cord in between the segments of the spine. When the spine becomes misaligned, it can result in interference in the nervous system. This could occur due to direct compression on the nerve root itself from the spinal segment, or it can occur from indirect compression of the nerve root due to inflammation. Inflammation can form around the spinal segment as a result of misalignment and undue strain. The bottom line is, it's the misaligned segment causing the nervous interference here. This interference acts like static in the nervous system, stopping messages from clearly getting through to their intended destination, with their intended and complete meaning.

If the brain and the body are not communicating clearly with each other, you can't expect the body to function at its highest potential. You can't expect the different systems in the body to work well all the time. Remember, the nervous system controls every system in the body. That includes the immune system. If there is interference in the immune system, how are you supposed to fight against infection from bacteria and viruses? If there is interference in the reproductive system, how do you expect fertility and all the associated functions to occur in the orderly fashion that is needed? And if there is interference in the respiratory system, how do you expect to easily breathe and exchange oxygen into the blood?

We don't think about all this communication going on within our bodies every second of the day, but that's what's happening. Keeping the spinal segments in proper alignment, with regular chiropractic adjustments, helps to reduce or eliminate this nervous interference. Therefore it allows the brain-body communication to occur clearly, and allows the body to do what it was designed to do—regulate and heal itself. That's probably why research shows that children with chronic ear infections, who have been under regular medical pediatric care for the same condition, have responded positively with excellent outcomes with chiropractic care.

This was documented back in 1996 in the *Journal of Clinical Chiropractic Pediatrics*. It's also why research shows that some women who are suffering with fertility issues have gone under medical interventions unsuccessfully, but yet they have had excellent outcomes following chiropractic care. This research was done in 2003 and documented in *The Journal of Vertebral Subluxation Research*. Also, studies have shown that some children suffering with asthma were able to reduce or discontinue their medication after receiving chiropractic adjustments to their spine. This was documented in the *Journal Chiropractic Pediatrics* in 1995.

These are just some of the reasons why I say that the single most important thing a person can do to improve and maintain good health is to see a chiropractor and have their spine adjusted regularly. Reducing or eliminating interference in the nervous system will allow a person to function at a much higher level. This enables a person to express themselves to their full potential.

Chiropractic has had so many great advances in the last one hundred years. There are so many new techniques available in chiropractic that weren't available before. Many techniques used today involve gentle adjusting of the spinal segments. Once people are adjusted this way, they can't believe that it was ever anything to be worried about. Sometimes the pressure used to adjust a segment is no more than what they would feel if they were getting a massage.

When I'm adjusting a baby, the pressure I use is about equal to what you would apply to a tomato to check it for ripeness. I utilize many of these gentle chiropractic techniques such as NRCT, ART, TRT, and many more, on a daily basis in my office. When performing these soft gentle techniques, the patient doesn't feel or hear the popping or cracking sounds often associated with chiropractic adjustments. Instead, patients feel a soft gentle pressure applied to an area in a very specific way. There are many gentle techniques like this available today, and they can provide relief of pain or symptoms; sometimes immediately.

WRIGHT

Why is the REACH Wellness Program so unique?

MCCABE

Many wellness programs focus on one or two things. Sometimes the focus is on weight loss or exercise or possibly both. These are often called wellness programs. As much as weight loss or exercise can be important factors incorporated into a wellness program, just those two alone cannot be considered a comprehensive wellness program itself. Focusing on one or two things in your life is not the answer to achieving a state of optimal health and wellness. As I mentioned before, you must reach a state of physical, mental, emotional, and spiritual wellness in order to be truly well. That's exactly what REACH Wellness does. That's what REACH Wellness was designed to do. That's why there are five core components that make up the program. Each of the five components plays a role in helping to develop or improve the physical, mental, emotional, or spiritual factors that have to be addressed in order to reach that level. Some of these core components play a role in helping more than one of them at the same time.

Let's look at the first component of REACH Wellness—Relaxation. Relaxation involves meditation as well. Everyone knows that the body heals best when it's at rest. When the body is calm and resting, it's better equipped to heal because of the way that the nervous system is working at that time. You have two responses in your nervous system, the sympathetic response and the parasympathetic response. The sympathetic nervous system response is the excited stress type of response. It's called the "fight-or-flight" response. It's how your nervous system responds when your body encounters stress. That stress could be physical, chemical, or even emotional stress. This is the nervous system response, which can explain why stress is the number one cause of disease.

Think about taking a nice relaxing walk in the mountains. Suddenly, a bear comes out from behind a tree. Do you feel the stress? Do you feel the fear build in your body? Of course you do. That's "fight-or-flight." That's the sympathetic nervous system kicking into high gear. At that moment, you have to decide to stay and fight the bear or turn and run from the bear. That's fight or flight. But either way, no matter what your decision, your body undergoes certain neuro-physiological changes at that moment. There are certain neuro-chemical changes taking place in your body because of the stress that just occurred in your life. Your nervous system is preparing your body to do what needs to be done at that moment in order to survive.

Your nervous system stimulates glands in your body to secrete certain hormones—typical hormones that would be secreted during this response would be adrenaline and noradrenaline. One of the functions of these hormones is to divert blood flow from the internal organs of the body, or the organs that are not essentially important at that time, in order to save your life. It sends this blood to the skeletal muscles where it's needed more—the muscles of the arms, the shoulders, the legs, etc. These are the muscles that are going to need more nutrients and oxygen and glucose for energy. These are the muscles that will be used in order to fight or run from any alarming situation. Therefore, stress causes a sympathetic nervous system response that diverts the blood that is carrying all of these important lifesaving nutrients and oxygen to the muscles of the body and away from the internal organs. This type of response is necessary, of course, when the body is faced with an emergency situation that requires the body to perform extreme physical tasks.

The problem occurs when the sympathetic nervous system response tends to be firing in the body on more of a constant basis rather than an emergency situation. When a person is suffering from chronic stress, think about what is happening in his or her body on a frequent basis. The person is constantly secreting these stress hormones that are diverting blood and nutrients to the skeletal muscles of the body and not to the internal organs. Therefore, the internal organs are not going to be receiving these vital nutrients they require in order to function and be healthy.

The internal organs of your body are extremely important to your life. If these organs become overwhelmed and not able to protect themselves and heal properly, they become diseased. This is the reason why chronic stress causes disease. There are many hormones released during stress. Another is cortisol. When a person suffers from chronic stress and maintains high cortisol levels, more problems can occur. Blood pressure can rise and blood sugar levels increase because insulin is blocked from doing its job, fat starts to build in the abdomen, gastric acid production increases, and bone formation is hindered. You can see how disease will start to set in when under chronic stress.

The second nervous system response is the parasympathetic response. This is when the body is calm. We refer to this type of response as "rest and digest." This is when the blood is diverted more to the gastrointestinal tract and enhances digestion and absorption of nutrients into the body. It plays a role in enhancing sexual functions and aids in excretion. When the body is in a parasympathetic state, it is calm, and the nutrients and the oxygen of the blood are diverted to the internal organs of the body. This allows those body parts to be able to function better.

The key to providing yourself with the opportunities for your body to heal in this parasympathetic state is by incorporating a relaxation program, or a meditation program, into your daily life. REACH Wellness does that by providing simple breathing exercises and relaxation techniques that teaches how to relax the body, calm the mind, and free the spirit.

REACH Wellness utilizes the Body Scan Meditation Technique. This enables a complete novice to become perfectly at ease with meditation in just twenty-four minutes. Research has proven the benefits of meditation. Several studies have demonstrated that high blood pressure is reduced after practicing meditation alone. There was a teenager study documented in the *American Journal of Hypertension* in 2004, and another study on elderly adults in the same publication in 1999. By incorporating these relaxation techniques, research showed that the need for hypertensive medication had been reduced and sometimes eliminated. Relaxation and meditation are a huge part of becoming truly well.

The second component of REACH Wellness is exercise. This of course is the "E" in REACH. When you mention exercise, most people think of going to a gym and working out for hours, and lifting weights or running on treadmills. I'm not saying that those types of exercise programs aren't beneficial, but what I like to concentrate on is another type of exercise that is much easier to incorporate in your daily lifestyle. It doesn't cost any money, burns calories, and doesn't take hours out of your busy schedule. It's stretching. Stretching is the most underrated part of exercise there is. Yet as we get older, the first thing we lose is our flexibility and our range of motion. When a joint is kept from moving, degenerative processes can occur. Tendons and muscles shorten, and joints can be more prone to injury. Maintaining joint flexibility and performing range of motion stretching exercises daily can help prevent this loss of flexibility. Maintaining flexibility in your joints will not only make you less susceptible to injury, but may also help in slowing down the progression of arthritic types of conditions.

Think about this: If you could increase the flexibility of your joints, and have a larger range of movement, doesn't it make sense that you could do more with less effort or stress on your body? Of course it does.

A professor of kinesiology, Arnold Nelson, at Louisiana State University in Baton Rouge researched the effects of stretching. He mentions in a study that stretching appeared to do more than just increase range of motion. These findings were published in a journal called *Sports and Exercise.* Nelson stated that stretching not only improved flexibility, but strength and muscular endurance as well. Stretching is an integral part of REACH Wellness, and it helps to relax muscle tension. Incorporating stretching in your daily exercise routine is an excellent way for you to improve your state of fitness, and your state of well-being. Almost anyone can start stretching today or tomorrow. The key is to stretch on a regular basis. Remember, when you are stretching, you're also burning calories.

Another vital component of REACH Wellness addresses your appetite. This is "A" in REACH. This third component considers what you eat on a daily basis. This is where nutrition, supplements, and diet are addressed in the REACH Wellness Program. I'm sure you've heard the statement, "You are what you eat." Remember, the body requires certain nutrients. The foods you eat and the nutrients you provide to the body will be broken down to become the building blocks of all the hormones, neurotransmitters, and enzymes. These are all substances your body will need at sometime. If you're not giving your body what it needs, then how do you expect it to perform to its full potential? How do you expect your body to digest your food properly without causing indigestion or heartburn or allow you to exercise without getting muscle cramps or build new cells in your body when fighting a cold or the flu, if you are not giving it what it needs?

What you eat is the energy source for your body. What you eat provides the body with the building blocks it requires for it to be able to produce and manufacture all different types of cells and hormones and enzymes. Without these things, your body will start to malfunction. Your body will not function to its highest potential. This is the beginning stage when disease processes start.

Our diets have become depleted of the nutrients our bodies really need. Just look at the fast food industry. It's a billion-dollar industry. Fast food and processed food have become the majority of many people's diets. Most fast food chains hardly ever supply a vegetable with their meals. Their main vegetable, the potato, is provided in the form of greasy French fries and only adds to more unhealthy eating habits. Sure, they may offer a salad on the menu, but that's not what most people are ordering. Most people pull up to the drive-through window and order a burger or possibly a chicken sandwich, fries, and a soda. Often, even more unhealthy items like desserts are ordered with that same meal as well. With this being the norm in life, few people are eating vegetables, let alone five servings in their daily diets. Vegetables are power foods, and are some of the most nutrient dense foods available. Vegetables are what you look for when seeking vitamins. They're packed with vitamins, but they also contain protein. That is actually what provides them their structure. Some vitamins are not able to be manufactured by the body itself, so we need to consume these vitamins in the food that we eat. Not providing vitamins to the body on a regular basis causes the body to become stressed. If you're not eating a balanced diet, you should seriously consider taking good quality vitamin supplements.

The REACH Wellness Program examines your diet, what you are eating, how often you are eating, and if you're getting the nutrients your body requires. The REACH Wellness Program addresses what supplements might benefit you, and what manufacturers you can trust to get them from. The REACH Wellness Program discusses weight loss or weight gain, and the importance of maintaining a healthy weight. It helps you determine what weight is healthy for you. REACH Wellness has answers for people who have gone on yo-yo diets their entire life, or have unsuccessfully traveled down numerous diet paths. Many people seeking to lose weight have had great success with the REACH Wellness appetite protocol.

REACH Wellness understands that being on a diet for only a period of time, which usually involves sacrifices and cravings, is not the answer to long-term healthy weight management. Instead, REACH Wellness teaches you how to transform your eating habits in a way that becomes a normal lifestyle. This way, people are able to reach their weight loss goal and maintain it for life, rather than lose the weight and then gain it all back again. Diet, nutrition, supplements, etc., all play a very important role to achieve and maintain good health and wellness.

The next part of REACH Wellness is what I referred to as the single most important thing a person can do to improve and maintain good health. It's the one thing someone can do to start on the path of wellness. This is the "C" in REACH. In this part of the REACH Wellness Program we address chiropractic and all its health benefits. We thoroughly explain the brain-body connection and the importance of eliminating or reducing interference in the nervous system by adjusting the segments of the spine. We explain the body's innate ability to regulate and heal itself. Once people hear this explanation, they better understand the human body and the innate life force within it. They realize that they need to put more faith into how our bodies were created. They realize the unbelievable power the body possesses, and they start to treat it the way it should be treated. They allow it to do what God created it to do—regulate and heal itself.

This amazing organism that we call our body has such incredible ability we often take it for granted. We eat food and never think about all the processes that have to occur in order for that food to be broken down to provide us with the energy we need to function. We catch an object thrown at us, even though we may have only seen it at the last second. We accidentally cut ourselves on a piece of glass or a knife and we heal to a point where months later we can't even tell where we got cut. Two people get together and in nine months there is another one us who has a perfectly functioning brain and nervous system, beautiful flawless skin, and full of life. This is an absolute miracle, and probably why we refer to it as the miracle of life. Our bodies have been created to produce these miracles repeatedly. We need to acknowledge that, and remember it, and start putting more faith in what our innate intelligence is capable of doing. Chiropractic is exactly that—chiropractic is about reducing or eliminating interference in the nervous system, facilitating our bodies to communicate clearly, and allow our innate intelligence to flourish and heal us.

Now, also understanding that many of us do not take care of ourselves in the way we should, many of us are not following the REACH Wellness Program, and understanding that disease and disorders can and will occur in life, this section of REACH Wellness also addresses other care. We also go into the importance of regular checkups and exams. REACH Wellness is based on natural ways of living healthy by making better lifestyle choices. That's what the REACH Wellness Program is based on. By lessening the amount of bad stuff you put in the body, by giving the body what it needs, and by exercising the body, and by exposing the body to as little nerve interference as possible, the body should function at its highest potential and be much less stressed. But there are always going to be times when disease occurs. This is the reason why this section addresses other forms of care as well.

In today's high technologically advanced world, we have the ability to detect diseases and problems earlier than was available before. If we didn't take advantage of this technology, we'd be foolish. Therefore, following certain guidelines will help you avoid worse situations. Knowing that statistically it's advantageous for a male over the age of forty to receive certain examinations in order to possibly detect early disease processes and initiate early treatment; these exams are discussed as well. Knowing that women can also benefit from certain diagnostic tests performed at different times in their life, this section of REACH Wellness addresses that and educates them on the importance of receiving regular checkups and exams.

The final part of REACH Wellness, "H" is Hydration. In this final section we also address pH balance, but we focus heavily on hydration. There is a book titled *Your Body's Many Cries for Water* by Dr. Batmanghelidj. For simplicity, I'll refer to him as Dr. B. In his book, Dr. B explains how dehydration alone sometimes causes a person to suffer from symptoms that mimic certain diseases or disorders. The patient may not be suffering from a disease or a disorder at all, but could simply be dehydrated. Hydration is a vital component to reaching and maintaining good health. This is an aspect of everyday life that so many people take for granted, yet it often goes neglected.

The REACH Wellness Program alerts you to the body's needs for hydration. The Program educates you on the recommended daily intake that your body should receive and how less than this could make you sick. Along with learning about hydration and how it affects your life, REACH Wellness addresses pH levels and how imbalances matter to the body. REACH Wellness explains the importance of how maintaining proper pH levels are vital to achieving excellent health and what foods tend to jeopardize this balance. REACH Wellness shows you how to effectively test your current pH quickly and easily. Understanding the importance of hydration and pH can provide that final piece to the puzzle and allow you to break through whatever resistance you had toward your eventual goal of total wellness.

WRIGHT

Will you tell our readers about people who have influenced you most in your life?

MCCABE

There have been many people who have had a great influence on my life as I grew up. My father died when I was only twelve years old. Therefore, my mother had to do everything for us. Watching her change from a stay-at-home mom to entering the workforce and putting her kids through school was something I wouldn't appreciate until much later in life.

I remember my mother grieving over the loss of our dad. I later realized that the overwhelming medical bills had taken all that Dad and she had saved. But my mother never let it get the best of her, and certainly not her kids. She continued to do whatever she had to do to make things work. That was a real lesson to me on how hard you need to buckle down sometimes and start forging ahead if you plan on surviving.

I don't know if my mother is the strongest woman on this planet or she just realized that she didn't have a choice if her and her children were going to survive. My mother did everything she could possibly do and never quit. As I write this book today, my mother is ninety-two years old and still drives. She is very active and my children love having their Mom-mom around. I'm very proud of my mother when I think back on what she had to endure all of those years. I don't remember hearing her once complain about it. When I think about that, it provides me with internal strength and makes me feel that I can achieve any goal if I maintain my focus and determination. Thinking of her makes me determined to never quit.

Throughout the years, I have met people who have touched my life greatly and had an unbelievable influence on me. Some of these people have opened up not only my eyes, but my heart as well.

When meeting people like this in your life, it's like feeling the bright light from the sun warming you. It's a great feeling and one that I hope all of you experience. Once you have, I believe you become a better person because you strive to do the same for others. I am so grateful to have had these people in my life.

I could not complete this section if I didn't mention another person who has had a big influence on my life. His name is Tony Robbins. I really enjoy listening to Tony, and I feel that he has touched my life in great ways.

Knowing how he has inspired me at times, I wanted to share this same experience with my wife, Dina. I decided to give her Tony as a birthday gift one year—I booked us both on a four day event with Tony Robbins titled, "Unleash the Power from Within." It ended up being a great time for both of us. Dina was completely thrilled and thought it was one of the best times she's ever had. My wife was not alone with that feeling. Although I had already listened to Tony on several occasions, and this event was given as a gift to my wife, it ended up being a gift to both of us. Again, Tony made an impact on my life and revealed something to me that I would've never believed was even possible

During this particular event, Tony finished one of his days by having us walk across two-thousand-degree red-hot burning coals with our bare feet. If someone would've told me that was possible before listening to Tony, I wouldn't have believed it. To become a doctor requires years of studying science and biology classes. I've had years of studying anatomy and physiology. I currently teach anatomy and physiology at the college level. I am very well aware of the tissues of the human body. I know what two-thousand-degree heat can do to human skin. So of course, I knew that there was no way someone could walk across two-thousand-degree red-hot burning coals with his or her bare feet without suffering severe third degree burns and experiencing excruciating pain. But after this night was through, my thoughts would be forever changed.

Tony explained that you have the ability to change your physiology by the way you think. He calls it "Putting Yourself in State." We finished up that night with the fire walk. When I woke up the next morning to start the next day of his event, I couldn't help but be amazed at what I had accomplished. Here I was, lying in my hotel bed with my wife. I had no burns on my feet whatsoever. I was completely healthy. Yet I had done something that seemed physically impossible. That changed me forever. I already knew that the human body was amazing, but there was so much more to it. The human body is not just a physical entity by any means, and that's why REACH Wellness addresses the body, mind, and spirit.

WRIGHT

Today I have been talking with Dr. Chuck McCabe, designer of REACH Wellness. He has discussed the five core components that must be addressed in order for anyone to live a life of health and vitality.

Dr. McCabe, thank you for being with us on *Concrete Jungle.*

MCCABE

Thank you very much. It's been my pleasure speaking with you, and I wish everyone great health and wellness.

About the Author

Dr. Chuck McCabe resides in Moorestown, New Jersey, where he is the president of REACH Wellness, P.C., a chiropractic and wellness center focused on helping and educating others in gaining true health and wellness. Dr. McCabe has holistically treated patients suffering from various illnesses and disorders for twenty-three years, and that still remains his first passion on a daily basis in his office today.

Dr. McCabe enjoys donating his time and speaking with various groups, corporations, and government offices in order to spread awareness and the need for wellness programs. He blends his real-life experience with his innovative teaching technique to help individuals navigate their own path to better health while easily incorporating the REACH Wellness Program.

Dr. McCabe and his wife, Dina, are blessed with four children who are all actively involved in sports and community events. Dr. McCabe enjoys coaching, community service opportunities, and teaching. He also currently serves as a professor at Burlington County College teaching Anatomy and Physiology.

Dr. Chuck McCabe

REACH Wellness, P.C.

63 East Main Street

Moorestown, NJ 08057

856-866-0711

Chuck@reachwellness.com

www.reachwellness.com

Chapter Ten
The Forgotten Laws

An Interview With...
Bob Proctor

David Wright (Wright)

Today I'm talking with Bob Proctor, featured in the blockbuster hit, *The Secret*. Bob Proctor is widely regarded as one of the leading masters and teachers of the Law of Attraction and has worked in the area of mind potential for more than forty years. He is the best-selling author of *You Were Born Rich* and has transformed the lives of millions through his books, seminars, courses, and personal coaching. He is a direct link to the modern science of success, stretching back to Andrew Carnegie the great financier and philanthropist. Carnegie's secrets inspired and enthused Napoleon Hill in his book *Think and Grow Rich,* which in turn inspired a whole genre of success philosophy books. Napoleon passed the baton on to Earl Nightingale who has since placed it in Bob Proctor's capable hands.

His wide-ranging work with businesses and industries around the world extends far beyond the pep rally syndrome. Instead, it encompasses working with business entities and individuals to develop strategies that will assist individuals at all levels to grow, improve, and adapt to the ever-changing nature of today's world. His company, LifeSuccess Productions, is headquartered in Phoenix, Arizona, and operates globally.

Bob Proctor, welcome to *Concrete Jungle.*

Bob Proctor (Proctor)

Thank you very much, David. It's my pleasure to be here.

Wright

Perhaps a quote from Doug Wead, former Special Assistant to the President of the United States in the Bush Administration, will better describe you for our readers. He said, "Zig Ziglar may be the master motivator, or Mark Victor Hansen and Jack Canfield, master storytellers and co-authors of the Chicken Soup for the Soul series, Anthony Robbins may be the guru of personal development, but Bob Proctor is the master thinker. When it comes to systematizing life, no one can touch him." That's pretty heavy stuff. How did that make you feel?

PROCTOR

I was a little flattered with that and humbled coming from Doug. Doug is a great individual. It's what I've done for the last fifty years—all my adult life. I've made a study of thinking and why we end up where we are or why we do what we do.

My life went through such a dramatic change at the age of twenty-six. I had no formal education and I had no business experience. I was losing and picking up speed. A good friend of mine, Ray Stanford, who was really the first mentor I ever had, suggested I read *Think and Grow Rich*. So I did and I began to study it. Everything in my world changed. My income went from $4,000 to $175,000 and then I took it to over a million. I started a cleaning business cleaning floors. I started with a bucket and a mop, cleaning one office and in less than five years we were cleaning offices in Toronto, Montreal, Boston, Cleveland, Atlanta, London, England. It was such a dramatic shift that I wasn't satisfied with just accepting it and enjoying it, I wanted to know why I changed because everything I had been taught indicated that what happened with me couldn't happen. But, it did happen.

So I started to study. I wanted to find out how I changed and that led me to the mind and why we do what we do and why we don't do many of the things we want to do and should do. It took me about nine years to figure it out. I was really looking; I was a very serious student. I came to the conclusion that the information I had learned was lacking in our educational system and, oddly enough, it's still not taught.

So, when I finally figured it out, all I wanted to do was share it. I'm a firm believer that we don't really enjoy something until we share it. I don't care if it's a new suit, a dress, a new car, or even a sunset. You want to say, "Oh my goodness, look at that," and then you enjoy it a little more. Well, I had this information and all I wanted to do was share it, so

I decided that that's what I'd do—that's what I'd spend the rest of my life doing. And, that's what I've done.

WRIGHT

So it's been several years since the revolutionary movie, *The Secret*. It made such an impact and you were one of the key figures in that endeavor. Would you explain to our readers what the film was about?

PROCTOR

The film was created by Rhonda Byrne and it was such a phenomenon. Yet, there was a lot of criticism of it because it talked about the Law of Attraction. It created an awareness that there are laws that govern our universe. And, although it didn't get into the laws in any depth, it focused on the Law of Attraction and it made people think.

The Law of Attraction is actually a secondary law, the law of vibration is the primary law and whatever vibration we are in is going to dictate what we're going to attract. But, I still think *The Secret* did a phenomenal job. It's estimated that two to three million people have been affected by that film and/or the book, worldwide. It's been translated into just about every language.

It really woke people up and made them stop and think—why do these things happen? Why are things as they are? So I think *The Secret* did something that nothing else has ever done, certainly in my lifetime. I was just extremely fortunate to be asked to participate in it. Oddly enough, many people think I created it. I had nothing to do with the making of it, aside from the contribution I made.

WRIGHT

So over the years there have been many speakers, trainers, and educators who have introduced me to the Law of Attraction theory but now I find that you believe that the Law of Attraction is incomplete, and for the first time you reveal eleven forgotten laws that finally uncover the laws' true potential. How did this knowledge come about?

PROCTOR

I don't think the Law of Attraction is incomplete. I think the Law of Attraction is a part of but inclusive of everything. The Law of Attraction is one aspect of the laws that govern life. You might be thinking, how did these laws come about? Well, I see the law as God's modus operandi. I believe in God. I believe that there has to be a first cause, a primary cause, and I see the laws as the modus oprandi—how all work is done. You see it in all of life. The sad part is that we're not taught this as children.

You see, I believe if you can teach a child three or four languages before he or she goes to school (many kids learn several languages before they're five years old) we should be able to teach children some of the basic laws that are going to govern their life. But, we don't and the laws are not part of our formal educational system, so when you start talking about the laws of the universe, people laugh at you.

I recall being on *Nightline* with Cynthia McFadden. Cynthia was asking me questions about *The Secret* and the laws. She brought in a couple of professors from one of the universities in New York to refute what I was saying. They were mocking and criticizing it and she said, "Well, what do you have to say about that?"

"They obviously don't understand it," I replied. "Anything we don't understand we have a tendency to criticize or ridicule and rather than doing that, we should try to understand it. The Law of Attraction is an absolute law, energy attracts like energy. That's why a carrot grows. Not all the energy in the Earth is in harmony with the vibration of a carrot seed, just those particles of energy that are in harmony with it are attracted to the seed. And, of course, the attraction continues. Over a period of time, governed by the law of gender, in about eighty days the carrot is ready to eat. This doesn't happen by luck, it happens by law."

When I began to study Earl Nightingale and his Lead the Field Program, I remember him saying that as you begin to move toward your goal, it will begin to move toward you. I really didn't know very much at the time but I thought, "Wow, I wonder if he is right." Well, he was right. As you move toward the goal, the goal moves toward you because you are in harmony with whatever you are attracting into your life, so it's coming to you and you are going to it.

WRIGHT

Will you explain to our readers the original Law of Attraction blueprint on which you based your eleven forgotten laws in an effort to uncover the true potential of the Law of Attraction?

PROCTOR

Well, there is a Law of Thinking. Think about it. What is thought? Thought is energy. Thought is the most potent form of energy in existence, it penetrates all time and space. Edgar Mitchell, the Captain of the Lunar Landing Module (one of the Apollo flights), was doing thought transference exercises from the other side of the moon. It was well documented.

Our thoughts are omnipresent and the thoughts that you think and internalize instantly begin to move into form because of the Law of Transmutation of Energy, which moves your thoughts into form. We should be very cognizant of what we are thinking because most people are thinking what they don't want. I've heard it said that many people treat life as a deep mystery—a complex and incomprehensible problem. Mystery is just another word for ignorance, but as we start to understand it, it's not really a mystery.

Thinking is the highest function of which we are capable. Every great leader who has ever lived has been in complete and unanimous agreement that we become what we think about. They disagree on virtually everything else, but on that one point they're all in agreement. Solomon said, "As a man thinketh in his heart, so is he" (Proverbs 23:7). He's referring to the heart of hearts—the mind. The thoughts that we entertain are going to control the vibration we're in because it's energy.

Our body is energy, our mind is movement. Our body is the manifestation of that movement. So as we think, we impress that energy upon the cells of our being and if they're negative thoughts we'll move into a negative vibration, if they're positive and good thoughts, we move into a positive or good vibration.

As we become consciously aware of the vibration we're in, we don't say, "I'm consciously aware of being in a good or bad vibration." That's where the word "feeling" comes in. We say, "I feel good" or "I feel bad" or "I'm not feeling that good." If we're not feeling that well, all we have to do is adjust our thoughts and our vibration will change and we'll feel differently. But I don't believe that the vast majority of people have any understanding that they have such control of their life.

In his little book, *As Man Thinketh*, James Allen said, "A man becomes calm in the measure that he understands himself as a thought evolved being, for such knowledge necessitates the understanding of others as the result of thought." So, if we see a person acting in a certain way that is not very pleasant and they're directing that energy toward us, when we understand we're a thought-evolved being, we're not going to let what the person is doing or thinking control our thoughts. Instead, we might look at people's bad behavior and wonder why they are acting that way. Would they deliberately upset themselves if they were in control of their thoughts?

Wright

Perhaps we should state the eleven laws. Will you give us a brief overview of each one?

Proctor

There's The Law of Supply. There's a Law of Thought. The law of Perpetual Increase means progress and growth. We see it in everything in life and when we understand that everything in life is expanding and growing, we'll want to get in harmony with that so our life moves in that direction.

There is the Law of Attraction. We just spent some time on that. You will attract to you whatever is in harmonious vibration with you and if you don't like what's coming into your life, you'd better start to see yourself receiving what you want. Most people hold the image of what they don't want. I hope this doesn't happen. If you go back to the great sufferer in the Bible, Job, he said, "Lo, the things I fear have come to pass it upon me" (Job 3:25). The fear is nothing but the thought you've internalized that you are giving emotion to. Fear is the next step from doubt and worry, but that's a conscious exercise we get involved in and it turns into fear.

The Law of Receiving is the other half of The Law of Giving. Remember, give and it shall be given unto you, good measure and running over. In learning how to give, we learn how to receive. One of my mentors taught that to me very well. He said that we should willingly give and graciously receive. You see, as we give, we open ourselves up to receive. This is all based on law. Emerson said that The Law of Cause and Effect was the "law of laws," meaning that what you put out is what is going to come back.

We spoke about The Law of Increase—everything increases. Everything we give energy to grows. To quote Emerson again, he said the only thing that will grow is the thing that you give energy to. So The Law of Increase is a definite law and we are in control of what does increase in our life, what grows, and that is whatever we give energy to.

The Law of Compensation is another great law. You might hear someone way, "I don't deserve this. Life isn't fair. It hasn't dealt me a fair deal and why are they getting all that and I'm not." I personally think the law of compensation is very clear. It clearly states that what we receive in life is going to be in direct ratio to the need for what we do, our ability to do it, and the difficulty there is in replacing us. Realize that no one is indispensible but some people are very hard to replace. I think that if we just make up our mind we're going to become very good at what we do, then things are going to start moving in the right direction.

We've got to have direction in our life, without it we're lost.

I am reading *Churchill Defiant: Fighting On: 1945–1955*. He was a great man. Churchill was on the Queen Mary sailing from England to New York. It was just after the second world war and the ship was filled with veterans who were returning from battle, Canadians and Americans.

He was up on the bridge one night speaking to the troops over the loud speaker and he told them that what was going to happen in the future was now in their hands, their life was theirs and they could make out of it whatever they chose, but he suggested that they have a definite purpose that they follow.

He told about being on the bridge the night before and looking down and seeing all these massive, angry waves smacking against the ship and there were so many of them but the ship just kept on going.

He asked himself why was it that the waves could not stop the ship, even as violent as they were. He said, then he realized the ship had a purpose and the waves had no purpose. Some people live like the waves at sea and others like the ship. We've got to have a definite purpose and really throw ourselves into it and love what we're doing. If we do that, we'll be very well compensated.

The Law of Non-Resistance is another law. Whatever we resist persists. So, it's best to just let it go. I think that is where forgiveness comes in so well. To forgive is to let go of completely.

I just mentioned forgiveness in The Law of Non-Resistance. Well, there actually is a Law of Forgiveness and it's very clear—to forgive is to let go of completely, to abandon. Michael Beckwith, who also appeared in *The Secret,* said something one day in a seminar I was attending. He said, "When anything happens in our life, it doesn't matter what it is, there is a three-step strategy to handling it. Number one: it is what it is, accept it. It doesn't matter what it is, accept it. It's either going to control you or you'll control it. Number two: harvest the good. The more you look for it the more you'll find. And, number three: forgive all the rest.

As we look at these laws and start to dig into them, we might change our thinking and say that these aren't just cute sayings that have been passed down from one generation to the next—these are laws and they work every time for everyone. It doesn't matter where you are. You can be in Singapore or Sault Ste Marie, you can be in Montreal, or anywhere—you're going to get exactly what you attract, what you are. The law responds to your paradigm, not your wishes or wants.

The Law of Sacrifice is next. A lot of people, myself included, thought sacrifice was losing something or giving up something. In truth, it's letting go of something of a lower nature to receive something of a higher nature. We're merely making room for greater good in our life. Sacrifice is a very positive forward step and it's something that we should all start to understand. It has nothing to do with losing something, it's about gaining something.

The Law of Obedience is a matter of being obedient to the law. I think this is where discipline comes in. Discipline is, as I see it, giving yourself a command and then being able to follow it. As we become more obedient and live more in harmony with these laws we, of course, will experience greater rewards.

I like the way Raymond Holliwell talked about The Law of Success. He said, "God intended every individual to succeed. It is God's purpose that man should become great. It is God's will that man should not only use but enjoy every good in the universe. The law of God denies man nothing. We're born to be rich. The powers inherent in him are inexhaustible. Each normal person is endowed with a complete set of faculties which, if properly developed and scientifically applied, will ensure success—ever-growing success." You see, success can be and is an absolute law if we understand it.

So these are some ideas that I have worked with, that I've grown up with, and I've been teaching for more than forty years. I've seen some phenomenal results come from people attempting to apply them to their lives. I don't know anyone who does it perfectly; I certainly don't.

WRIGHT

One of the questions I have goes back to The Law of Receiving. I've been here for a whole lot of years and it seems I never get better at it. In your opinion, why is it much easier to give than it is to receive for a lot of us?

PROCTOR

Well, I think we're raised with the wrong idea as children. I don't think our self-image or our self-esteem is properly established as a little child and unfortunately we grow up and we don't get into it the way we should.

I know my own self-image has grown tremendously over fifty years but there is still room for improvement because I still find myself putting myself down. Our paradigms are very powerful. They're genetic; they go back for generations. Many of the things you do, you don't decide to do consciously. Consider some of the foods you eat—you didn't consciously decide you liked them, it was decided by an ancient ancestor and it's been passed along in genes; it's genetic conditioning. If we paid attention, we would notice that some of the little idiosyncrasies we have can be found in our parents and grandparents. This genetic conditioning is so strong. It's the same with why we don't feel worthy of the good that we desire.

When working with Earl Nightingale, he shared something with me one time that I absolutely loved. He said that when you're going after a goal, don't ask whether you are worthy of it, ask whether it's worthy of you because you're going to trade your life for it.

So I think we've got to realize that all we have to do is open up and we'll receive. Just ask and it's given to us and it's all here. We don't have to get anything, it's all here. It's a matter of becoming aware of its presence. Nothing is created or destroyed.

I guess it's part of the eternal journey that we're on and we're attempting to gain a better understanding. I believe, spiritually, that we're perfect. I believe our spiritual DNA is perfect. I don't think it requires any modification or any improvement. What we have to do is become aware of its perfection and the more aware we become, the more it's reflected in our life.

WRIGHT

Wesley said that we're moving toward perfection, and you think we've reached perfection already and we just don't know it?

PROCTOR

I believe we are a soul. I don't think we have one, I think we are one. And, I believe the soul is perfect and the soul is forever seeking its awareness of its oneness with Spirit, with God, with that which is. So the perfection is there but we're not aware of the perfection. So Wesley is right, but it's an intellectual statement that we haven't understood on a deep emotional level.

Intellectually, you may say, I believe I can do thus and so. I believe I can. And yet, your behavior would indicate that you don't believe it at all. Well, that's because we believe on two levels of consciousness—our conscious level of belief and our subconscious level (that's where the paradigm is). Our paradigm is controlling our behavior. That's where the word "Praxis" comes in. Praxis is the integration of belief with behavior. We've got to take some of these beliefs that we have created in our conscious mind through study, through paying a price, and then internalize those beliefs so that they become part of our everyday behavior.

WRIGHT

Praxis?

PROCTOR

It's a beautiful word.

WRIGHT

You have defined Matrixx as an incubator, a place of growth. So, for the first time as a Secret teacher and renowned business mentor, you are personally providing six full days of your time in a small group setting to help people develop their ideas and business. How do you deliver this unbelievable information?

PROCTOR

We bring people together for six days and it's pretty intense. The program goes from morning to night, and we help those who attend to understand that they are capable of executing a dream, an idea. If they come with an idea, we help them give birth to the idea, to execute the idea. If they attend and don't have an idea in mind, we help them create one. We put them in brainstorming sessions and mastermind sessions and they get into the energy of creating something special. Typically, it's a small class of 25–50 people. They are together for six days. On the last two days, we bring in suppliers I use, some of whom I've dealt with for fifteen years. They are very trusted and wonderful suppliers and we have them attend to work with the participants. We don't pay the suppliers to come in; they come in on their own dime. We allow each supplier to give a ten-minute presentation on what they do and then we allow the participants an opportunity to set up individual appointments with a supplier, where they sit down for thirty minutes with suppliers of interest to them to discuss their idea. If there's a good connection between the two, they set up a time to work together. We don't make anything on the back end. We just bring them together. We've seen some wonderful work get done.

We help the participants better understand themselves and the creative process and how the creative process actually works. The creative process starts with a fantasy. It then moves to a theory where you mentally play with it for a while and ask yourself two questions: Am I able? Am I willing? If you can answer yes to both of these questions, then you can turn it into a goal. It's at that point where we bring in the suppliers/experts to show them how to execute the goal and work with them. I believe the program is built on three Cs: Consciousness, Creativity, and Connections.

WRIGHT

So you don't just say go home and read a bunch of stuff, you actually introduce them to people who can help them.

PROCTOR

Oh no, it's not just, "Here are a bunch of books, go home and read them." We have students re-audit several times. We had one fellow, Joakim from Sweden. Joakim went back home and turned his idea into a multimillion dollar idea. Now, he comes back as a facilitator and helps out with the class. He shares his experience with the people, what he did, how he learned it, got the idea, and got it going.

It's a great environment and something I have a lot of fun with. I wanted to put something together where we got the participants to take action on their idea before they left the class. So it's a special environment.

WRIGHT

I can almost imagine some of the suppliers who might even come for some of the guests you have coming and mentors, as it were, in the future.

PROCTOR

Absolutely. It's an environment where you make great connections and learn some great information. If you're going to execute a big idea, you're going to want to be associating with other thinkers who are moving in the same direction as yourself. We have a tendency to be attracted to people who are much like ourselves. And, if we don't begin moving ahead, start thinking differently and hang around people who think differently, we'll probably stay where we are, or worse, fall back. The paradigm always wants to hold us back.

WRIGHT

This has been such an exciting conversation. Do you mind if I ask you one more question?

PROCTOR

Anything at all, David.

WRIGHT

One of my mentors many years ago told me that if I were ever walking down a country road and saw a turtle sitting on top of a fence post, I could bet he didn't get up there by himself. I'm just wondering who are some of the people in your background, going all the way back, who have made you the person you are?

PROCTOR

I love that. Well, Ray Stanford was my first mentor. He's gone now. In fact, they're all gone now. Ray Stanford was the person who introduced me to *Think and Grow Rich* and I really owe so much to him because he saw something in me that I didn't see in myself and I believed in his belief in me, because I didn't believe in me.

Then Earl Nightingale and Lloyd Conant. I went and worked with them and spent five years working with them. It was such a rich, rewarding experience just being around them and they were so different—they were as different as night and day in their personalities. Lloyd was a great businessman; Earl was a great philosopher, teacher, visionary. So I learned so much from both of them. I worked at their side for five years.

I was introduced to Nightingale Conant and then to Val Van de Wall from Western Canada and he, in turn, introduced me to Dr. C. Harry Roder. Val and Harry were the two men who taught me about the mind. In fact, there is a psychiatrist I worked with in Florida, Dr. John Mike, and he said I taught him more about the mind in a year than he had learned in four years of medical school and five years of psychiatric training. When he said that, I thought, "Wow, what I taught him was simply what Van de Wall and Dr. Roder taught me." They were absolutely brilliant and they took the complex subject of the mind and reduced it to something that was really simple for me to understand.

I think my effectiveness as a teacher and communicator of this type of information is largely due to the fact that I have had great teachers who communicated to me in a very simple way. I read one time where John Kennedy said he prepared his speeches so a ten-year-old could understand them. I thought, "Wow, what great advice." That's probably the way I communicate the information because that's the way I received it.

Last but not least, my sixth mentor was Bill Gove. Bill Gove was the Frank Sinatra of public speaking. He was the greatest guy in the world. I was very shy but I had studied so diligently. I had such a desire to teach the material I'd learned, but I was too afraid to raise my hand to ask a question, let alone stand up in front of a crowd and speak. I remember going to hear him speak. I was in the back of the room. We were at the O'Hare Hyatt and it would have been around 1968. He was on stage and he held up his hand. He was looking out into the audience with about a thousand people in front of him. He said, "If I want to be free, I've got to be me. Not the me you think I should be, not the me I think my wife wants me to be, not the me I think my kids think I should be. If I want to be free, I've got to be me." And, then he said, "But I'd better know who me is." I was watching him and thinking my goodness he is so good at this. I thought, if only I could do that.

Now, on Earl Nightingale's Attitude recording from the "Lead the Field," there is a part where he says, "Now right here we come to a rather strange fact. We tend to minimize the things we can do, the goals we can reach, and for some equally strange reason we think other people can do things we cannot. Understand that's not true. You have deep reservoirs of talent and ability in you." If you had asked me whether or not I understood that, I would have said of course I understand it. After all, I must have listened to that a thousand times. But here I was at the back of the room and I'm thinking, "If only I could do that," and at that moment, Earl's recording started to play in my head, "Now right we come to a rather . . ." and I thought, "That's exactly what Earl meant." I made up my mind that I wasn't only get to know Bill Gove, I was going to get him to teach me what he was doing.

Bill and I were great friends for a long time, right up until he passed away. I think the last time he spoke was at an event that my company had invited him as guest speaker in Florida. It was late September and I think Bill passed away around the twelfth of December. If he had lived to January, he would have been ninety. Fortunately, we had the event professionally filmed and we've got his last public appearance on film. It was just weeks after that he passed away and I thought, "Wow, that footage is worth something." So I gave it to Bill's business partner, Steve Siebold, and Bill's wife, Ada. He was such a phenonomenal speaker; I loved him so much. I miss him.

WRIGHT

He was absolutely my favorite speaker, and that is saying a lot.

This has been a pleasure for me. It has been such an interesting conversation and I know the readers of this chapter are going to get a tremendous amount of information from it. I also hope they'll follow up on what they learn.

PROCTOR

David, it's been my pleasure, I have enjoyed chatting with you.

WRIGHT

Today I have been talking with Bob Proctor. Bob is widely regarded as one of the living masters and teachers of the Law of Attraction and has worked in the area of mind potential for more than forty years. He is the bestselling author of *You Were Born Rich* and has transformed the lives of millions through his books, seminars, courses, and personal coaching.

Bob, thank you so much for being with us today on *Concrete Jungle.*

PROCTOR

My pleasure, David. Thank you for having me.

About the Author

Bob Proctor was featured in the blockbuster hit, *The Secret.* Bob is widely regarded as one of the leading masters and teachers of the Law of Attraction and has worked in the area of mind potential for more than forty years. He is the best-selling author of *You Were Born Rich* and has transformed the lives of millions through his books, seminars, courses, and personal coaching. He is a direct link to the modern science of success, stretching back to Andrew Carnegie the great financier and philanthropist. Carnegie's secrets inspired and enthused Napoleon Hill in his book *Think and Grow Rich,* which in turn inspired a whole genre of success philosophy books. Napoleon passed the baton on to Earl Nightingale who has since placed it in Bob Proctor's capable hands.

Bob's wide-ranging work with businesses and industries around the world extends far beyond the pep rally syndrome. Instead, it encompasses working with business entities and individuals to develop strategies that will assist individuals at all levels to grow, improve, and adapt to the ever-changing nature of today's world. His company, LifeSuccess Productions, is headquartered in Phoenix, Arizona, and operates globally.

Bob Proctor
LifeSuccess Productions
8900 East Pinnacle Peak Road, Suite D-240
Scottsdale, AZ 85255
800-871-9715
customerservice@bobproctor.com
www.bobproctor.com

Chapter Eleven
Lost in Your Own Office:
A Path to Productivity

An Interview With...

Anne McGurty

DAVID WRIGHT (WRIGHT)

Today I'm talking with Anne McGurty. Anne is a keynote speaker, productivity coach, organizational consultant, and author. Anne believes it is important to be a leader with the ability to innovate and drive an organization whether you are a business owner, business unit, a CEO, or even as an individual in a personal or professional setting moving toward new ideas and directions. Her ability to persuade, influence, model integrity, communicate, motivate, innovate, implement strategic vision, and demonstrate drive and tenacity are skills and attributes that she uses daily. In addition, she is constantly working on her own personal and professional development.

Anne McGurty is the CEO and Founder of Strategize & Organize. Anne shows people how to work more effectively with less effort. Her entrepreneurial upbringing and corporate background mesh with her experience to get results. Anne's company, Strategize & Organize, improves productivity for individuals as well as organizations of all sizes and within all industries. She is the author of the book, *Lost In Your Own Office*, and a contributing author to *Speaking Your Truth*: *Courageous Stories from Inspiring Women, Volume II*.

Anne, welcome to *Concrete Jungle*.

ANNE MCGURTY (MCGURTY)

Thank you, David. I am pleased and honored to contribute to this book.

WRIGHT

Anne, you speak of personal productivity. I find as a business owner that my time is being more and more strained with more and more access points. For instance, I have a cell phone, I have a land line, I have voicemails on my phones, and I have several e-mail addresses, just to name a few. I am bombarded with information and get stumped on where to check first when I need to access it. It's hard to prioritize all this incoming information. From your personal productivity perspective, how would you be able to help?

MCGURTY

David, you know just the right questions to start. This is a conversation I have every day with clients. Many people give me examples and scenarios exactly like the ones you've posed in your question. People look at me strangely when I tell them what I do. Then they say, "Boy, everyone needs those services!" or, "Holy cow, do I need your help!"

For those who are willing to work with a professional, I find that one of the first steps in beginning our work together is to help them see the value of actually doing something about their inefficiencies. Statistically, executives waste 150 hours per year retrieving misplaced information. One hundred fifty hours is six weeks—six weeks of lost productivity. Lack of organization is costing companies millions of dollars every day. I ask clients to stop and think about an inefficient person in their organization, and it could be them. I ask them to think about how much they are spending on payroll over those six weeks for that one person. When they look at the numbers, and that's just for six weeks, then they are a little more eager to talk to me about how they can make some changes to make their business processes more efficient.

WRIGHT

Once you get the client to understand that they are losing money through lack of productivity, how do you address their problems? It seems to me that each scenario would be different because each industry or business has its own proprietary ways of doing things. Anne, it seems that you really have to be an expert in an awful lot of different businesses to be helpful.

McGurty

Ironically, David, there's a common thread to the majority, if not all, work environments. There are generic checklists for general areas to address, no matter what industry or size. Very quickly, we are able to identify where there are missing links. We then refine the checklists to address their specifics.

I once heard a story that I now incorporate into my basic "getting organized" training. If you have a car sitting in the garage and it has three flat tires, a dead battery, and expired plates, chances are you're not going to be using it. People often have stuff in their office, or even staff in their office, that are just taking space and not being fully utilized. They throw ideas at the employee to get him or her motivated, hoping the employee will be more productive, and they are surprised when it doesn't help. If you compare that scenario to the stranded car in the garage, it would be the equivalent of getting a new battery. Sure, the car will start and sound alive. The question is, how far will it go when the tires are still flat? And what other problems would you encounter with those expired plates? The key is to continually look at the big picture while working with a client. Understanding and assessing where clients want to go and what resources they have to get there gives you a foundation to start. This holds true for all businesses and industries.

Wright

That sure seems like a lot more than "just getting organized!" I think of organizing as getting the papers off my desk, maybe going paperless, or maybe buying some filing cabinets. It seems that it's a lot more involved. How do you even start with a client?

McGurty

I learned a long time ago that there has to be a system for working with each client. I have several areas we address, and not all clients need to address all areas. We focus on what makes sense to their situation. That being said, it's rather simple. As I ask in my keynote address, I pose the question, "What's going on here?" What is happening is not always as obvious as they think it might be. In posing the question, we begin to dig deeper to ultimately identify root causes. The question registers in their mind that something's not working.

Then we go about "checking in" by using assessment tools. Once they check in with themselves, we are able to identify the problem or problems. In my book, *Lost In Your Own Office*, I give tips for focusing on some main areas common to most of my clients:

Space

An inefficient workspace can significantly affect your productivity. Studies show that each year 1.8 million workers develop injuries related to ergonomic factors. That translates into an annual productivity cost of more than $60 billion.

Paper and files

Pilers and filers

Everyone has his or her own work style, and these work styles have now expanded to virtual workspaces. Creating systems to store information—paper and electronic—and make it easily accessible are an ever-increasing demand for all businesses. As I mentioned previously, the average person spends 150 hours retrieving or redoing misplaced information.

Contact information

When I wrote my book, social media hadn't been in everyday conversation, so I focused primarily on managing business cards and creating systems to maintain relationships. Today, however, contacts and depositories for their data are multiplying. People not only have business cards, customer databases, such as Outlook, they also have LinkedIn profiles, Facebook, Twitter, and now Google+. I'm sure that by the time this book goes to print, there will be even more. Managing relationships is probably one of the most critical parts of running a business. So, having systems to manage contacts is part of being well organized.

Time management

This area is more about priorities. We all have the same amount of time, so it really can't be managed. Most clients can benefit by evaluating their life passions and looking at what they really want out of life. I can then help them address their commitment to focus their time on what really matters.

The stuff

This means clearing the clutter. "Containerizing" what is essential along with simplifying or eliminating what's not necessary.

E-mail

This pertains to synchronization to a central location, such as your smart phones. It also involves making decisions on how and when to address e-mail, along with learning how to use e-mail as a tool rather than the driver of your daily business.

Maintenance

How are you going to do your business and your life differently so that you can stay on the path of organization and improved personal productivity? My coaching programs may kick in at this point to set up a long-term relationship of accountability and address new goals as my clients' life priorities and interests change.

My experience with clients is that each of these areas are common denominators and once we assess them, then we get the right key (tool or process) to improve that area of inefficiency. Hotel keys come in all sizes and styles—some are simple manual keys, some are more sophisticated electronic card keys. It's the same with organization and productivity solutions. Depending on the sophistication or style of your environment, you'll need a key that is best for you.

Once my clients have the right key, then they can freely open the door to the opportunity for relaxation (or at the very least, the opportunity for better efficiency). Finding the right solution for each of the main areas allows the client to move forward and get the relief he or she needs so the client can check out at times. In the business sense, it means checking out of the office for a break.

WRIGHT

It's curious that you use the analogy of a hotel. People are in such a rush these days, and they are bouncing all over the place multitasking.

How do you decide what will work for them? How do you help people get focused?

McGurty

As a consultant of personal productivity, I have to quiet them down and start to look at what is going on in their world. What is their vision? It's up to them to set up the systems by defining how they want to communicate and have people reach them.

We all need to take responsibility for how the world communicates *to* us, and we need to have the appropriate tools so that we can synchronize incoming information. In that way, we can be as efficient and productive as possible, maximizing all the benefits of these technologies and not getting ourselves overwhelmed in the process. Every day, there is something new that comes out—something bright and shiny. People don't want to get behind the eight ball, so they grab it. I just have to tell them to pull in the reigns—tame them down a little bit and tame their technology. Did I just coin a new phrase? I think I did. It used to be "tame the tiger." Now, it's "tame the technology!"

I also use the example in my webinars of using a day planner or a calendar. Some people still carry around a planner because they like to see their calendar, and it often makes sense. If, however, they also use an electronic calendar and don't synchronize the two systems, there will be havoc. And it can get even worse if they have a family calendar on the refrigerator. You see where this is going. The solution is to get one system and stick to it. Consolidate all the information in one place—one container, so to speak. You'll always know where to go when you need to make an appointment.

It's the same with all the new devices out there. You need to stop and look at what you need to stay on track and make sure that all your technology talks to each other and can be accessible in one container. Document management systems are all about keeping your information in one place and being able to collaborate with others so they can find it. Too many businesses spend too much time resending e-mails, redoing documents, or using outdated documents because they don't have synchronized systems.

I took a huge turn in my business this past year educating people on how to organize their electronic information. I've known about it for years, having been an information systems major in college. I'm just happy that my clients are finally open to hearing about how to use them.

WRIGHT

How would your clients describe your consulting style? Give me examples to support your answer.

MCGURTY

When I first worked with someone on my keynote speech, my mentor, Pam Gordon, immediately identified that the key question I ask clients is, "What's going on here?" When it comes to personal productivity and managing clutter and chaos, I believe it's important to identify what's causing the problem—what is the root cause. If you don't change or address the behavior, nothing will be sustainable. It's not always easy for the client to accept the depths to which I like to address their current behaviors. Those clients who are willing to accept that they might be doing something to cause the problem and who are willing to do something about it, tend to be my greatest success stories.

My clients would most likely say that I easily adapt to their personal style and look for solutions that make sense to their personal mission. I like to stay within the integrity of their organization and find a mix that works for them. Many of my clients will often confess that it's almost like therapy working with me, as I'm able to dig deep and find out what's really going on.

WRIGHT

One of the most important values to demonstrate as a consultant is in the area of ethics. Can you give me an example of these in practice?

MCGURTY

Well, as a leader, I believe that integrity, and being truthful and trustworthy, are all essential qualities to possess. I have a strong conviction about the message I convey to my clients. I feel that as a consultant I need to be an effective leader and demonstrate my values and ethics through my personal behavior. It's important that I integrate these values and ethics into their organizational practices and activities. Congruency is a word that comes to mind here. I tend to take chances with my convictions and state my truth at the risk of not being liked. Sometimes that happens—some people go away, and then they sometimes come back.

One of the early lessons I learned was that I wasn't qualified in all areas. In those instances, I recommend other professionals for my clients. I make several recommendations if the client wants a choice and try to be unbiased in my recommendations.

While I am open with my clients and I model honesty, transparency, and fairness, I don't violate their confidences or divulge potentially harmful information. When I work with clients, chaos tends to cross lines between business and personal, and I sincerely respect the need to protect that confidence. It's critical to their success and development that they trust me with that information.

WRIGHT

Tell me about a time when you failed as a leader.

MCGURTY

When I first started my business in 2002, being a consultant was new to me. I had been in the corporate world for twenty years, and I wanted to please everyone. I wanted to learn how to solve all of their problems. I found there were a number of factors, though, that fell outside my skill set. Physically and mentally, and with time constraints, it was very difficult to do everything. It was also challenging to do all the research for the areas that were beyond my skills, and my budget for learning or acquiring additional certifications was a little lean at the time.

I realized I couldn't please everyone. I needed to be realistic about my abilities and stay focused on my purpose—to help individuals with their personal productivity. I also found that if clients were lethargic and negatively oriented, it created a situation ripe for failure, so I needed to be aware of those touchy situations.

I learned to deal with difficult challenges. Now, I'm able to identify how to analyze setbacks, seek honest feedback, and learn from failures within our communications as consultant and client

I now address clients when they are not as willing to move forward. Although I risk losing the client, I will express when it is not working or suggest that clients move on and work with somebody else. That can be a big ego blow. It's humbling when you get to the point where that's okay—it shows growth as a leader. My goal has always been to make a difference and for clients to see a difference. If that isn't happening, I want them to take their time, energy, and money to someone else who can serve their particular needs. I've often said, and I've learned over the years, that my business in consulting is like a twelve-step program. My services are for those who want it, not necessarily for those who need it. They must admit they have a problem and be willing to change. That's where I can be the most successful leader and when we're not setting ourselves up for failure.

WRIGHT

What role do you play as a leader to your clients? I mean, how have you demonstrated this with your clients?

MCGURTY

I think a leader's role is to communicate the strategic vision to the client with clarity. One of the first questions I ask clients is, "What is your vision?" or "How would success look six months down the road?" To transform their vision into concrete directions and plans is what I do with that question. I identify and communicate priorities, short-term objectives, timeliness, and performance measures. I use clear accountabilities and performance agreements. Every client truly is different. I wish it were as simple as a template that I could wrap up in a package with a pretty bow on top. But the truth is it's more like a gift bag that has a little surprise inside for each person; everything I do is specific for them.

Being persistent with clients is also a way to be a role model for my clients. I can think of a client who was going through a particularly difficult time—a loss in his family. Business was down because of the economy, and staffing was an issue. He was floundering and unable to move forward. There was a time when his business might have even been in jeopardy of staying afloat. He needed an assistant. He has ADD (attention deficit disorder) and needs a certain type of administrator. Keeping him focused on the bigger plan of his business mission and keeping him on track to hire the right assistant became my job. I took the responsibility of hiring that right person for him because he wasn't the best person for the job.

A good leader delegates appropriately, and sometimes as a consultant, having a client do something outside of his or her skill set just doesn't make sense. He now has an assistant who is amazing! She is the perfect fit for him. The bittersweet truth, though, is that I worked myself out of a job. He doesn't need my services anymore. I'm not complaining, though. I've helped him, created a job, and made a friend with a happy client.

Wright

Well, tell me about an innovative solution you developed to address a non-traditional problem.

McGurty

I've always considered myself to be an incredibly curious person, and just recently, I heard journalist David Brooks being introduced. I believe he said he was compulsively curious. I really resonated with that description. My unique solutions to unique problems are facilitated by encouraging a constant information flow in all directions and emphasizing my client's need to be responsive to changing demands.

I spend a ton of time on the Internet researching the latest productivity tools, including apps for smartphones. I'm reading about them daily and installing them on my own Droid, trying to figure out what works. It's not unusual to find me at a local bookstore scrambling through books to figure out how to implement a new solution and to take those to my clients to help them be more productive.

This question goes back to when I was practically a kid. My story is that my parents bought a hotel when I was fourteen years old. I did not want to be cleaning the rooms, so I became the hotel manager. I share this story when I present my keynote. The hotel was a chaotic mess when we bought it. The previous owners were using an old shoebox for the keys to the rooms. It was a problem when we were busy and people checked in before all the rooms were cleaned and sometimes before the previous night's guests checked out. You can imagine what happens when you give two keys to two different guests at a hotel. Well, at fourteen it seemed rather innovative to create a cubby-hole box with numbers on it representing each room. When there was a key in the slot, the room was available. When there wasn't a key there, don't go digging into the old shoebox, because the room is either occupied or not yet cleaned.

Innovative solutions are sometimes very obvious or even rudimentary solutions. We can be too smart for ourselves and over-complicate how to get things done simpler and faster. It doesn't have to be that way. We can create simple solutions to improve the quality of our life at work.

WRIGHT

Tell me about a time when the going got really tough. How did you rally the client and build morale?

MCGURTY

Well, as a consultant, I see myself as a leader where I am building a sense of common purpose by promoting the organizational vision both internally and externally. As a professional dealing with the person, rather than a team, I have found the need to develop and implement effective communication strategies. That being said, it's not uncommon for clients to completely break down in tears or experience fits of anger when I first start working with them.

Right now I can think of one person. This gentleman was really resisting. I finally said to him, "We are just not going anywhere." I started thinking about my own personal experience—times I rejected someone and wondered what it was that he was seeing and didn't like. I was able to get him to relax and finally tell me what was going on.

Ultimately, I need to remove the barriers that are holding clients back from their personal success. I take my personal years of growing up in what may be defined as a fairly dysfunctional family environment. My experience has turned out to be a gift that I share with my clients. I offer honesty and communicate my personal story to inspire trust.

You see, I grew up in a family where my father was driven to develop a strong work ethic in us kids. I had three sisters and two brothers. We were all over-achievers, but it *didn't* feel that way growing up.

We were living in Spring Lake, New Jersey, and my dad came home from work one day, making the announcement that he'd bought a hotel.

That was how he was going to teach us kids to work. He promised us that we were going to love the place, the town, and the schools.

When we showed up, though, it wasn't a slightly-worn palace—it was a dump. There was a mess everywhere! So we rolled up our sleeves and went to work. As I dug through what was supposed to be our family livelihood, I uncovered a certain truth—things don't clutter, we clutter. When we understand why, we can make simple changes to improve the quality of our lives at work. The *experiences* I learned when I was only fourteen years old were the beginning of what I teach my clients today. We eventually did experience some great rewards as the dream of being a success was accomplished. We even were designated a four-star hotel with AAA.

Oftentimes, clients are the same way when they start a new job or take over a new business. They may not be getting all they bargained for or they may not be totally happy in their work or home environment and they let their daily routines or performance slack. I feel that I need to work with them to show them their personal value and build hope again so that they can value themselves and have pride in their personal space.

I worked with a client who told me about the book, *The Dream Manager*. The book is about allowing your employees to be free or flexible in their work environment so they can have life balance to pursue their dreams. It made so much sense to me that when I work with clients, we look at whether they may not be fulfilling their personal dreams and life ambitions. This lack may be causing them to be unproductive, and this is where I feel like a counselor. I use time management skills to look at their life and business purpose and have them address their personal as well as their business goals each week. Most people don't get their goals accomplished within a week or even a month; however, identifying them and keeping them front and center each week creates a new sense of purpose and hope.

I have a client who is an engineer at a public utilities company. It has been an absolute delight to watch her incorporate her personal goals. I ask my clients to prepare their goals the beginning of each week and then send me an accountability update on Friday. I was thrilled to hear this woman share how she landscaped a water feature for her backyard in one weekend—a project that had been on hold for more than two years. Talk about morale—she has transformed during the time I've worked with her.

She used to complain about the people she worked with, she was in a state of fear all the time, and wondered what was going on. I asked her about her conversations with peers. Apparently, she never said hello. She just grunted hello or ran by them because she was often late coming into work. She finally saw her part in the poor morale and sheepishly started to make changes to her patterns—saying hello, getting to work on time (or as best she could being a mom and teetering so many balls in the air with family life and a demanding career). I look forward to her weekly e-mails because she is now enjoying her life and accomplishing more work at the office. When work doesn't get done, it's not always her fault anymore. That has taken a huge weight off of her. In the past, she would blame herself because she really didn't know if it was her fault or not.

WRIGHT

What methods have you used to gain commitment from your clients?

MCGURTY

I gain commitment by influencing and persuading clients about several objectives and by having them buy into the process. I have a plethora of methods. As I said earlier, every client is unique. I figure out what works for each individual one.

I do have one client in particular, and even though her company is no longer keeping me on retainer, she still e-mails me weekly. I worked with this company for about eight years, and due to a reshifting of their priorities, my services were put on hold. Even though I'm no longer on retainer, this individual still e-mails me every Friday with her successes for the week and a quick note about the lessons she's learned that week.

I had just started working with her prior to the budget cuts, so we really wanted to keep this going. We established a spirit of cooperation and cohesion for goal achievement. I couldn't let her go because I saw how much she wanted to change. The method I used with her was for her to write an "accountability" every week of what her goals were, what she'd accomplished, and what lessons she'd learned.

I inquire which methods my clients have previously used or considered using and what they want to accomplish in using those resources. In the process of questioning them, I validate and acknowledge their desire to learn more, to do things more efficiently, and to help themselves. I then help them identify which resources will best address their needs, taking into consideration ease of use and cost-effectiveness. Once we establish that I'm listening to them, understanding their needs, and looking at what's best suited for them based on where they are, then they're ready to make the time commitment to learn and incorporate these new methodologies into their work practices.

I have heard many speakers throughout the years and recently have been on calls with Michael Bernoff. He talks about asking people to commit to the time they schedule with you. I learned from him that just using the words, "Do I have your commitment that you will accomplish such and such?" has a strong emotional affect for people. They hear the word "commitment" and know they need to show up.

I've also found that if a client isn't committed to keeping appointments, I have to fire them. I guarantee my clients that I can help them and if they are not willing to commit to the work or systems that we define are best for them, then I tell them that they are setting me up to fail in helping them. If that's the case, then either they get on board and become accountable or we work together to get them help elsewhere. Sometimes, they are just not ready, and I let them go with love.

Wright

Let me ask you a follow-up question. Do you find that you have to look at your clients' business and personal lives as a whole rather than separate the two? In other words, do you feel you have to weave their personal and business lives together in order to aid your clients in their personal productivity?

McGurty

I thought at one point in my business a couple of years ago that the corporate client was all business and the entrepreneurial client, or small business owner, was a little bit more of both. I found after working with one large healthcare organization for a couple of years that their general managers worked around of the clock. I would receive e-mails from them that had been written in the middle of the night. Although their work required 24/7 responsibility, these managers found it difficult to stop working and to create some personal balance. Their minds were always on the patients as well as the efficiencies of the business.

It was only natural that their personal lives were intertwined with their business lives. This actually took some pretty delicate coaching because they needed permission to know that even while they were on a 24/7 business responsibility, they could take some downtime for themselves in the midst of their scheduled duty time. My job was to help them create awareness around their life passions and to build in time for those passions during identified downtimes without risk to patient care or business practices.

Many people seem to fall into the reality that there are very few boundaries between our personal and professional lives. There are ways that we can help people define those boundaries and work them systematically into their day. These boundaries need not interrupt their business processes, their desire to make money, or what they need to do to have their career. And their personal life need not suffer.

As I said previously, however, it is different with everyone. Some executives find that their personal life is just as important as their business life because their personal relationships realize into professional relationships. It's looking at the vision of what that individual wants, what his or her personal commitment is, and what his or her values are. We then incorporate systems that make sense for the person to achieve balance, which is reflected in how the person sets up his or her productivity system.

WRIGHT

How do you help people see the value in investing in personal productivity?

MCGURTY

I learned to be very focused on what I am truly passionate about and to concentrate on the outcome and the completion of what it takes for individual personal productivity. Like my clients, I strive to not get distracted by the shiny objects. Just as I coach my clients, I avoid the peripheral "things," the "maybe we should look at that, too," or "look at this!" I focus on the simplified methodology for the issues they are dealing with, and that is really where I am the most successful.

I have clients who ask me to do things that are off my radar screen and although I may have a good experience—professional or personal—but it's really not in the mainstream of my core competencies. In those instances, I've learned that I have to say no and work with my wonderful network of colleagues from mastermind groups, The National Speaker's Association, and other associations. I find other professionals and recommend my clients to those individuals and let it go. That's where I feel I can be most of service, and I learn from that. It doesn't have to be all about me; it's really all about the client.

People sometimes feel ashamed of where they are, and they are embarrassed to say that they need help. Oftentimes, they think they should have figured it out by now. At other times, they believe that someone in their organization, who already shares in their pain and knows the challenges, will be able to fix things. They consider using someone from the inside rather than bringing in an outsider. The issue with using insiders is that they may be enmeshed in the problem themselves and lack a sense of objectivity. Having an outsider, such as me, come in and take a look offers the organization that objective, non-judgmental, bird's-eye view. I am there to assess and analyze the problem, identify the root causes, and offer solutions that, once implemented, will result in consistent, positive, and efficient outcomes.

I always like to remind people that they're in business because they wanted to do something they care deeply about. Maybe they run an international nonprofit organization or want to be a physician heading up a healthcare company. That's what their passion is, and my passion has always been analyzing methodologies to help people be more efficient. I've worked with so many different people through different industries—entrepreneurial to large organizations—that I can make more expedient decisions and not just set up little packages of quick fixes or Band Aid containers for how things should look. I can give them systems that are repeatable and transferable to other people. Once those systems are in place, they will be there for the long haul. Their investment in me and my services is really a significant and worthwhile value to them and their organization.

McGurty

Do you think we answered all the questions that might be helpful?

Wright

I certainly think so. Obviously there is unlimited potential for individuals who work with you.

Today we have been talking to Anne McGurty, a business consultant who focuses on personal productivity for organizations and individuals.

About the Author

Anne McGurty is the CEO and Founder of Strategize & Organize. Anne shows people how to work more effectively with less effort. Her entrepreneurial upbringing and corporate background mesh with her experience as a professional business process consultant, trainer, and keynote speaker to get results. Anne's company, Strategize & Organize, improves productivity for individuals as well as organizations of all sizes and within all industries. She is the author of the book, *Lost In Your Own Office*, and a contributing author to *Speaking Your Truth*: *Courageous Stories from Inspiring Women, Volume II.*

Anne McGurty
Strategize & Organize
303-881-0174
amcgurty@strategizeandorganize.com
www.AnneMcGurty.com

Chapter Twelve

How to Market While You Sleep:

The 10 Keys to Leveraging the Internet, Selling More, and Working Less in Your Small Business

An Interview With...

Clifford Jones

DAVID WRIGHT (WRIGHT)

Today I'm speaking with Clifford Jones. Cliff is the Founder and President of WealthNet Partners, LLC. WealthNet Partners was founded in 2002 with the intention of helping small business owners, professionals, and entrepreneurs worldwide to more effectively start, fund, market, and grow successful businesses thereby creating real wealth through entrepreneurship. In addition, Cliff is a small business marketing consultant, a best-selling author and speaker, husband, and father of two incredible sons.

Cliff, welcome to *Concrete Jungle.*

I understand you've committed your entire professional life to helping small business owners, entrepreneurs, and professionals to create real wealth through entrepreneurship, starting, funding, marketing, and growing successful businesses. So how did you come up with the concept of how to market while you sleep?

CLIFFORD JONES (JONES)

When I started my business coaching and consulting company in 2002, I was focused on sales, marketing, and business planning. The focus was to help specifically with sales acceleration and development, primarily. Everything I knew was based on my personal experience as a corporate marketing and sales executive, and later as a small business owner. As you know, I built from scratch a very successful wealth advisory and financial planning business and sold it to a Wall Street firm in 2000.

The knowledge and experience I could deliver to clients at the time was based on what I consider to be more traditional planning, marketing, and sales tactics. This includes how to buy and build lists of leads, prospects, and close business. I knew how to get results with direct mail. I knew how to be effective at trade shows. I had a ton of experience with cold calling. I knew how to buy advertising. I knew how to write and present workshops and seminars. I was great at knocking on doors. I could work an office tower better than anyone. I also knew how to recruit, hire, manage, and coach salespeople.

Taking a look back on my early career as a marketing and sales executive, which started in 1983, there was no Internet, as we know it today. There was no Google. There was no Amazon. There was no e-mail. The concept of eCommerce was a pipe dream for some guy sitting in his garage. Our younger readers might find this to be unbelievable, but we used typewriters and word processors. I even had an assistant who did shorthand at one point.

Yes, I guess you could say I was "old school." Looking back on these days, I remember that we had a saying about interruption-based sales and marketing tactics—they worked but they just didn't work well. What I mean by that is when we measured results on direct mail for example, or cold calling, if we achieved even a 3 to 4 percent conversion rate, we could consider that a success.

Fast forward to 2002 when I launched WealthNet Partners. It was clear to the world that the Internet was here to stay and a real game-changer for business. However, when a client would ask me for my opinion about their Web site, I was not well equipped to advise them. Back then I routinely suggested that we bring in a Web site designer and/or developer.

So we would bring in the person who built the client's Web site, or someone new. Our goal was to get specific advice about how to make the site look better rather than a more effective element for generating leads and new business. I didn't know what I didn't know.

After several instances like this with clients, I learned a very powerful lesson that transformed my business model. What I learned was the Web site designers and developers we met knew or cared very little about sales and business results. Here I was, in the trenches with each client trying to figure out how to fire up sales and grow the business. What drove me absolutely nuts at the time was the Web site people my clients had hired knew one thing at best—how to build a Web site that amounted to nothing more than an online brochure.

WRIGHT

So what was the shift that took place in your mind based on what you were learning?

JONES

The shift was that my clients needed to learn how to leverage the Internet better. Very few people I met, who built Web sites for small businesses, were focused on business and sales results. It's not that they didn't care. The truth is virtually every Web site designer and developer knew what they knew. But they didn't know how to align with my client as a trusted advisor to get new business results. They didn't know what they didn't know.

When we looked at what was happening with bigger businesses, it was clear that much of the best talent in online marketing was working for larger businesses. I noticed a gap in the talent that was dedicated to small business. So I committed myself to learning as much about Internet marketing as I could. Then I built a team of experienced, results-oriented professionals to work on my projects as well as client projects.

WRIGHT

What happened next?

JONES

Honestly, it was a very steep learning curve. I dove in headfirst and searched for people who knew how to design and develop Web sites that get business results. I learned the difference between a Web site designer and a Web site programmer. These are two distinct skillsets. Most people are not good at both disciplines. If they are good at both they typically were not working with the small business owners I was serving.

While I read as much information as I could get my hands on, the most valuable learning was doing for myself what I would help others to do eventually. I started blogging in 2006. Since then I have published hundreds of articles online. I learned about search engine optimization (SEO). I learned about search engine marketing (SEM), also known as pay-per-click advertising. I learned about Web-based customer relationship management (CRM) software. I learned as much as I could about social media. I learned about the power of effective e-mail marketing. And I learned about software as a service (SaaS).

Truthfully, the most important work I did was recruiting and hiring the best talent my money could buy in each area. At first, I hired people who turned out not to be very effective. I was not a good judge of this talent. I am not a programmer. I am not a designer. So I was not very good at determining up front whether the people I was hiring were really good at what they said they could do. This was a huge lesson for me.

WRIGHT

How so?

JONES

Results, or lack thereof. I would almost always hire someone, whether a Web site designer, developer, or search engine expert to work with me on my own projects before letting them work on a client project. The lesson learned was that anyone I hire—anyone you hire or anyone a business owner hires—needs to get measureable sales and business results to be worth their fee.

WRIGHT

I think I see the picture you're painting here, Cliff.

JONES

Here's the bottom line. If a business has a pretty Web site and it doesn't generate and new leads or sales results, then what purpose does it serve? Not much.

So what matters most? What matters most for any small business owner are results. Small business owners have limited capital when it comes to growing their business. So they can't afford to invest a boatload of money into Web sites and other marketing campaigns if they don't get measureable results.

WRIGHT

That makes complete sense. So how do you and your team at WealthNet Partners approach this?

JONES

We start by asking about sales and business goals. We start with a plan to grow the business. We look at the metrics each client sets for their definition of success. While small businesses in general live and die by their cash flow, it's critical to be crystal clear about goals and measuring results.

Here's a question I ask prospective new clients: "When your Web site designer took you through his or her Web site design profile to help you get laser-focused on your business plan and goals, how did the conversation go?"

The typical response is, "What the heck are you talking about? So and so never asked me anything about my goals or my business plan."

Therein lies the key. Every sales and marketing campaign and the related tactics boil down ultimately to results. I can't tell you how many times I hear business owners complain that they just aren't getting results from their online marketing efforts. It's also true for offline marketing because small business owners don't generally measure results enough.

This is why our business is booming. We focus on planning, setting goals, defining a budget, and implementing super-affordable technologies to test each campaign and measure results. A small business owner works directly with me or one of our consultants as his or her most-trusted small business growth expert. As a team we focus on sales acceleration and high-ROI Internet marketing. This is our niche.

WRIGHT

So how do you blend what you describe as your "old-school" marketing disciplines with teaching people how to market while they sleep?

JONES

Great question, David. Virtually every business owner we consult and advise needs to integrate what you refer to as "old school" tactics with their online strategy. Direct sales calls, advertising, direct mail, seminars, and tradeshows are still important for most of our clients. However, all this "interruption-based" selling and marketing must be complemented by the work we do on the Internet. We refer to this as "attraction-based marketing."

Let me give you an example. One of our clients owns a very successful incentive travel company. They sell high-end cruises and group and incentive travel for big companies. The owner of the company has been very successful leveraging radio advertising. The radio ads run, people listening to the radio show hear the ads and do one of two things: They call the toll-free number to speak with a travel consultant or they go to various Web sites and landing pages to check out the offers.

By deploying both marketing campaigns—radio, and Internet—we capture more leads and help him convert more sales. Now it may be that one day, as we refine his marketing to be more focused online versus the radio, that we could eventually stop spending money on the radio ads. But right now we can't. We need to keep testing and building the success he's having online and see if these efforts will generate enough business at the right cost to acquire each new client. It's all about testing and doing and learning from the data we collect. Eventually we want him to be able to market while he sleeps using the Internet 24/7.

The other element that has been very powerful for this, and virtually all of our clients, is e-mail marketing. I am a certified consultant with Infusionsoft, which is a Gilbert, Arizona-based software company focused on small business growth. They deliver their software over the Internet as a service. This means the Infusionsoft software is delivered over the Web. You don't buy it and install it on the servers in your office. When you hear the term "cloud," this means the software is delivered over the Internet. Infusionsoft is one of the most powerful tools on the planet for small business owners. And it costs only a few hundred dollars a month for most clients.

WRIGHT

Okay. So I understand what you're describing here in terms of integrating more traditional or interruption-based marketing with online marketing tactics. But what do you mean by helping your clients, market while they sleep?

JONES

It's about helping business owners work smarter, not harder. It's about leveraging incredibly powerful and affordable technologies to help us attract more business, converting people into paying, loyal customers. We deploy attraction-based marketing campaigns integrating them with very dynamic marketing automation software. The Internet, the client's Web site, the search engine optimization, the pay-per-click advertising campaigns, the social media, and the automated e-mail marketing software are all working for clients while they sleep! I use this phrase metaphorically really.

The truth is our clients can also play golf, travel to various corners of the world, or sit on the beach sipping a Peña Colada while our online marketing campaigns are working for them. Small businesses can compete much more effectively with these strategies and tactics. The Internet is transforming the way small business owners can grow their businesses while working less and selling more.

WRIGHT

Wow. I get it. What you're saying is you've figured out how to grow and transform small businesses leveraging the Internet. You also integrate the more, "old school" elements when appropriate.

JONES

That's it in a nutshell. And this is precisely why I wrote an eBook to teach business owners all over the world how to market while they sleep. We practice what we preach and we continue to get better at what we do. We consult and advise our clients to do what we practice for ourselves each and every day.

I am compelled to help others do this by teaching them the fundamentals so they can do the work themselves, hire my team and me or find another company focused on the strategy, planning, and tactics we deploy. The education and consulting we provide is all created with the desire to help small business owners be more successful.

WRIGHT

Sounds like you're on a mission here, Cliff.

JONES

You bet I am. I strongly believe the key to economic success and prosperity lies in the success and growth of small businesses worldwide. And Internet marketing is simply too powerful, too affordable, and too dynamic to ignore if you want to compete in any industry or vertical market.

There are three primary groups of business owner out there, David. The first type of owner understands the power of Internet marketing. But he or she has no interest in doing the work. So they hire companies like mine to do the work once the plan is in place. We refer to these owners as the "Done-for-You" people.

The second type of business owner is the "Do-It-Yourself" person. This business owner may not have the budget to source the work so they choose to learn it the best they can and do it themselves. We provide education and coaching services for this group.

I refer to the third group as the "Ostrich Group." They've got their heads in the sand when it comes to believing in the power of online marketing. These are the people who tell me, "I won't/can't do anything until you prove to me that it can work for me and my business."

The latter mindset is the real crusher. I just don't get it. But I accept it for what it is. My only hope of showing this type of business owner is to fire up one of my browsers, do an online search for what they sell and show them their competition sitting on the first page of a search result. If that doesn't convince them, nothing will.

WRIGHT

So what are the 10 keys to leveraging the Internet, selling more and working less?

JONES

Actually there is a lot to it. I wrote an eBook on the subject and our readers can download it at www.wealthnetpartners.com.

Here is an overview of How to Market While You Sleep:

Key #1: Understand the new rules of the game when it comes to marketing. This means you've got to learn the fundamentals of how the Internet, search engines, Web sites, lead magnets, conversions, and automated marketing follow-up work together. Otherwise you're less likely to succeed.

Key #2: Commit to learning and investing. Learning how to market online and leverage the many amazing and affordable technologies available to small business today will not happen overnight. This is a process. You must commit to the process of learning and investing. If you are not willing to put your time, energy, and capital into learning, doing the work, testing, and measuring results as you go, you might as well not start.

Key #3: Build your foundation on research and data. One of the most amazing aspects of Internet marketing is the data we can collect and from which we learn and adapt our strategies online. What is your competition doing to beat you today? How are they doing this exactly? What search engine results do they get and what can you do to beat them? We teach you how to use very powerful technologies to build your research and competitive foundation. And some of the best software we teach you to use is free.

Key #4: Build your Web site with purpose. Your Web site is one of the most, if not *the* most, powerful marketing weapons in your arsenal.

You must build or transform your current Web site with solid planning and specific purpose or goals. Too many business owners simply wing it on this one. It's a shame because they end up with a Web site that's nothing more than a static, online brochure. This is mostly a waste of digital space if the site is not serving the growth of a business. Web sites should be lead magnets built for conversions.

Key #5: Learn and deploy search engine optimization (SEO). Think about your own online search habits. You fire up Google in most cases, you search for something, and you get search results or a search engine results page (SERP). What do you do next? Where do you click? The vast majority of us will click on the top three or four organic search engine results. We generally won't click the paid search results. So the question is, are you on the first or second SERP? If not, why not? And if so, what happens next? The art and science of SEO can make a huge difference for any small business. SEO is not a one-time marketing endeavor either. It's an investment you make each and every month until you achieve your business and sales goals.

Key #6: Learn and deploy Search Engine Marketing (SEM). This is how Google and other search engines, even Facebook, make their big money—online advertising. You pay for clicks in the most simple sense. This is also called pay-per-click advertising. Pay-per-click isn't for everyone. It can be a very effective component for driving instant traffic and generating big sales numbers when executed well. But it should be deployed with caution, otherwise you can waste a lot of money and time.

Key #7: Automate your follow up with e-mail marketing automation. E-mail and other types of automated follow-up campaigns make the difference between fast growth and no growth for small business automation. E-mail is a very powerful and vastly overlooked tool for growing a business. The automation capabilities with certain e-mail marketing software are often overlooked. If you are a business owner reading this right now, take a moment to ask yourself how much money you're losing for lack of proper follow-up with leads, prospects, customers, and past customers. Be honest with yourself. You probably have no idea. When we measure this it's generally in the thousands and thousands of dollars for small businesses. If you go to our Web site, www.wealthnetpartners.com, and you choose to "opt in" to one of our offers, you will get immediate and personalized follow up by e-mail. We call this Marketing Automation. We love and use Infusionsoft. *But th*ere are a number of other software programs that help you automate your follow-up. It's this simple: if you're not automating your marketing follow-up, you're losing money.

Key #8: Learn how to create great content for blogs, eBooks, special reports, Web sites, video, infographics, and more. It's sad that most businesses completely fail when it comes to content. The biggest excuses or reasons people don't do this is they feel they don't have the time, they can't write, they don't believe it works, etc. The truth is you need great content to stand out from the competition. If you can't create it yourself, pay a professional.

Key #9: Be active and consistent with your social media. I've got to admit that I resisted social media for a long time. At first I felt as though I could not be effective with it. The truth is we get great results with social media. It's also true that there's a lot of hard work to it. And it takes time to get results, even if you're really good at it. The real key here is to tie it into your business metrics so you track and measure results.

Too many people will tell you how many followers on Twitter they have, how many friends they have, etc. Yet they don't know how to translate this into meaningful business results.

Key #10: Here's the last and most important key. I call it the Golden Key. It's Kaizen. This is the Japanese word for constant and continual improvement. Without this you will fail to evolve, learn, and adapt your online or offline marketing strategy. What works well today may not work well tomorrow. The search engines engineers change their algorithms constantly. Technologies come and go. You need to focus on measuring results, testing new online marketing tactics, and investing in what works well to keep your return on investment as high as possible.

WRIGHT

Cliff, this is amazing. You've done a great job of breaking this down very well for our readers. How can people learn more about, How to Market While You Sleep?

JONES

Thanks, David. The first thing I would suggest is for the "Do It Yourself" business owner or professional. Go to www. wealthnetpartners.com/marketwhileyousleep and download my free eBook. You can also go to our blog at www.wealthnetpartners.com/blog. I've written more than two hundred articles on the blog so there is plenty of free content to help our readers climb the learning curve. People are also always welcome to e-mail us or call our office.

WRIGHT

Cliff, it's been a pleasure to learn about your dedication to serving and teaching small business owners about the power of Internet marketing for transforming virtually any small business. Let's summarize your key points for our readers today.

JONES

Thanks. Here's the best way I know to summarize How to Market While You Sleep:

Small business success is crucial to the sustainability of our national and international economies.

Small business owners commonly overlook the sheer power of the Internet to transform their small business marketing budget to attraction-based marketing upon which How to Market While You Sleep is mostly based. It's also known as Inbound Marketing, Internet Marketing, Interactive Marketing among others. Far too many people continue to struggle with ineffective Internet marketing because they have chosen not to get educated and make informed decisions to properly test and adapt to more attraction-based marketing campaigns.

Small business owners can truly learn how to market while they sleep if they commit to learning, doing, and measuring results with online, attraction-based marketing.

In leveraging incredibly affordable, Web-based software, small business owners can grow their businesses more successfully. Just as important, they can choose to live their dream. Whether this means spending more time with their family, contributing to their communities, or focusing on their mental, spiritual, and physical well-being.

In the end, we no longer need to be held hostage by our businesses. We can be more free and create real wealth through entrepreneurship.

WRIGHT

Thank you very much for you passion and vision, Cliff.

About the Author

Clifford Jones is the founder and president of WealthNet Partners, LLC, an Internet marketing and business development consulting firm based in Scottsdale, Arizona. Cliff founded his consulting business in 2002 after selling his financial advisory practice to a major Wall Street firm in 2000. Cliff's greatest passion is teaching entrepreneurs that starting, funding, and growing successful businesses is the absolute best investment most people can make.

Cliff is a highly sought-after speaker, author, and small business marketing consultant who works with entrepreneurs globally. He and his team consult and coach entrepreneurs, helping them to create real wealth through entrepreneurship. Cliff is a certified consultant with Infusionsoft, a Web-based E-mail and Customer Relationship Management (CRM) software application for small businesses. He has been a dedicated business blogger since 2005 and currently shares his insights and thoughts at www.wealthnetpartners.com/blog.

To learn more about Clifford Jones and how his team at WealthNet Partners, LLC can help you, visit www.wealthnetparters.com and download a free copy of, 30 Ways to Grow Your Business in 90 Days or Less.

Clifford Jones
WealthNet Partners, LLC
Grow Your Business. Live Your Dream.
888-501-9216 (fax)
cjones@wealthnetpartners.com
www.twitter.com/clifford_Jones
www.linkedin.com/in/wealthnetpartners
http://facebook.com/cliffordjones3
Read our blog at:
www.wealthnetpartners.com/blog
Connect on Skype with me at: wealthnetguy
Connect on Yahoo Messenger at: wealthnetguy

CHAPTER THIRTEEN

Empowerment and Hidden Strengths

An Interview With...

Diana Robinson

DAVID WRIGHT (WRIGHT)

Originally from England, Diana Gardner Robinson has been empowering people for almost twenty years, as a personal coach, motivational speaker, counselor, and an instructor of future addictions counselors. With a doctorate in Social Psychology and a dissertation on creativity and motivation, she has developed a vast admiration for the potential of people to discover strengths that they do not know they have. She believes that, just as we are all empowered by the discovery of these strengths, so too can the strengths empower us as they grow, creating an ever-growing upward spiral of self-discovery, personal growth, and achievement.

Diana, welcome to *Concrete Jungle.*

Why are Empowerment and Hidden Strengths important topics?

DIANA ROBINSON (ROBINSON)

Abraham Maslow summed it up well when he wrote, "The story of the human race is the story of men and women selling themselves short." There are many reasons why people believe themselves to be powerless to make improvements, either in their own lives or in society. The result is that the strengths and talents of those people remain hidden, unable to contribute to society and unable to bring fulfillment to the lives of those who have them, because they do not know that they have them. There is so much more to life when we begin to realize our potential.

When people believe that they are lacking in talent, in the ability to take charge of their own lives, then they often continue to live Thoreau's "lives of quiet desperation." I believe that an important part of the path that I am on is to help people to discover that they do not need to remain trapped—they can climb the ladders leading to personal growth and empowerment, they can be the captains of their own ships. I want them to know that even if life has crushed their childhood dreams, each of them still has a ship of dreams, and it can still take them on voyages of discovery and achievement far beyond those original childhood dreams.

Un-empowerment leaves us feeling helpless. When un-empowered, we believe that whatever we attempt to do will be unsuccessful; often we do not even know what we want to attempt. If we are un-empowered, we have to wait for others to take action because we believe that our attempts to take action will fail. The belief that other people have the power to control us and our circumstances, and that nothing "I" do can change that, leads to the belief that no action or effort is worth taking. Why bother? Why not stay home and watch television? "Nothing I do is going to make a difference anyway." There is a psychological term, self-efficacy, that refers to people's belief in their own competence. When we are un-empowered and unaware of our own strengths, then we could say that we lack self-efficacy, which leads to lack of motivation, which leads to lack of action.

Being un-empowered brings us dangerously close to learned helplessness. You might remember the horrible experiments in which animals were placed in cages, the floors of which could carry an electric shock which the animal could not escape, or, in some conditions, could escape. Those that could escape learned to escape the shock. Those that were unable to escape learned to be helpless. They stopped trying to escape, so that when the condition was changed and they *were* able to escape, they did not even try. Similar results showed up in helplessness research with humans. Using this work as an analogy for undesirable conditions in our lives, we can see that if people have no sense of being able to change their environment or their situation, they, too, may learn that they are helpless, and give up trying to improve things.

WRIGHT

What are some examples of how life can improve through self-empowerment?

ROBINSON

Empowerment can powerfully affect our lives, even when it leads to quite small steps. Let's start with psychiatrist Viktor Frankl who was imprisoned in concentration camps in Europe during World War II. What he saw there suggested to him that those prisoners who lost hope of being able to maintain at least some small area of control, did not survive. As an example, cigarettes were one form of currency that could be traded for coupons with which one might obtain soup. Soup provided extra nutrition, a crucially important element of survival in the camps.

Frankl saw that those who chose to smoke their cigarettes often died fairly quickly. They no longer believed that they could do anything to create a better future, and so their behavior ensured that they would indeed have no better future. In contrast, the prisoners who did not give up sought every opportunity, however small, to increase their chances of survival. Their chances of survival were greatly increased, even by such a small step as not smoking a cigarette, but instead using it as currency. They saw that there *was* something they could do, and they did it.

Today doctors see parallel behavior in people who are HIV positive and who choose to maintain their regime of medication and exercise, such as Magic Johnson, as opposed to those who, feeling helpless in the face of their diagnosis, give up and go back to whatever their previous lifestyle had been. They often die relatively quickly. That they had other options is shown by the fact that Johnson, who discovered his diagnosis over twenty years ago, is still living an active and otherwise healthy life.

Less extreme examples can come from people who have grown to adulthood in environments where circumstances combine to un-empower. I teach part-time in the city campus of a community college. Many of the students who choose my courses do not fit the "average student" description. Most are older, and many are choosing to take or re-take control of their lives in what is, for them, a huge first step. Some originally dropped out of high school because they saw no point in staying on to graduate. They did not see themselves as capable of succeeding in college, perhaps because of family situations or environment, messages of "You'll never amount to anything" spoken repeatedly by parents or other relatives, or even, sadly, by teachers. Perhaps the message was given in other ways, by abusive relationships, or failures in life itself. Overcoming those messages, they are now taking back the power that has in the past slipped away from them. They are reclaiming their dreams. They are getting off social services and finding meaningful work, or moving on to higher education or, in some cases, doing both at once. The un-empowering burdens of their lives are being transformed from heavy weights into stepping stones on which they can climb toward their goals.

To put it in a nutshell, the empowered person knows that he or she can take useful action—action that has at least a chance of bringing about results. This leads to a feeling of confidence; you know that you can achieve what you want to achieve. Because of that you also know you have some control in your life. The stride lengthens, the head is held high, and a smile comes more readily when we feel confident and at least reasonably in control.

WRIGHT

You put empowerment and hidden strengths together. Do they really relate to each other?

ROBINSON

The two play into each other, each supporting, and encouraging the other. Un-empowered people will not look for their hidden strengths because they don't believe they exist. In fact, if some of their strengths were to jump up and down in from of them they would probably ignore them, muttering "Oh, I could never do that," or some other "Yes but" type of response. However, if they are gently encouraged to take notice of their strengths, one small step at a time, their feelings of empowerment can grow. Equally, becoming more empowered will encourage people to seek, find, and have confidence in the strengths that used to be hidden.

WRIGHT

Babies seem to be quite helpless—are we born disempowered?

ROBINSON

Although, obviously, there are tragic exceptions, usually relating to mental health issues of the parents, most babies have huge power to unwittingly re-organize an entire family. In the early stages, a baby is the center of its own universe, and families usually respond in ways that reinforce that. Babies cry, people come running to fulfill their needs. Good parenting can start to convey a feeling of empowerment even to infants. It is what comes later than can empower or un-empower the little person that the baby will become.

Let's take one of the earliest examples. A baby lies in its crib, and just above it dangles a cord from which hang assorted colored shapes. One is a plastic ring that, when pulled, causes music to play. In one family, whenever the baby reaches toward the ring, a family member reaches over and pulls the ring down to start the music. In another, when the baby reaches for the ring, it is allowed to take hold of it and try to pull it down. If help is needed, then someone may gently help, but does not completely take over. In a little while the baby reaches for the ring purposefully, and is able to pull it down by itself.

Which baby will have learned that it can have an effect on the environment—can make the music play? Obviously, in most cases it will be the one who is allowed, even while being gently helped if necessary, to do it for itelf. Very early in life, the baby discovered that it could control its environment by crying, which brought a big person into the room to do something to fulfill its needs. Now, however, it has learned that it can control something in its environment *by itself*—by pulling the ring, it can create music! No intermediary is needed! That is empowering!

Unfortunately, some children do not receive this kind of empowerment but instead learn that they cannot (or, in some situations, must not) attempt to exert control, so that, unless others do something for them, no music will play, or no other change will come about. This can be one source of un-empowerment. Obviously there are situations and activities that children must not be allowed to handle alone or at all. However, the tendency to hold them back from learning new (and appropriate) things can be as stunting to growth as forcing them too early into situations in which failure is inevitable. Forcing growth and allowing it are two different things, and create very different mind-sets.

I remember some research that was being done by the Developmental Psychology folks when I was in graduate school. They found that the behavior of mothers of very young children predicted how confident and self-sufficient (relatively) the child would be about eighteen months later. As I recall, the experimenters watched as the mom sat with the baby, who was given a set of blocks. The extent to which the mother *refrained* from interfering with what the toddler was trying to do, encouraging it but letting it do its own thing instead of doing for it, predicted the child's self-confidence and willingness to explore on its own, without clutching at the mother, about eighteen months later. Again, indications are that knowing help is available, if needed, is helpful to a child, but having that help imposed on it makes the child feel less empowered. The same thing applies to adults. Help that is offered without pressure, and accepted by choice, is helpful. On the other hand, however well intended, help that is thrust upon us when we thought we could do something ourselves implies that we "need" that help, which carries with it a message of incompetence. As a result, we may discard something that we had previously thought was a strength. That strength becomes hidden when we cease to perceive it as strength.

WRIGHT

That takes us to hidden strengths—and how they become hidden.

ROBINSON

Some strengths may never have blossomed because they never saw the light of day. A child, raised in a home where there is no music and who goes to a school where there is no music education, may never learn that he or she has a latent musical ability—or it may blossom later in life as the growing individual learns to follow his or her own feelings. However, even strengths that do begin to blossom may suffer from the best of intentions and shrivel nearly to invisibility. Parents or teachers may believe that a child's interests are not in its best interests. We may have read of musicians or artists who were told that they would need to get "a real job" when they grew up, so that they should study science, or math, or law rather than the thing that was their real strength. Someone may believe that a particular field of interest is not "gender appropriate" and try to guide a boy or girl away from the field in which they show real talent because "boys [or girls] don't do that." Yes, even in this day and age, that happens.

There are girls in some families who are treated as less important than their brothers. There are boys who are less valued if they do not excel in sports. Both of these groups may also become members of the "un-empowered" who may not ever reach their potential for living rich lives and contributing to society if they are not able to change how they see themselves.

A parent who fears the "sin of pride" may have a fear that a child will get "too big for its boots." This was a major concern of my own mother, and although she was eager for me to succeed, any praise that she heard directed toward me from other people tended to be countered with something that came over as disapproval, as a put-down, even if it was not so intended. I am self-aware enough to remember a couple of strengths displayed as a child that I still have difficulty using even today. If, in later life, we partner with someone who has similar "put-down" tendencies to those of one of our parents (not an unusual occurrence), then resurrecting these gifts can be made even more difficult, for the message may continue to be heard into adulthood

Our strengths *are* gifts, and we all have them. Those who discover, acknowledge, and welcome our gifts are most likely to claim our loyalty and it is to be hoped that those people are healthy and well intentioned, and that it would happen early in life. Unfortunately, though, not all of them have our best interests at heart, and some may take advantage of the young one's vulnerability.

A young boy who feels that he is not valued for anything will be hugely vulnerable to anyone who praises him and focuses on his strengths. That "anyone" could be a drug dealer who values him as "part of the team" when he has never been able to make a team before. It could be a child molester who seems to value his company as the child has never felt valued before. Similarly, a young girl who does not feel herself valued or empowered might discover that she has huge power (temporarily) over boys if she has sex with them. Though we can see that these paths are damaging to them, and potentially dangerous, only they can know how powerful the glow of warmth and the feeling of importance are that they may experience in those situations *and that they do not experience anywhere else*. In these cases, they may later come to see those strengths as their downfall, and try to hide or deny them. This form of hidden strength, too, can be revived, brushed off, and rechanneled later in life, rather than allowing it to molder as a source of shame that must be left hidden.

WRIGHT

Where do we start this process of finding what is hidden?

ROBINSON

First, remember that there is no shame in starting from scratch when working to develop a strength. Ogden Nash wrote that before you can have a pianist in the family you have to have a beginner, and beginners are expected to make mistakes. Some people believe that once they are adults it is shameful to make mistakes as one begins to develop a new skill or strength, but Nash's point holds good for adults as well as children.

As to where to start . . . anything that helps an individual to know and connect with the self is good. I encourage self-exploration. My first step with coaching clients is usually to ask them to go back to times when they felt good about something they had done. What had just happened? What had they done? How did they get to that point? Where did this good feeling come from? Then we move on to what might recreate those feelings in the adult, here-and-now world. We might also look at what stopped those situations from recurring back then, and at erasing negative messages they may have received in the past. We look at what their dreams were and are.

Journaling about oneself is always a useful process in the self-exploration and personal growth area. One of the most self-aware people I know has been journaling since childhood. It has not only helped her in her personal growth, but it has led to extraordinary articulateness and skill with words. The important thing about journaling is to go back and read past journals that show us how far we have—or have not—come since that time. There's an addiction recovery book called *The First Thirty Days to Serenity* in which the writer originally wrote daily in his journal for the first thirty days of his recovery. A year later he went through the journal commenting on what kinds of mind-games and manipulations he could see that he had been playing at that time. That is an amazingly powerful use of journaling; one might call it meta-journaling.

Some people come to empowerment through the route of 12-step recovery from addiction. There they were not asked to aim for some high and apparently unattainable goal that would only set them up for failure. Instead they were asked to set a goal "just for today"—just a small step, not a huge and terrifying leap. Others have received small-step messages in some other way, from an individual, a situation, or perhaps a spiritual experience of some kind. They received some encouraging small-step message that says "You can do this. You do not have to try to change the world, but you can change just this small thing" (whatever that may be). When they succeeded they were ready for another small challenge. As a result, they are taking charge of their own lives, making plans, taking action, and moving forward.

Other, less direct but still very powerful ways of becoming aware of what is inside ourselves are exemplified by what some people think of as Eastern techniques, and these work for many people. Martial arts, yoga, meditation, and breathing exercises all work to bring our conscious thinking more in touch with what is internal, and more difficult to reach. Breathing is an example. It is one of the very few processes the average person can control and yet it continues unconsciously when we are not controlling it. Some say that becoming more aware of our breathing hence brings us closer to our unconscious processes—which is where our hidden strengths are often hiding.

Another useful technique can be what I call the "180 reframe." Sometimes we have developed un-empowering viewpoints that are not helpful to us, and that may even portray our strengths as weaknesses. If looked at from all angles, we may discover that what from one viewpoint was a weakness can also be seen as a strength. This is why "the strengths perspective" has become a powerful aspect of therapeutic work. When I worked as an addictions counselor, often with people whose early lives had been quite traumatic, I saw this often and found that reframes can be truly a steppingstone toward growth and acceptance of one's strengths.

A grown man who looks back at his childhood with disgust because he, as a six-year-old, was not able to protect his mother from being physically abused, but instead hid in the closet or under the bed, is typical. He may continue to berate himself for cowardice that actually indicates a true survival skill, since nothing he could have done would have prevented the violence. His creativity in surviving, and perhaps protecting a younger sibling, indicates strengths that he has never noticed.

The young woman, who since childhood has carried the blame for "breaking up the family," may still believe that she did something wrong and, as a result, is unlovable. A reframe, looking at the situation from all angles, may help her to see how courageous she was when she got her younger siblings dressed that cold winter day and walked them to the police station to seek help. You see, her mother's repeated abandonment, leaving the nine-year-old in charge of three smaller children while mom went out on yet another drug binge, may truly have endangered the children. The young girl's action may not only have found food and safety for herself and her siblings, but also led to mom getting into rehab and putting drugs behind her. We reframe "unlovable" as courageous, nurturing, and perhaps even wise.

We may not have experienced such drama, but even minor incidents from childhood can still resonate into the present. I once knew an elderly woman who still talked of incidents in which her much older siblings played tricks on her as an innocent young child. Though funny to them, those tricks made her feel foolish and left wounds of humiliation that, sadly, still resonated in her memory ninety years later. Was that why she had such difficulty in making friends?

Overall, any technique that enables us to go back over our feelings and experiences from the past and see them in relation to what is happening now can speed the process of self-knowledge. Self-knowledge includes getting to know where our strengths are and what has been keeping them hidden.

WRIGHT

It sounds as if quite a lot of courage may be needed. Is that really the case?

ROBINSON

Definitely. The un-empowered see little choice but to go with the flow. Swimming against the stream is not essential to empowerment, but it will probably become necessary sooner or later. And, yes, swimming against the stream does take courage, and it takes strength.

You may meet with situations where everything is working just fine for other people, but *only* because you have been going along with it. If *you* change, then everything will change. People may not want that. You may be told that, if you think things are not okay when they have been okay for so long, you must need to see a mental health counselor. While it is true that a counselor might help you to explore your options, it does *not* mean, as is being implied, that you have mental health problems.

We must deal also with the "nibblers"—those who nibble away at our empowerment with a comment here, and a back-handed compliment there, spreading a general miasma of doubt throughout. Make it clear that it stops or else. And stick to your "or else."

Note who tries to block the changes you want to make and who encourages you. Who has what agenda, and how does it fit with yours? That is information you need to know because changes that have the cooperation of the folks around you are very much easier to make. That does not mean they are more worthwhile than those that are difficult. It just means they are easier. Marching to the beat of our own drum is not easy when other people are trying to beat theirs even louder. It is not easy, and it certainly does take courage, but it can be very rewarding.

I've mentioned my teaching work with people who, as mature adults, come into the classroom in fear and trembling as to whether they will be able to "cut it" in college. I remember too well my own fear when I, too, having left school when I was sixteen, walked into a community college classroom for the first time. A stay-at-home mother with two children, I knew that I had done reasonably well in school (and could have done better had I really tried) but after all the years that had passed, I did not expect to be able to compete with young people who had just finished high school. I took my courage in both hands and signed up for only one class, just to dip my toe into the water. I was fortunate in that the water was neither too cold nor too hot, and now I have a doctorate and a couple of master's degrees, but back then I could not believe that would be possible. I was lucky because that first professor helped me to discover that I could think, and my opinions had value.

Courage is important, but common sense is also involved. There are usually costs and risks involved in making changes, and empowering yourself, though very worthwhile, can involve a few losses and struggles. As the old saying goes, it is important to look before you leap. Again, think about the very first thing you want to change. Decide if the cost is worth it. Yes, there may be costs. Make your choice. Then either prepare to make the change or work on getting comfortable with not making it.

In other words, recognize that your choice is indeed a choice. If you choose to not make that change because you choose to not pay the cost, be sure that you recognize your part in making that choice. Do not run around blaming other people, because that only turns you back into an un-empowered victim, in your own mind at least. And it is what is in your own mind that matters most. Make the change externally, or make the change internally in your attitude. Then look to see what else may help you to reach for another hidden strength, or for another step toward empowerment. You will find that having made the first choice, in either direction, if it was truly a choice, will already have you feeling a little more empowered. If you have just given up, then you will feel less empowered.

WRIGHT

When the self-searching is done, what comes next?

ROBINSON

What comes next is decision making, followed by action, as we've already been discussing. What those decisions and steps are depends on what the individual's situation and mind-set are. A person who feels helpless in a situation, but helpless to leave it, may need to stay in it, at least for a while. That does not mean he or she cannot begin to make changes. Usually the earliest changes have to be internal anyway. People who feel helpless may have found, while connecting internally, that yes, they are creative and have the ability to write, paint, compose, play an instrument and that the next step needs to be to take a class, or read more about the topic. Others may seek a way to stand up for themselves against verbal abuse or against someone who is not abusive in any other way except to be controlling. (It should be remembered that not all controlling people are working from ill intent. Often they want what is best for the person they are controlling, but they are unable to understand that what they perceive as "best" may feel far from best to the other individual.)

Whatever steps are needed, it is wise to have a trusted person walking beside you. It should not be someone who has his or her own agenda. People may have their own vision of who you are based on the past, and it may not be easy for them to encourage you if they cannot share your vision of who you are trying to become. An aunt or best friend may have very different ideas about how you and she or he may relate to each other if you become more independent of your current situation. Nevertheless, an objective person whose only agenda is *your* agenda may help you to see your vision and yet to keep you grounded in reality.

For most of us, one small step at a time is the most advisable when it comes to change. Changing "people, places, and things" all at once, though necessary in some situations, is an extreme move if one does not already have a few connections that will remain solid. A huge leap into a 180 degree turn-around of your life may occasionally work out, but it also involves huge risks. In rock-climbing there is a rule of thumb that advises against moving more than one extremity (hands and feet that are anchor points) at a time. In this way, that one move can be made, contributing to one's progress. At the same time, the other three extremities remain grounded until that one move has been made. Extreme life changes seem often to be easier for young people, but to become more difficult as we grow older. It may be that most young people usually know that they have their parents and home to fall back upon, and those two major anchor points remain relatively stable.

One word of warning: It is too easy, when contemplating change, to focus on the negative complaints about the present and the positive hopes and dreams of the future. This can distort our thinking. We have many needs, but the difficulty of addressing our needs comes mostly from the fact that once a need is fulfilled, we tend to forget about it. I have seen people who have ripped apart a current life because it does not fulfill certain needs. Let's call them needs A, C, and E. These unfulfilled needs (or wants) can become so important in a person's thinking that they overpower all else. However, we may be forgetting about needs B, D and F, and perhaps an entire alphabet, that are *already* being fulfilled in the life that we are choosing to leave. It is important to be scrupulously honest about the pluses and minuses of what we already have, that we might be giving up, before we make some great leap toward change. Not that change is something to fear, it is just important to survey the territory from which one is leaping as well as the destination.

Another problem that can occur if we try to make huge changes with little practice, or without giving warning to others, is that we may overshoot the mark. When we aim for something, whether in golf or target shooting or in behavioral changes, the first adjustment tends to overshoot the mark. If we were told we aimed too far to the left, then we adjust too far to the right, and so on. If we are told we need to become more assertive we may sometimes go beyond assertive to aggressive. Someone who decided to become more independent may go way past independence to the extreme of lonely eccentricity. Making changes takes practice, and practice is best done with small steps.

Take small steps. Set a boundary as to how you will allow someone to treat you and stick to it. Have a discussion with someone who discounts your opinions about how it feels to be discounted. Ask that the behavior stop. Do not accept "you have no sense of humor" as a response, for you are entitled to your feelings. Read a book about a topic related to that previously hidden strength you want to develop, and bring it into the open. Journal about what your perfect life would be in a year's time—or two or three years. Think about what you would need to do to reach that vision. Imagine the vision as being the top of a ladder. What are the rungs on which you need to climb? There are two ways to do this. You can mentally start at the bottom, considering your next step, and then the next. Or you can start at the top, considering the vision achieved, and looking back to see what was the very last step you took to get you there. And what was the step before that? Do this all the way down to the bottom, which is, of course, the very next step you need to take. Which way works best for you? Only you can decide.

WRIGHT

Lives can be happier even with small changes, if people choose not to make a total transformation?

ROBINSON

Absolutely! We've seen that total transformation can be scary and can involve dangerous leaps. It can also be deeply distressing to other people who are involved in one's life. I do see that it sometimes occurs very successfully and wonderfully, but growth into self-efficacy can be achieved with less drama and potential for serious upset if it occurs gradually, step-by-step, rather than in one total 180 degree turnabout.

We can all make adjustments. Sometimes just a small tweak can make more difference than we had foreseen. At the start of our work together, a client once told me of her dream house, planned for the far distant future. In the meantime she kept making small improvements to her existing home. Much later she reported a discovery that to her was amazing. Apart from the unchangeable floor levels, her existing home now included everything she had hoped for in her dream home. Life can be like that when we stay true to ourselves and honor our strengths.

It may be that small steps can achieve all that is needed. If not, having succeeded in small steps can give confidence to move forward and take more and perhaps bigger steps in the future.

WRIGHT

How long does this take?

ROBINSON

Change may be as slow as the movement of tectonic plates beneath the Earth's surface, or as swift as the fall of leaves after first frost. What is important is that you make progress and keep changing until you are comfortable. In the meantime, keep checking. Is the cost to you changing? Is the value changing? Is it still worth it? Is it still what you want? As we make changes *we* change, and we may decide to change our goals. That is all right. There is nothing wrong with allowing our goals to change as we change. Indeed, it is foolish to stick to a goal, or a plan, if it is found to be unrealistic as circumstances change. Figure out what makes you feel good, what attracts the empowerment enhancers, the cheerleaders for your goals. Spend time with them.

Above all, keep track of your progress so that you can take pride, and gain confidence as you see how far you have come. If we do not take note of small successes we may not realize we have achieved them and begin, once again, to lose confidence in ourselves.

WRIGHT

And then?

Robinson

And then people who are empowered and aware of strengths that were previously hidden can feel confident, and can march to the sound of their own drummers. They do not feel dependent on the approval of others. They do not spend their energy worrying about how they look to others or justifying their actions and opinions to everyone they meet.

They are free to be autonomous. They make decisions based on what seems right to them. They are empowered to honor who they are and the strengths they have. And, of course, to encounter and conquer the new challenges that will no doubt appear.

About the Author

Author Diana Gardner Robinson is originally from England. Despite leaving school when she was sixteen, she now has a PhD in Social Psychology, having done her doctoral research on the interaction between creativity and motivation. She believes in continuing to grow as a person and a coach, and has extensive training and experience in empowering people who want to enhance their own growth and inner strengths, the topic that is dearest to her heart.

Robinson now lives in Rochester, New York, has had an international coaching practice for more than fourteen years, teaches addiction counseling at a local college, and tries to find time to write. In her spare time she is also a Distinguished Toastmaster and a volunteer in several local organizations. She recently renamed her business "DGR Coaching." She says that, although it might stand for Diana Gardner Robinson, she prefers that it stand for "From DREAMS to GOALS to RESULTS!"

Diana Gardner Robinson
2604 Elmwood Ave., #230
Rochester, NY 14618
Diana@ChoiceCoach.com

Chapter Fourteen
Life Transformation

An Interview With...
Dan Morand

David Wright (Wright)

Today I'm talking with Dan Morand. Dan is a seasoned life transformation expert, having worked from coast to coast. His "Get Over It" approach to overcoming adversity has helped thousands shift their perspective and continue on a path to building fruitful and productive lives. He is a motivational speaker and humorist whose messages kick you in the gut and send you into fits of laughter at the same time. His passionate heart and work has translated into a thirty-year career as an advocate and coach for those with life-controlling self-esteem and general productivity issues. You can check out his weekly blog at www.DanMorand.com.

Dan, welcome to *Concrete Jungle.*

Dan Morand (Morand)

Thank you, David; it's a pleasure.

Wright

So what exactly is a Life Transformation Expert?

Morand

I believe we all possess the power within us to do anything we want. Regardless of ability, it begins from infancy as we discover, adventure, and journey forward into life, initially having no fear or judgment toward anything. We find our world fascinating and exciting, we simply just appreciate life.

Did you ever watch young children play together? They get so excited at the simplest of things—the things we now take for granted—and can become great friends in a moment regardless of race, religion, creed, or economic status. Unfortunately, however, the older we get, the more distorted our view of the world and what we can accomplish becomes as we receive information from others that limit our thoughts based on what they tell us, subsequently through their own fears and prejudiced viewpoint.

As a life transformation expert, I teach people to become the leader of their own life, so they can push past their critics and the messages they have received through the years that hinder belief in their own ability to do anything they set your minds to do.

Look at most inventors in history—if they had listened to their critics instead of believing in their ability or vision, even the seemingly impossible, we would still be sitting in a cave trying to figure out how the whole concept of fire worked.

In order for all of this transition to take place, we must have the willingness to decode ourselves and learn to believe in our abilities. In the past we were taught it was wrong to be strong willed or self-reliant or confident but that kind of thinking doesn't create leaders, it creates followers. In order for us to be the leader in our own life we have to learn to be confident in who we are and trust in our abilities.

I have worked extensively with people identified as at risk, all desperate, hopeless in their own situations, as they believed they had no control over their life whatsoever. This is similar to the many professionals I have coached and mentored through the years. They, too, had the same kind of mind-set of feeling a lack of control of their abilities. It is like setting out on a trip and you forget your GPS unit. How will you know where you're going or, more importantly, when you will arrive?

To be the leader of your life means to know what you want, not to be fearful of the roadblocks that get in your way. It means to learn to adapt to life's curve balls so even though you don't have all the answers, you will enjoy the adventure along the path that takes you to your desired destination. A life transformation expert is similar to a guide or coach who teaches you to read your internal GPS.

WRIGHT

What are some of the key skills to remember in order to become the leader in your own life?

MORAND

One of the key skills to help people survive their own concrete jungle and even thrive in it is to remember where you come from. Our roots help keep us grounded, regardless of the experiences in our past—positive or negative. We still learned from those experiences and if we remember what brought us through that to the present, we can continue to build on them so that we can continue to move forward in life; it also keeps us humble. Think of some actors, musicians, and professional star athletes whom we admire. The quality we admire most is that these people, regardless of how popular or talented they have become in their own trade, did not forget where they came from and what it took to get where they are now.

To be the leader of our own life, it is important to remember that some of these people refused to give into the fame and fortune by remembering where they come from. For any of us, it helps to appreciate what we went through and what it's taken to get to where we are now. It also provides us with an opportunity to inspire other people.

Attitude is another key skill. I love this quote from Albert Einstein, "If you don't like something, change it. If you can't change it, change your attitude." This is where I got my whole "get over it" philosophy from. There are lots of things that maybe didn't quite happen the way I may have wanted them to. Some call that the cards we've been dealt in life, but at some point you have to get over it and move forward. Very often we're the only person holding ourselves back by hanging on to things that limit our success and destroy any chance of feeling that we're in control or the leader of our own life. We can't change our past but we sure can change our future, all by adjusting our attitude. Some of the most difficult situations in history were overcome by having the proper positive attitude.

Now this is a big one for me, and I have used this in my professional career as well as my personal life—the power of humor or just being real. In most situations, be it the workplace or life in general, nothing is worth getting so stressed about that you risk your mental health because of it.

An old retired army general friend once told me this (I was probably in my twenties at the time), "If it's not worth going up the hill to die for, don't sweat it." I never really understood what he meant by that at the time but as I got older and gained more life experiences, it became clear and I understood those hills in life. We need to take a step back in this busy life once in a while to reassess our situation and see it for what it really is. It's equally important to learn how to laugh at ourselves and put things into perspective.

We get this message that we have to be perfect. Newsflash—none of us are. People are so afraid to show who they really are for fear that they won't be accepted by others, so rather than being a leader in their own life, they become an unwilling follower. Humor is a great tool to get comfortable in your own skin and to allow people to see you for who you really are. I laugh at myself all the time and share my silly antics and stories on a blog or when I speak to audiences; it makes me vulnerable and yet it's freeing at the same time. If you don't have the ups and downs in life, there is nothing to appreciate, so keep your humor.

Recently I went for some routine blood work at the hospital. An admissions clerk directed me to follow a color on the floor to my destination, simple enough right? This hospital has an amazing system for directing people by using different colored circles, squares, and arrows on the floor to take you to your destination so you don't wander off to someplace like the morgue or somewhere like that. Now, the system is simple enough, unless you are color blind like I am, and that's what made this a funny story.

When I reached my destination I was met by a room full of women, young, some not so young, but nonetheless, all women. In fact, there wasn't a man in sight. I knew that standing there with a foolish expression on my face, paperwork in hand, and everybody grinning at me that I was likely in the wrong place.

A nurse approached me with a slight grin, do you need any help?

"Well, obviously I'm not in the right spot," I whispered. "I don't want to know where I am, just where I need to go."

She grinned saying, "fair enough," and redirected me to the "other" orange color that led me back to the blood clinic where I was supposed to be in the first place.

When I was finished, I couldn't resist leaning over to the admissions clerk on the way out, saying, thanks for sending me to the morgue. She began to laugh when I shared my story of what happened and promised that next time I came in she would have me follow a shape instead.

Sometimes just sharing a funny, silly little story like that exposes our flaws and our faults in a positive way. I could have been frustrated with that clerk for sending me on a wild goose chase but it wasn't her fault—she had no idea I was color blind or feeling embarrassed by the situation I found myself in. I could have became impatient with the nurse who attempted to help me, instead I chose to be the leader of my own life by making the best of the situation and by having the right attitude and humor for the situation. It turned into a positive learning experience. So, next time, I guess I will definitely follow a shape when I go there.

WRIGHT

You mentioned about remembering our past. Why should we remember what we have learned from the past rather than just relying on the latest trends?

MORAND

Our past, positive or not, is what forms our belief system. It's what we've learned through experience that shapes us, so we can survive our own concrete jungle as adults.

I remember one such experience. I grew up amid racial tensions in the city of Detroit, Michigan, in the mid-sixties. As a young boy from a small rural village in Ontario, Canada, directly across the river from Detroit, my brother and I used to spend a lot of time in Michigan with relatives for long weekends and holidays; we loved going there. During those visits, I witnessed lots of these racial tensions that I couldn't understand. Why was discrimination based merely on the color of someone's skin such a big deal? It seemed so ridiculous to me; it just plain didn't make sense.

Through those years I witnessed a number of incidents, but even at a young age—I couldn't have been more than eleven years old at the time—a single event stood out for me that taught me the important lesson of being the leader in your own life. It was another hot sunny afternoon, one of those really muggy Detroit days where the air just hangs and you labor for every breath. My aunt sent me out to the local variety store to purchase some ice-cream so we could cool down. I was also to get some milk and a loaf of bread for lunch the next day.

Entering the store, I caught the end of a conversation between a clerk and an elderly black man. He was being told that the store was out of bread for the day. The customer just smiled at the clerk, said, "Fine." As he turned to leave the store, he looked down at me and smiled saying, "Don't worry son. You'll get bread if you need some." That made no sense to me, because the clerk just said there was no more bread for the day.

Confused by his comment, I made my way to the refrigeration unit in the rear of the store, got my ice-cream and milk, and then headed back to the front counter to pay for them. The clerk asked if I had everything I needed. I told him I would send my aunt the next day to pick up bread. To my surprise, the clerk produced a loaf of bread from behind the counter and handed it to me. I was confused by this because I had heard him tell the other customer he had no more bread. I asked him why he said he was out of bread. The clerk smiled saying, "That's the way it is, son."

"That's the way *what* is?" I wondered to myself.

As I walked back to my aunt's house I couldn't stop thinking about what had happened and how unfair it was. When I reached the house I told her the story and my aunt was disgusted and outraged. She explained to me why the clerk did what he did. The only thing I can remember that night as I lay in my bed trying to fall asleep in the heat, is how calm that older man seemed. Regardless of the situation, regardless of what had happened, he maintained his control. He was the leader of his own life—he refused to let that situation belittle him. In the end the store clerk lost respect and the store lost money for the lack of a sale and a customer.

Funny and weird that an eleven-year-old thinks that way, but that single event changed my entire perspective on life. I spent my early adult life living in Vancouver where I volunteered on infamous East Hastings Street. It is filled with drug addicts, prostitutes, and homeless people. I delivered meals or was just an ear for the ones whom society had tossed away. I saw them as human beings, deserving love and guidance as they begged for a way out of a life that circumstances had seen them fall into.

I was working full-time and attending part-time business courses at Simon Fraser University while I volunteered.

Through those experiences I decided that people were my business and dropped everything to devote myself full-time to work with at-risk youth and people with disabilities for the next number of years. Remembering the early events in my past fueled my passion to what I felt drawn to in the future.

Once I was into my forties, I worked with a ministry that was devoted to helping people with varied addictions. It was during that time I was asked to move with my wife and two young children off mainland Canada to Newfoundland, an island off the east coast, to establish a long-term drug and alcohol center for men. However, this was no simple task. I quickly realized the local drug dealers were not going to just roll over and let us clean up their customers. This was going to be a major crunch on their livelihood and they planned not to go down without a fight.

I spent countless hours looking for locations, only to be asked to leave town by the locals too afraid to deal with these hapless drug-dealing thugs. After all, some of these people were related! Despite the situation, the organization I worked for refused to give in and wanted a center established. I was taunted on the daily radio show and on the front covers of local papers for five or six months with the clear message that I had to leave. We were threatened twice that our house would be burned down. We also received some personal threats. Yet in all of that, I knew this was something that was going to free people from their addiction and I was determined to try as hard as I could to help this center become a reality.

With little support, other than from a group of local churches, schools, and my spouse, the fight became too much because the threats had become too risky for my family. After one year, almost to the day, we moved back to the mainland where I established a center within months that still operates to this day.

Being the leader in your own life, means sometimes you have to really believe in what you're doing, believe in what you're called to do, and not listen to anything else that might throw you off track. Gathering experiences from your past for strength to pull you through situations is easier than trying something new.

WRIGHT

Why is it important to always maintain our integrity in all we do in life?

MORAND

People are often afraid to be themselves—to be real—because they believe they won't to be accepted. Ever hear the phrase, "That person is the real deal"? People like that are happy with whom they are. They are leaders in their own life. When you meet them, there is no pretense—they're exactly who they are and they maintain a high level of integrity. Others are willing to compromise their integrity so they are accepted.

This next story comes to mind—my one and only traffic court appearance. I felt I had wrongfully been charged with a speeding violation while driving a company vehicle. To avoid coming under question from my employer, I decided to fight the ticket. Case by case was called up, now it was my turn. The court bailiff signaled me to step forward. I stood behind a microphone and the officer was seated at a table full of paperwork beside me. The judge motioned the officer to explain the offense as he gave me the once over with his eyes. I felt as I was going to get life!

The officer began to explain that I had been travelling south-bound when he spotted me from his location and that I had been speeding twenty-five miles per hour over the limit. No mention of the hill I was coming down or that the speed limit sign changed. That would have reduced my crime to speeding only ten miles per hour over the limit. No, he has to bring up that fact that there is a school in the area! Yeah, several blocks further up the road. Seriously? The judge looks over at me with disgust.

"Gee whiz," I think to myself. "My record is spotless." I keep my mouth shut because my boss was seated behind me in the courtroom for support. The officer continues to describe his routine of setting up the speed trap, the fact that he was trained on three models of the equipment, trained other officers, and in his spare time, read up on changes.

Not being able to keep my mouth shut at that point, I whispered, "Of course you do!" Unfortunately for me, I was standing in front of a live microphone and my whisper filled the courtroom! Awkward!

The officer stopped speaking, my boss stared at me, and the judge looked over sternly saying, "Don't worry son, you will get your chance to speak."

I could have crawled under a rock. I apologized to the officer and he continued. Now, I came in that courtroom ready to beat this ticket, but as I listened to the officer explain what he did and the things he had witnessed due to speeding, I realized that he was just doing his job. I was ashamed for trying to get out of the ticket just because I didn't want to get in trouble with my boss. Yes, the conditions may have not been totally fair, but at the end of the day I was still speeding.

When it came time for me to speak, I told the judge that I changed my mind and didn't want to fight the ticket. I said I realized why the officer pulled me over and that he was just trying to keep our streets safe. The judge was impressed with my honesty and gave me a substantially reduced fine, with no points off my license. However, the officer looked over at me and winked. Oh my goodness, he thought I was working the system! That's the danger of compromising your integrity—people never know when you are being honest or working an angle. It was a valuable lesson for me that day! My boss was also more impressed with my honesty than if I had beaten the ticket.

When people know the real you, they know exactly where you stand; but if you're not real and compromise your values, then your integrity will be in question.

Wright

Why is it so important to maintain an integral balance when it comes to being competitive in life and the workplace?

Morand

When I speak to audiences, I like to tell this story about my friend and me. It is more a fishing tale than surviving the concrete jungle. Each year my friend and I met up once during the summer months, halfway between our cities, which were twelve hours apart. We would just hang out and compare our successes with one another. Even though we had grown up together, we were very competitive guys who always put on a front that everything was perfect in our lives. Although we had gone through many trials, the other never knew for fear that the other would be seen as weak. He was a part time firefighter and worked as a maintenance person for his small picturesque community in the Rockies. I owned a small business on the West Coast. No matter what we did, it was always a competition.

One year it was decided that we would go fishing, even though I'm a lousy fisherman. We found this little spot and were maybe an hour into fishing when this older gentleman in a rust bucket of a boat approached us and asked how the fishing was going. I told him it was fine and he asked us if he could take a peek at what we caught, I said, "Sure!"

I had cut the tails and heads off already, although these were legal size fish and we were under the limit, the wardens don't like it if the heads and tails are cut off. As I opened the container, I looked up and saw that the guy was a game warden and had his badge out. He could have confiscated our boat, our truck, and our equipment, but he didn't because the fish were legal size and we were under the limit allowed, he just took our fish and let us off with a warning.

A little deflated by our experience, we began to leave when I spotted a rickety sign on a native reserve across the area where we had been fishing that read: "Fishing—no limits." We looked at one another and smiled. What the heck! So we decided to pay the fee and not leave empty handed. As we headed to the lake, my friend yelled out, "Usual bet!" This meant that the person who lost paid for dinner. We would usually get the most expensive dinner we could come up with such as steak and lobster and the trimmings.

We began to fish but it became apparent, by the seventh or eighth fish he had on his string already, that I would be buying dinner.

Suddenly in the distance I spotted some natives fishing up the shore and an idea came into my head. I looked at my buddy and said, "Listen, pal, we're too close. You're scaring my fish away. So I'm going to go fish up a little bit and see if I can't catch something," to which he smirked and said, "Okay, whatever."

So, concerned with losing, I approached the men and immediately went into my sales pitch explaining my dilemma and asked to buy their fish. They laughed and sold me the fish. I placed them on my stringer and threw them back into the water.

About an hour later my friend, wearing a smug look on his face, holding a stringer full of fish comes up singing, "Big, juicy steak and lobster, salad, dessert, and a drink." Hang on a minute—I hadn't even counted my fish yet! I pulled my stringer out of the water as I counted, "Nine, ten, eleven, twelve, thirteen." My friend cried out, "What the heck!" Raised to be honest, I said, "Honestly, it was so easy; it was as though I bought them!" Needless to say, I enjoyed a free steak dinner, including lobster, salad, drink, and dessert. But the story doesn't end there.

About ten years later, we're sitting at a barbeque with friends, trading off stories when I decide to tell this one. Now, although everyone was laughing about the story, my friend realized that he had been cheated. The moral of the story is that the steak and lobster, salad, drink, and a dessert cost a heck of a lot more ten years after it happened. The real lesson here is that if we hadn't been so competitive and more transparent with each other, our times spent together would have been more honest and genuine.

We need to be real in the way we work and in the way we play. Competiveness can be healthy and even fun—if it maintains an integral balance.

Wright

Is it important to stay connected and relevant in today's fast-paced world?

Morand

Absolutely. It is so much easier to stay connected and relevant in todays fast-paced world than ever before. Things move so quickly—we have e-mail, instant messaging, Facebook, Linked In, Twitter, Skype, and so on. The world has become so small now. In the past it would have taken days, even months to catch up on the information that now takes seconds. And sometimes we complain that it isn't quick enough!

You are never too old to jump onto the information highway. At the flick of a key on your computer you can be instantly connected to someone across the globe.

My parents are a great example. In their seventies, I finally talked them into getting a computer because most of their children live away from home now. As I connected their computer, lo and behold there was an unsecure Internet access from the school across the street from their house. My mother refused to use it because she thought she was stealing. I tried to explain to her about the Internet and how it worked. I had to get my nephew who is tech savvy to explain to his grandmother. There are lots of courses and information out there, often free, so it is inexpensive to stay connected and relevant in today's world. It is easy to grow your network of business or friendships with the use of this technology.

WRIGHT

What do you think is one of the oldest most common mistakes to make in the workplace or in life or in general, for that matter?

MORAND

If knowledge is power then lack of knowledge is weakness. Don't be afraid to ask questions, never assume that you have all the answers, and even though you may know something ask anyway because you may learn something new. That is something my father drilled into us as children. So many people are afraid to admit that they don't know something. Well, you are going to look foolish if something bad happens because you didn't ask.

I have coached and been an accountability coach with many people through the years. Most of the core issues were related to the fear of asking questions because they didn't want to appear incompetent. This often got them into a huge mess.

There was a case I worked on where an individual cost his company $25,000 because he didn't ask questions; that was a huge mistake! He lost his higher paying position to a lower-paying entry level position and only because he had years of service with the company. If he would have asked the questions that he should have, he would have avoided the demotion and embarrassment, not to mention the cost to the company.

As a teen I worked part-time at a Chinese restaurant, one day the owner was displaying his culinary genius by sautéing onions in a cast iron pan in front of some customers. He called over to me to take the pan to the kitchen as he finished. Assuming he would never hand me a hot skillet, I grabbed it from his hands! It burned the first few layers of skin and the back of his head when, startled to be holding a hot skillet, I threw the skillet back toward him. That was the shortest job I ever had because I didn't ask questions. (I still love Chinese food.)

Ask, ask, ask the questions, even if you think you know the answer. You are never too skilled or too professional not to ask questions. Asking questions clarifies things, and you can still learn other angles. It's the oldest, most common mistake people make—being afraid just to ask the question. Never be arrogant enough to think that you know everything.

WRIGHT

You talk about coaching, and you mention accountability. Why should on have an accountability person in one's life?

MORAND

I have an accountability person—my latest one for six years now. An accountability person can be a friend or someone you respect and trust to keep you accountable, to keep you on track, to keep you humble. That neutral person that is going to tell you something like, "You're totally off on this one" or "I think you should really take a step back and look at this again." You need that someone to do that double check for you, but you also have to be mature enough, open enough, and honest enough to listen to that person if he or she is going to be an accountability person for you.

While lying on the ground with another forty-six students during an elementary school protest about having to wear school uniforms in grade eight, I ignored my best friend and very first accountability person who cautioned me that I may not be taking the best course of action in protesting. I chose to ignore his advice and inadvertently laid in a patch of poison oak! Needless to say I was "itching" to get back to class. I should have heard my accountability person out.

Your accountability person is the best person for you to double check those ideas you have for work and life. He or she is your check and balance person. A spouse or close family member is not always the best choice to be an accountability person because that intimate, personal relationship can get in the way of being honest and saying exactly what needs to be said at times.

WRIGHT

So why is it important to remember what worked in the past?

MORAND

Often we are so busy "reinventing the wheel" that we forget that it has already been invented. Remember, what worked for you in the past will sure save a heck of a lot of time and effort.

To be the leader in your own life, you need to remember where you've come from. I think it's very important to remember the mistakes you have made, not necessarily celebrate them, but understand what you learned from that mistake. It builds our confidence in solving the current issues that we face in life.

I was blessed to come from a loving home, but didn't always appreciate it; I took it for granted at times. It is important to remember when you were successful in the past—forget about the times you weren't, even those things you will learn from. Failure is not falling down, it is refusing to get back up and try again. Remembering our past, both good and bad, puts everything into perspective, keeps us humble, and saves time and money.

WRIGHT

How important do you think it is to take quiet time for yourself?

MORAND

This is hugely important and will save your mental and physical health. There is a lot of information out there to support the importance of shutting down for at least twenty minutes per day, be it in your office, or wherever you are, which includes unplugging from all your technology. I have practiced this for a few years now and it's been wonderful just taking that twenty minutes in a day just to center yourself, to think, and to take that time to reflect or pray or whatever. Just to have that time for you and just shut down. We are not doing anything any faster or any better than we have in the past; however, we probably make our mistakes faster with our advanced technology. After a twenty-minute break, you will come back rejuvenated and ready to tackle anything with a rested, clear mind.

Taking that time just to relax also means taking that vacation day without any guilt—just take that one day once in a while to shut down and spend time with yourself. You should also take those true vacations with your family so that you can appreciate your family; we don't live to work. This means leave the company phone, emails and paperwork at home – they call it a vacation for a reason. If you want to be the leader of your own life, you need to know that proper rest enables one to make sounder decisions because you have had the opportunity to have the time to think things through. Many successful people make an undisturbed twenty-minute break mandatory in their routine because they realize the benefits of taking the time to be quiet. If you can learn to be quiet and content with yourself, you will be better equipped to handle life.

WRIGHT

What a great conversation, Dan. Thank you for your input.

Today I have been talking with Dan Morand. Dan is a life transformation expert and an advocate and coach for those with life controlling, self-esteem, and general productivity issues. He is a motivational speaker and humorist whose messages kick you in the gut and send you into fits of laughter at the same time.

Dan, thank you so much for being with us today on *Concrete Jungle.*

MORAND

Thank you David, it's been a pleasure. I have had some amazing mentors in my life and these principals are simple to adopt, but take discipline to master.

About the Author

Dan Morand knows people. His thirty years of working with populations at risk is impressive, whether it is for life-controlling, self-esteem, advocacy, or productivity issues, Dan has impacted thousands of lives with his unique "get-over-it" sense of humour style and passionate heart. Dan trains with purpose and leaves his audiences with information that is both inspiring and useful.

Dan makes no apologies for his life journey. Working in environments as a factory worker, a salesmen, a clerk, a cleaner, a youth worker, an entrepreneur, a business consultant, an executive coach, a college instructor, a minister, director, author, actor and comedian – Dan believes the real core to his success is relating to people where they are at – and in most cases, he has been there himself.

Dan Morand
15 Glen Abbey Court
Moncton NB E1G 2C6
888-502-6317
dan@jumpstart720.com
www.danmorand.com

Chapter Fifteen
Your Job Is Not Who You Are

An Interview With...

Steve Rizzo

Make conscious choices to periodically step away from your job and experience other parts of yourself that are yearning to be expressed.

—Steve Rizzo

DAVID WRIGHT (WRIGHT)

Steve Rizzo is a motivational mechanic who tunes and tweaks each member of his audience to succeed at his or her full potential. With a delivery that is poignant, hilarious, and inspiring, Steve, affectionately known as the "Attitude Adjuster," teaches methods for improving opportunities and provides skills people need to get to a better place at work and in life. He is Executive Producer of his own PBS special, author of the award winning book, *Becoming a Humor Being,* and a "Speaker Hall of Fame" inductee.

Steve, welcome to *Concrete Jungle: Survival Secrets for the Real World.*

In your experience, is there a difference between being successful and enjoying inner happiness?

STEVE RIZZO (RIZZO)

Years ago I was watching a Barbara Walters special on television. She was interviewing a major personal comedic influence of mine, Johnny Carson. Of course, Johnny Carson was an inspiration to an entire generation of performers. As the host of *The Tonight Show,* Carson spent thirty years as the "top dog" in television comedy. To me, at least, it seemed like no one on Earth could have been happier and more successful, and I tuned in eagerly to hear what such a fortunate man might say.

The interview came during Mr. Carson's last year as the host of *The Tonight Show*. As you may know, Barbara Walters has a reputation of being very direct when interviewing celebrities, but if anyone could handle "The Woman Who Pulls No Punches," I thought surely it would be "The King of Late Night Television."

In the end, I was surprised, shocked even, at the way Johnny responded to Walter's questions. I expected the carefree attitude of a man having "conquered the world" going out on top. Instead of the usual barrage of rapid-fire jokes and wisecracks, when he was questioned about his personal life, he gave short, awkward replies that didn't at all suggest confidence. There was an aura of melancholy about him that I believe even took Barbara Walters by surprise.

At the end of the interview, Walters alluded to Carson's fame and long list of accomplishments, any of which were far more than any that I, as an up-and-coming comedian, could have imagined attaining. Then she asked one last question:

"Are you happy?" I couldn't help myself. I blurted out, *"What a stupid question! Of course he's happy—he's Johnny Carson!"* I was shocked when he stumbled over what seemed to be a very simple question. It was obvious that he was uncomfortable giving his answer. *"I don't know,"* said The King of Late Night Television. *"I honestly don't know."*

Why, I wondered, was someone who gave so much joy and laughter to millions of people four and five days a week for almost thirty years unable to answer the question, "Are you happy?" Of course you could say that he was in a low mood because he was leaving the show that was a great part of his life. I could buy that. Surely anyone would be sad under similar circumstances. But even after being reminded of his accomplishments in the television and entertainment industry and the monumental impact he made in people's lives, he still couldn't answer the question.

WRIGHT

Based on your observations, did you come to any definitive conclusions?

RIZZO

On the final episode of *The Tonight Show*, Johnny gave his farewell address to the millions who were watching. And it was then that the reason why was evident. Let me explain.

Most people would say then that Johnny Carson had "the world in the palms of his hands." But perhaps having the world in the palms of your hands shouldn't be the point of focus. What really matters is the realization that you always hold your own world in your hands, and the choices you make as you are holding it. Your entire life is based on the choices you make. It is important to know that some choices are made consciously, while others are made unconsciously. Either way, there are always consequences for the choices you make. This is not a threat, but a universal fact.

We would all stand a better chance to live a happier life if we were more conscious of, and put some thought behind, our choices. The problem is that many of our choices are made unconsciously, therefore we don't think they are choices. Believe me, they are. In fact, everything that is occurring in your life at this moment is a result of choices you made in the past. Those choices that were made, consciously or unconsciously, are key factors that determine your quality of life right now. I have you thinking now, don't I?

On that final episode of *The Tonight Show*, Johnny Carson said, *"I am one of the lucky ones in the world. I found something I always wanted to do and enjoyed every minute of it."*

I'm sure he did. But not too long after that statement he revealed deep regret, and apologized to his sons Kit and Cory for "not being there enough," adding that he loved them. He also expressed sorrow and guilt about the death of his son, Richard, who died in a car crash in 1991.

Let us not forget that Johnny was married four times. His ex-wives were often the butt of his jokes. Behind the mask of humor, was there someone who truly wanted a lasting relationship? It was apparent that he was so caught up in his role as The King of Late Night Television that he had difficulty identifying himself with anything or anyone else.

It's obvious that Johnny Carson gave much and received much, but paid heavily. It makes one wonder, is there always a price to pay when what we do for a living becomes our whole life, no matter what the level of success that's achieved? We have to ask ourselves, is the price worth it? And, is there a way to find a happy balance?

WRIGHT

What you are saying is that he was married to his job, right? Do you consider that to be a bad thing?

RIZZO

Not too long ago, I was sitting on a beach in San Juan, Puerto Rico, and noticed a couple holding hands, walking along the shoreline. They looked so peaceful, like an advertisement for an island getaway. And then it happened—his cell phone went off. She gave him a look as if to say, "I dare you!" I couldn't believe it. The idiot took the dare. Not only did he answer the phone, but he let go of her hand, walked away and talked for about ten minutes. She shook her head, walked over to their beach set-up, which was about twenty feet from mine, and sat down under their umbrella. By now the couple who looked like an advertisement for an island getaway were about to become prime candidates for the *Dr. Phil Show*.

He walked over to her and tried to explain. I grimaced. In my head I heard the booming catchphrase popularized by announcer Michael Buffer that boxing fans know so well:

"Let's get ready to ruuuumble!"

Ding, ding! She came out swinging.

"How could you?" she asked. *"I can't even believe you brought your cell phone with you, but you had the nerve to answer it!"*

Now, what he should have done was listened to what she had to say. Of course, he didn't.

"Hey!" he jabbed at her in his defense. *"If it wasn't for my business, we wouldn't even be* on *this vacation!"*

She rebounded with a combination of blows that seemed to shake the champ. *"Vacation?"* she said, incredulous. *"Vacation? You call this a vacation? This is our anniversary! We've been here for three days so far and you can't stay away from your cell phone and stupid computer! You brought your job with you! You just can't stop yourself! It's like you're addicted!"*

She picked up her belongings and took a few steps toward the hotel. Then she stopped, turned, and delivered the haymaker:

"You know, you used to be married to me. Now you're married to your job!" The champ just stood there, looking like a real chump. I thought the wife used an interesting choice of words.

Does this story come as a surprise? Let's face it. We are living in a world that is moving at an amazing pace. It is easy to get lost and misplace our feelings and values. Most of us are conditioned to devote most of our waking hours on our jobs and professional goals leaving little, if any, time for other important aspects of our lives. Who can deny that we live in a highly competitive society that stresses the importance of being the very best, rather than simply to do the best we can? Many have bought into the grand deception of always wanting more, regardless of what they already have.

We have adopted the illusion that money, power, and fame can fill that self-created emptiness and make us feel complete. I am not suggesting that there is anything wrong with these things. It is the obsession with them that makes them dangerous.

WRIGHT

What are you getting at?

RIZZO

What am I getting at? (I have absolutely no idea. Just kidding—I'm still in control here.) I'll tell you. Maybe it would be wise for us to come to the realization that what we think we want in life may not necessarily be what we need in order to lead a truly successful and happy life. Maybe, just maybe, we are leaving out important factors from the equation of what truly completes us as individuals. Maybe it's just a matter of making a slight shift, finding your balance, and choosing a better way. Maybe there are too many "maybes" in this paragraph.

WRIGHT

Are you saying that in the final analysis it all comes down to making the right choices?

RIZZO

Yes indeed—our lives depend on the choices we make, but I believe that we can at least minimize our regrets just by being more consciously aware of our choices. This is what the habit of shifting your focus in order to be happy moment-to-moment does for you. Before you know it, you're actually happy. Then it becomes clear what you should focus on in the big picture.

There's a Spanish proverb where God says, "Choose what you will and pay for it." This proverb stresses that life holds no easy answers, only choices. And sometimes they are costly. We must live with and pay for the consequences. I don't know what type of business the guy on the beach was in that consumed so much of his time, but it was apparent that the scene between him and his wife was not an isolated incident. I would wager any amount of money that they have had this discussion many times before. After all, he was clearly unable to shift his focus. He *was* married to his job.

Here is a question I want the readers to ponder: I really want you to seriously consider what I am suggesting here before you answer. Are you ready? Is it possible that you are focusing so much of your time and energy on the success of your job or career that you are unconsciously leaving out important elements that would otherwise bring you joy and make your life complete?

WRIGHT

As you go about helping people on a daily basis, how do you envision your job?

RIZZO

My job is to show people how to acquire the attitude they need to succeed on all levels of life while enjoying the process. When I write, "success on all levels of life," I mean just that. Your personal and professional lives are parts of you that make up the whole of you. If you put most of your time and energy on one area, you run the risk of leaving the other unfulfilled. This is especially common with those who are high achievers, perhaps like you, dear reader.

Marianne Williamson says, "*Hectic minds create a hectic world.*" Every now and then we just have to stop the hectic world and get off for a while. We must never be too busy to take time out away from our job and experience sacred parts of ourselves that are so often buried and yearning to be expressed.

When our jobs consume us, eventually, in one form or another, there will be a price to pay. I'm not suggesting that we shouldn't love what we are doing for a living. In fact, it's important that we do. And it is essential that we devote quality time toward our job. The problem arises when what we do for a living interferes with our other precious core values.

A value can be something tangible or intangible that we esteem highly such as health and fitness, honesty, truthfulness, freedom, courage, spirituality, beauty, goodness, playfulness, self-sufficiency, wealth, time to spend as we like, and so on. These cherished values are sacred parts of our self that need to be experienced and expressed. They give us self-worth. If we ignore them for too long, it can only lead to unhappiness, regardless of how prestigious our profession is, how much money we make or how successful we think we are.

WRIGHT

Would it be possible to give our readers some examples of neglected values that have affected our lives?

RIZZO

Below are some examples of cherished values that are often neglected or buried because of our jobs:

To spend more time with my family and friends. I really enjoy spending time at home. I love quality time with my children—playing with them, helping them with their homework, and getting to know them. I love spending time with my friends. It's a time for me to unwind, let loose, laugh, and put my worries behind me. I also love my job, but it hurts that I am missing out on valuable time with my loved ones—time that I know I will never get back. I am going to have to cut down on volunteering for assignments and working late. I want to occasionally leave early so that I can have more time for them. Sometimes when I get home too late, I get this empty feeling that I'm missing out on something very special. And I don't like going to bed feeling guilty.

To take a weekend off from work, without interruption and free from e-mails, cell phones, and text messages. I'm sick of taking my job home with me! I just want to be alone, hang out in my sweats, and not care how I look. I want to be able to do what I want, read a book, listen to music, work in my garden, or just sleep. I miss this part of myself and I'm taking it back.

To do the things that connects me to my spirit. Yes, things are going great at work. I've been recognized as "salesmen of the year" three years in a row. I'm producing more than I ever could have imagined. I am truly blessed for the financial wealth I have accumulated throughout the years. But my spiritual reservoir is on "empty." Taking time to commune with nature is important to me. I can't remember the last time I went hiking or even walked through a scenic area. I barely have time to meditate or to appreciate a sunrise or sunset, the way I used to. I guess I just got caught up. Yes I'm successful, but I don't feel fulfilled. I have to bring that sacred part of me back to myself. There is no reason why I can't continue my success at work and fulfill this other sacred part of myself as well. I deserve to be happy on all levels.

WRIGHT

What happens when people become aware that their jobs are interfering with their happiness?

RIZZO

When people finally become aware that their jobs are interfering with these sacred parts of themselves, they can then choose to find ways to bring their values into existence. The result is that they raise their self-worth, increase their self-respect, reduce the gap between aspiring for fulfillment and actually feeling fulfilled that reduces the risk of burn-out. Now *that's* what I call nourishing the soul!

I understand that it's far too easy to ignore these valued parts of yourself when you're caught up in your job and struggling to succeed. Nevertheless, they could very well be the main ingredients that make up the recipe of your life. One of those ingredients could be the missing link that soothes your hectic mind and fulfills your world with the happiness you desire. The amazing thing is that most of the time, it's just a simple matter of becoming aware of what is missing and then making the appropriate choices to fix it.

WRIGHT

Why do you think it's so difficult to for people to become aware?

RIZZO

"She'll understand," you may tell yourself. "She knows how much I love her. We'll spend more time together when things settle down at work. After all, I'm doing this for both of us." I promise you that's what the chump on the beach was telling himself.

Are you nurturing your artistic talents or hobbies such as painting, photography, crafts, gardening, music, and so on, or have you lost your way on the road to success?

When your little boy or girl is saying, "Hey, look at me!" are you really paying attention or is your mind on what needs to be done tomorrow at the office? You will never have that moment again. Remember, it's not necessarily what you did that causes you to have regrets, it could very well be what you didn't do that comes back to haunt you.

Your soul is continually yearning to be fulfilled and nourished. It takes more than just driving to succeed in your profession and overcoming obstacles to feed it. We must also take time out from the hustle and bustle of our everyday lives and feel the joy and simplicity that life has to offer.

WRIGHT

As you see more of this kind of behavior, what do you suggest people do to improve?

RIZZO

Sometimes I think, if my soul had a voice, it would say, "Excuse me, Steve? I understand that part of soul-work is honoring your job, pain, and grief. I know you have responsibilities. I know you have goals and dreams. I know you have bills to pay. I also know that life has thrown many challenges your way and for the most part that you handle them quite well. In fact, it makes me feel wonderful that you're learning life's lessons. But can you please stop for awhile and remember and connect with what really gives you joy? Might I suggest that you go to the child within you who used to be so close to me and rediscover what truly makes you happy and gives you peace of mind? And can you please care enough about yourself to find a place for those things in your life? In other words, my friend Steve, what about my needs? And, if you think about it, my needs and your needs are one and the same."

Forget for a moment the fact that my soul sounds like James Earl Jones. I'm more than aware that there are many people who find great value and fulfillment in their occupations. My profession—helping people to shift their mind-sets in order to find success and happiness—absolutely fulfills a sacred part of me. However, my job does not make up the whole of me.

I want you to understand that I'm not asking you to ignore your professional goals, joys, and responsibilities. They, too, are sacred parts of you that foster soul growth. I know all too well that our professional goals and responsibilities quite often require sacrifice, dedication, and countless hours of overtime. I'm simply asking you *not* to ignore other sacred parts of yourself that complete you. It's called balancing your life, and it's often just a matter of adjusting or shifting your life to do things that you value and that bring you joy.

WRIGHT

It sounds as If most people could solve this problem by changing their priorities. So, how do we start?

RIZZO

Write a list of things that you truly value and bring you joy, such as quality time with family and friends, solitude, playfulness, spirituality, walking, nature, health, traveling, artistic ability, and so on. Spend at least half an hour, and dig deep to think of things that make you happy.

If you're thorough and honest with yourself as you're writing out your list, you may be surprised to discover that your current way of living doesn't make much room for the things that you value and bring you joy. If this is so, my friend, it's time to make different choices to tweak your life accordingly. Whatever you do, don't make this too difficult and don't berate yourself for screwing up. You didn't screw up. (Unless you answered your cell phone on the beach, moron.) For the most part, you were just caught up in the thing we call life. We all make unconscious choices and respond to situations without even thinking of the long-term consequences.

Now you have a wonderful opportunity to take some time and contemplate how you can shift your priorities to fulfill your needs. This may take a few mental adjustments such as picturing where your couch will go in a new apartment. Imagine what effort on your part it would take to find fulfillment in each value on the list. Imagine the benefits of taking a few extra hours out of the week to devote to an activity on the list and how good that might make you feel. Listen to your heart, use common sense and steer yourself toward the things that lift you up and bring you joy. What I'm telling you here is that you teach yourself to become consciously aware of what you truly value, and then make the appropriate choices to fulfill those needs.

WRIGHT

What about the person who is basically living the "I want to be me" lifestyle, giving no thought to what others might think?

RIZZO

This is where "free will" comes back into play. Whenever you are in a situation where you are trying to bring professional and personal balance into your life, I want you to ask yourself the three, free-will "will" questions:

- *Will* there be personal consequences to this choice I'm making?
- *Will* this choice affect others, now and in the future?
- *Will* this choice make me happy, now and in the future?

The answer to the first two questions will always be "yes," whether you know it or not. The third question, I don't have to tell you, is the most important. By asking yourself the first two questions, you've answered "yes" and thought about what the ramifications of your decision will be. The third question is all about you, though. Will it make you happy? It's simple. Answer it. Your answer may end up guiding you to a decision, especially after forcing yourself to consider the consequences that will arise from answering differently.

These three questions don't guarantee that you will always make the best choice; however, they are very empowering in that they allow you to stand behind the helm of your life and see more clearly how to steer the course of events, situations, and circumstances you encounter.

WRIGHT

What about the guy who constantly blames the lack of time for every problem in his life?

RIZZO

There are those who insist that they can't afford to spend time outside of the realm of their careers. In actuality, when you think of the consequences, you really can't afford not to. Taking time off is not a waste of time. It's a recharging of your inner battery. When you step away from the worry and chaos that so often comes with success, you are energizing your spirit.

My friend Victoria was so caught up in climbing the corporate ladder, deadlines, overtime, and working weekends, that she was neglecting something of great value that always brought her great joy and lifted her spirits—her friends. She couldn't remember the last time she spent quality time with them. It really was a simple matter of picking up the phone, inviting them to dinner and to spend the weekend together. Now they all make it a special occasion once a month or so.

By the way, Victoria is still climbing the corporate ladder. Only now, she does it without neglecting a sacred part of herself. She made the shift and is now spending time with people who are very important to her, nourishing her soul by sharing experiences with like-minded people. In her words, "I feel refreshed and complete whenever we spend time together."

WRIGHT

Let's talk about time for a minute. It really is a problem in our culture. How do you separate your life in order to "have your cake and eat it too?"

RIZZO

I put a great deal of time and energy into building my career. There always seems to be something that needs to be done—new projects to be worked on in the way of books, DVDs, CDs, and customizing programs for clients. The more engagements I complete, the more in-demand as a speaker I am. Now don't misunderstand me. This is not a complaint. I really do love and enjoy what I do. It feels good to provide services that are needed, and I believe I do them well. The important thing is what I choose to do when I'm not in front of an audience or working on new programs.

After a lifetime of worry, frustration, and disappointment in little shortcomings, I am now beginning to understand how valuable that time in between is. I call it: "My Time." And with My Time, I simply do what makes me happy. I have found that the amount of time I have for My Time isn't as important as the attention I give it. In other words, it's quality time that matters, not quantity.

This time can be a day or a few weeks at home in between bookings, or it can be a simple luxury of staying overnight at a hotel before I give a morning speech. Whatever the amount of time I have, it's what I choose to do with My Time that brings value to it. I try to make conscious choices to feed my soul and complement parts of myself that need fostering and make me happy.

For example, whether I'm home or on the road, I always find time to exercise. It simply makes me feel great—physically, emotionally, mentally, and spiritually. Sometimes when I'm away from home, I may choose to go for a walk through a historical neighborhood. I discovered years ago that walking is a form of meditation that always puts my mind at ease. Quite often, as I'm walking, solutions to problems hit me with such clarity that I have to laugh. (You might want to try that the next time you're all stressed out over a problem at work.) Perhaps I may choose to stay in my hotel room and take a nap or read a book. Both are something I have become accustomed to. Something else I love to do when I'm traveling is to meet with friends for dinner and indulge in great conversation, nonstop laughter and, of course, a great bottle of wine.

These are just some of the things that complete me as a person. To you, they may seem simple or unproductive, or even boring. But to me, they are essential to my wellbeing. My Time is when I let go of the hectic world and find my balance. Within this time, I have a profound understanding that I don't have to push life so much in order to experience it harmoniously but to be guided more by intuition than ambition. Some of my greatest insights have come to me when I have decided to simply break away and pay attention to who I am.

WRIGHT

That's a life changer. So, you're saying that you are not defined by your job, right?

RIZZO

Your job is not who you are, it's what you do. What you do for a living may be a sacred part of who you are, but on its own merits, it doesn't complete you. There's so much more to you than what you do to earn a paycheck. Deep inside, you know this is true.

By all means, dedicate a great amount of time toward achieving your professional goals. But for your sake, learn how to let go and honor those other sacred parts of yourself. If you do, don't be surprised if you find that you are more passionate and enthusiastic at work.

Allow yourself the freedom to use your time to love, laugh, and learn. Find your balance! Find your joy! Live your life with passion! Don't be afraid to shift your life in the direction of the things that you value and that nourish your soul. Shift your focus when you are feeling fragmented and upset to bring yourself back to your higher sense of being, and shift your priorities to allow yourself to focus on what matters.

Remember, when shift happens, your life changes. And trust me, my friend, it's for the better.

About the Author

Steve Rizzo is a "Hall of Fame" speaker whose mission in life is to show people how to be happy and successful, no matter what their circumstances are. With a delivery that is entertaining and inspiring, Steve, affectionately known as the "Attitude Adjuster," takes motivation and confidence building to an entirely new level.

Steve Rizzo

www.steverizzo.com

Chapter Sixteen

Lean Forward Marketing

An Interview With...

Eric V. Holtzclaw

David Wright (Wright)

Today I'm talking with Eric V. Holtzclaw. Eric is the Founder and Chief Executive Officer of User Insight. He has spent more than twenty years creating opportunities through the practical application of emerging technologies and trends in business. His professional experience includes founding multiple successful startup companies, including one of the first profitable Internet enterprises, and implementation of more than thirty consumer-oriented and internal use products and services worldwide.

Eric has the opportunity to interview and understand thousands of people annually and uses this knowledge of consumer behavior to advise the world's leading brands to prioritize strategic investments in technology, advertising, and marketing for maximum return.

Welcome to *Concrete Jungle: Survival Secrets for the Real World,* Eric. I appreciate your being in this book.

Eric Holtzclaw (Holtzclaw)

Good afternoon; how are you?

Wright

I'm fine, thank you.

I know you believe that the way traditional companies look at selling to their customers doesn't work today. Will you tell our readers a little bit more about what you mean by that?

Holtzclaw

Absolutely. During the past ten years, leaders in most of the companies that come to us for help view their customers through the lens of traditional demographics and segmentation. They want to break customers down into nice neat packages defined by factors like how much money they make, their gender, marital status, where they live, and how old they are. This is information you can gather about customers or prospects without necessarily having to ask them, which makes it an easy way to approach sales and marketing. And it's also easily quantified—you can determine how large the market is for a given product or service and you can justify the investment.

To quantify the market size, companies commission large segmentation studies that profile who their customers are, what their customers may own, and the vehicle they drive. Then they attempt to make strategic decisions based on that information.

For example, a company may define its customer as "a married Boomer woman between the ages of fifty-five and seventy, she makes a certain amount of income." The company will approach building a product or service that speaks to the demographic in that way.

At User Insight, we know through years of talking with people that their purchase behaviors, the company they buy from, or services they choose, have very little to do with this arbitrary demographic or segmentation approach. Decision-makers still follow this antiquated method partly because they are taught to create products by conducting focus groups and looking at large quantities of data to understand how big a market is and, more importantly, to justify the return on investment for creating something new. When attempting to apply this concept, they are finding that, especially during the past several years, there has been a shift in the overall landscape as it relates to the way people buy and what they expect from the companies they work with. Traditional demographics and segmentation are no longer valid indicators for success.

WRIGHT

So what is driving this shift in the way customers interact with companies?

HOLTZCLAW

Design and development is much easier. Traditionally, it has been very difficult to build a product or service for everyone because of the costs necessary in building it. The thinking was that a product had to include features and functions that worked for most users.

For example, if you were designing a telephone, you had to make sure that it would work for 90 percent of the people who were going to buy it. If you were building a Web site back in the '90s, you had to make sure the components worked or were appropriate for the majority of those who were going to use them. Every piece had the same common denominator, which could be the technology, tooling, design, and so on, so that these products could be mass produced. And a strong emphasis toward "best practices" was the norm.

As we have moved into the 2000s, technology has become more pervasive across all different types of platforms and locations. Consumers are used to customizing our experiences and we can get information and content in bite-sized chunks. Today, instead of being forced to buy a product that looks exactly the same as the company has produced it for everyone, we, as a consumer have the expectation that we can buy things customized to the way we want them.

It is difficult to realize how much technology has spoiled us. Technology today is so advanced, we now have the perception that everything we purchase should be customized and created in a way that is tailored to us and should give us the experience that we want from the source we are buying it from. This is called "many to many relationships"—many customers buying from many vendors. Instead of one giant company making a single product and distributing it to a large number of people, there are numerous people buying goods from several sources. The "sell" is more about community and growing connections. The complicated piece of the equation is no longer the technology, development, or creation of the good or service. Instead, the complicated piece to be understood is the customer—the person actually buying from you.

WRIGHT

So what are the signs a company can look for to determine the changing landscape?

HOLTZCLAW

Anytime there is a disruptive technology, companies should be aware of a changing landscape. In the '90s, the Internet was disruptive; people started using it, some transitioning to it very slowly. There were companies that could not decide if they needed a Web site or not, or if the Internet was a passing fad. As we know now, the Internet is not a passing fad and has fundamentally changed much of how we work, live, and conduct business day-to-day.

As we have moved into the 2000s we have seen the introduction of smartphones that allow you to customize the interface to any button layout you want or use any type of application you want to download. We also have social media that allows you to instantly talk with a company or talk about a company in small bite-sized chunks. Both of these disruptive technologies have been adopted at a much faster rate than the Internet.

As companies see these big changes—these big disruptions—they need to pay attention to what it is doing to their overall supply chain and, most importantly, their customer base. Companies often try to simply follow a "me-too" pattern—if something has worked for one product or service in a similar space, they merely follow this same formula for all of their offerings. Unfortunately, this cookie cutter type approach no longer works; consumers want individualization.

Companies need to understand why a customer is buying from them or what makes one customer buy from company A while another customer buys the same product from company B. It is less about feature function matrix than it used to be. It is now more about their feeling toward how that brand acts, what it stands for, or some affinity to a relationship with that brand.

WRIGHT

How is a company successful as the landscape shifts?

HOLTZCLAW

A company is not successful by looking at what has happened or at what people have bought or what they have—profile data about their customers. Instead, companies need to understand why people are doing what they are doing.

They need to understand that users and customers will lie and tell them they are doing something for one reason but there may be a base reason underneath that is very different and very powerful. Companies should look for what their customers are truly aspiring to be. If a company understands why and how consumers do things, then they can start to get within the ecosystem that already exists for that consumer. Meeting them where they are is a much cheaper approach than trying to change a consumer's behavior.

For example, if the company is a brand that needs to stay top of mind, something that consumers would buy on the impulse aisle at the grocery store, then leaders in that company would want to make sure they have the company's message available to consumers within their existing ecosystem. If it is something that the consumer has a relationship with—something they spend lots of money or time on and have an affinity toward—then the company needs to make sure its brand and affinity stays in line with what customers expect from the brand.

This sounds difficult, but it really is not. People claim to be very different from each other, but when you understand the true motivations and behaviors behind a group doing one task such as picking a bank or choosing where they are going on vacation, you find that people do things for a very specific set of reasons. Identifying these motivations rarely has anything to do with standard demographics or segmentation. Looking at consumers' "what" tells you what they have done in the past, but by looking at "why" and "how," you can predict future behavior— you can lean forward. As we know, technology changes every day, the world changes every day, if you're continually looking back at the what, you miss what is next, what is coming, how people are going to act tomorrow. However, if you understand how they have reacted in the past, you have a better chance of being within their thought stream moving into the future.

WRIGHT

What types of mistakes does a company make when its leaders use the tried and true ways of selling?

HOLTZCLAW

Companies will take features and functions that have worked for other competitors and say, "That worked for them, so let's rubber-stamp it and do the same thing for our customers." This rarely works. Customers are looking for individualization. They want to be understood, and they want authentic relationships or an authentic representation of the brand, service, or company they're working with. Customers become leery if a company or a brand does something outside of what it is known for. We have found that you can't make people do something. Instead, you have to meet customers where they are and convince them within their own context to act and buy something from you.

Companies put too much trust in numbers. Just because a group may be a small group doesn't mean that they are not significant or powerful. If a company is trying to sell a product or service, and its marketing department is only looking at the size of the group they are selling to, they may miss the fact that a group, though small, may be very influential. The small group may be people others listen to on a daily basis and would be the ones recommending your product or service to others. They are trusted advisors. In fact, the larger group won't act at all without a recommendation from the smaller group.

Tap into the smaller group to reach the masses. Start by selling something to the small group—the ones who don't want to follow the masses. If you are successful with the small group, the end result is that you have used that group's influence to sell to the masses.

This is an interesting approach as to how you roll things out. We used to call these groups early adopters, but I would now call them heavy influencers in a specific space.

WRIGHT

Does this apply to all companies, even startups?

HOLTZCLAW

It does, and people think that it is difficult to do, but it's not. It doesn't take much time to sit down with the users or the customers you are targeting, just start with what you know.

For instance, if you know the segmentation you are going after, those are still the people you talk to; however, you want to talk to them more in depth and on an individual basis instead of in groups. Companies like to use large focus groups because this is what they were taught in college, and then they wonder at the end of the day why it didn't work. It's because it is not individualized. You have listened to a group of people provide responses, but it's so much more powerful to hear the same number of individuals' responses and understand the driver behind the response.

Also, it is important that these conversations are done in person and preferably in context. There are numerous online testing systems these days, but you don't know who is actually taking the test. The incentives are very low, and there are serial testers who will come in and do things just to collect the incentive. This type of online information should be used with great caution. If you instead spend time talking to individuals broadly, following a standard set of questions and narrowing them to questions about your products and services, patterns will start to emerge. Look at those patterns and understand how they relate to what customers think of your product or service; then you learn how to tailor your message.

It doesn't take a ton of work to do it. It is very important, though, that it be done and done with a quality approach. You will get a quality result that allows you to talk to your customers or users in a way that resonates with the core reasons they buy your products and services and, more importantly, why they will buy from your company.

WRIGHT

I understand that the core behaviors are drivers for customers, but it seems like it would be very difficult to target. Will you explain how this can work?

HOLTZCLAW

Yes, I can give you a good, concrete example. We had a customer bring us a Web site for a travel company that was targeting Boomer women. They wanted to build a Web site directed toward this group. When designing a Web site or content for Boomer women, you would want to focus on messages about empowerment, being an empty-nester, and later stages of life. What we found as we talked with a large audience of Boomer women was that their decisions around travel had nothing to do with being a Boomer woman. They were actually making travel choices based on one of three things:

the destination—they wanted to go somewhere exotic or new;

the party—is there a disco, is there a casino, who they can hang out with, or

leisure—they really just wanted to get away; they wanted to have a lounge chair and a pool and be taken care of.

The messaging for that Web site should be more around party, destination, and leisure, not about being a Boomer woman.

When creating a Web site or a brochure or an advertisement in a magazine, talk to all three of those drivers as your initial funnel and then, as people self-select, because they will naturally gravitate toward the thing that is really important to them, you emphasize that driver more and more.

As a company promotes a product or service, it is crucial to focus on what the customer really wants and cares about.

Wright

So can you change customers' behavior, make them do new things or act in a different way? If so, what are some of the ways leaders in a company can shift their thinking to that of their customers?

Holtzclaw

The argument is probably no. If you think back to the Don Draper approach from the television series *Mad Men,* the thought was if we make and promote it this way people will buy. At that time, product and services were pushed toward the consumers and consumers had very little selection. Advertising told us what the American dream was and how we were supposed to live. It also promoted an idealistic way to approach life. That works when the messages to consumers are controlled. If you control messages to consumers you can tell them "this is how you should be" and "this is what your life should look like."

Today there is very little control over how a consumer is consuming content, when they are consuming it, where, under what mediums, when, and how. To be successful you need to know what consumers are already naturally compelled to select or participate in. If they like certain types of experiences or periodicals, their ecosystem—what they do naturally—then that is where you want to insert your messages so you can capture that person within his or her existing behavior.

If you have something that is completely disruptive, you can start to change behavior but you have to prove to them very quickly that it is of value. If it's not, they will move on.

One great example of this is in the apps you can buy for your smartphone. The cost of apps is typically less than a dollar or even free, so consumers feel they have very little vested interest in their purchase. The consumer thought is, "I'm going to download it, I'm going to use it, and if it doesn't work for me very quickly and it doesn't speak to something I care about, then I'll probably never use it again." The opportunity for capturing that person is very slim. In trying to change the person's behavior, you have to make sure you are within his or her ecosystem, resonating to what that person wants or cares about and then providing value very, very quickly.

There has long been conversation about how content is king, and this is becoming very true. We as consumers are given small nuggets of information throughout the day, which means the information needs to be good, quality content. Consumers are spoiled and are not going to slog through excess fluff to get what they want.

WRIGHT

When you were talking about selling travel to Boomer females, my first thought was a judgment right up front that they're probably the ones with the expendable income and they can afford it.

HOLTZCLAW

Yes, looking solely at their income and thinking about them from that perspective, you would think that the mistake would be to say, "Let's talk to who you are in your life stage." But that is very rarely why people make those types of purchase decisions. There is always some other core behavior that is driving them. You have to be careful because we are lazy with the words we use. We have done studies before where people would use a word repeatedly. For instance, they may say the word "convenience" and so you think, well, everybody does this because it's convenient. What you find out is that convenience means something very different to each group. You need to understand each group's definition of convenience.

When you hear something being said by your customers as to why they are buying a product or service, you want to get them to unpack it and define it for you. Don't just take for granted that they've used a particular word and think that this is common language for everyone because it may mean something very different to them than it does to you.

WRIGHT

Do core behaviors or attitudes change?

HOLTZCLAW

People would like to think that they do, but they typically do not. If I am a spender, I will forever be a spender. If I am a saver, I will forever be a saver. I may manifest that into a completely different way of spending or saving.

Take, for example, extreme couponing. It's a new trend that we are seeing, and it's actually a spending behavior. Automatically you think extreme couponers are saving money. However, they are probably people who really want to spend. At the end of the day, they are able to buy so many products because they use coupons as a currency for acquisition. The same is true for points or reward programs.

The key is to understand what the core behavior or driver is for that person and then you speak to it so that the person feels good about what they are doing. Once you have spoken to their core, you can influence micro changes in their eco-system and get them to help you push your message.

The bottom-line is that if we changed our core behavior, people would be much more successful with their New Year's resolutions than they are. To truly make good on a resolution, you typically have to have some kind of major change to your core.

WRIGHT

How can I find out if my customers are changing behaviors?

HOLTZCLAW

There are some good signs that occur, and if you are aware of them, you can get to the core behaviors of what your users are doing and why and how they're doing it.

Pay attention to when there are shifts in the space they care about. Think of banking, for example. We've had a movement toward online banking and we're seeing mobile commerce in such a way that we know it is going to be a major force in the next couple of years. If anything starts to change within a group's ecosystem, then that is a time to start looking for opportunities.

Disruption is a very good thing. Anytime something new is being talked about a lot, it is time to start identifying how your consumers are responding. You need to look at what they think of you within that ecosystem, where they think you fit, or if you fit. The key is to redefine yourself to work within the new paradigm.

This is important to survival. We've seen so many different industries go by the wayside because they weren't able to manage a disruption in their space. The closing of bookstores, music stores, and video stores are all examples of this. These closings all occurred because consumers are now receiving that type of information and content in a different way and the leaders in those spaces didn't react quickly enough to the changing landscape.

WRIGHT

So what else is important when considering the development of user groups?

HOLTZCLAW

One thing that is important is to know that you are looking at the user groups cleanly. When a customer is in context (i.e., the person is in the process of doing something), their ecosystem can change.

We did a large project last year on social media and television and the convergence between the two. We looked at why people used social media and why they watch television. What we found is that there is a group that really doesn't care about television, they don't watch it that much, and they don't talk to their friends over social media about television. You wouldn't really think they were that important, except when it came to football season, all of a sudden the television was extremely important to them. Social media also became important, from the standpoint of being able to talk to their friends who were fans of the same teams. Keep in mind, though, that it was only during football season. Because of this, you wouldn't want to build a product or app for them for television and social media for the entire year—instead only focus on the period of time they're very interested in these topics.

Be careful of the try-it-once-never-again phenomenon. A company will put out a new product or service and it becomes the hip thing to do or have. There will be a spike in sales around buying it. However, it is a fad and it's not something that is going to be a lasting and sustained for that company. You have to be careful that if you are doing these flash-in-the-pan things, that you have a good way of taking what you do during that period of time and moving it back to what that person's core behaviors are once they're finished participating in that singular moment in time.

The Super Bowl is a great example. Many people who watch the Super Bowl may not watch football for the entire year. If you are going to capture them at that point, then you have to know what their core behaviors are before the event, so that you can focus on those behaviors after the event is over. You can use the event as a great way of capturing people and introducing something new to their eco-system.

WRIGHT

Do you have any feel as to what new things are coming up that corporations might take advantage of in the next year or two?

HOLTZCLAW

Yes. One of the trends, I think, certainly revolves around social media. I believe that social media is going to finally start settling down. We have way too many players in that space. It reminds me of the Internet of the '90s—it was like the Wild West!

I also believe that social media is not going to be about tweeting with each other or posting on Facebook, but about location-based offers and knowing what people are doing and where they are. Tracking customer behavior is what you will hear about and marketing based on this knowledge will become more important. We won't think of it as an invasion of privacy; but instead, we'll like it because it's going to be about receiving reminders when we need them or knowing that there is traffic ahead—the types of things that will make our life easier.

Also, another trend is that we'll have an expectation of instantaneous information. We're going to see a big surge in mobile commerce— being able to pay for things with these many devices that we're carrying around. The United States is way behind in that area.

Finally, I really believe that we have too many screens. For example, there are iPads, iPhones, smartphones, laptops, desktops, and GPS. We are going to start to see those being consolidating into a more versatile device that's easier to carry and lighter weight. We have information in lots of different places and it's become confusing as to which device or thing somebody is going to pick up and take along. Those are some of the bigger trends. The cloud and some of that technology is just the Internet rebaked. We'll see where that goes, but it does lend itself to the storage of information. You don't have to worry about where you're putting your virtual information and it is always available to you, no matter what device you're using.

WRIGHT

I think I made a mistake on the last gift I gave my wife. She's an avid reader—five six books a week. I gave her a Nook, one of the better ones. I thought, "Boy, she's going to jump for joy just to find that the books she buys for the Nook are three and four and five times more expensive than the books that she buys. She will buy first-run books for five dollars, say, at a used bookstore or online.

HOLTZCLAW

I gave my wife a Kindle Fire at Christmas. She's never really been a huge reader, but she has read a lot more books since I gave it to her because it is so convenient for her to carry. I do think it's going to be interesting to see how tablet technology affects education. For instance, my daughter does not even carry her books home from school because they are available online. Wouldn't it be great if she just had them on her tablet and she could carry them with her everywhere?

It will be interesting to see how we adapt these technologies into education and moving forward. The United States needs to continue to put out well-educated young people and workers. That's where we could fail. We need to have smart people who know what to create.

WRIGHT

Well, this has been an exciting conversation for me and very educational. I can readily see why people hire you for your opinions and your research.

HOLTZCLAW

It's a lot of fun. At User Insight, we get to look at about 125 projects a year, across all kinds of verticals and industries. I've ridden tractors all over the world, I've looked at office supplies and cell phones—you name it. It gives me and my company tremendous insight into why people do the things they do and allows us to predict and influence their future behavior.

WRIGHT

Well, I want you to know how much I appreciate you being in this book and taking this time with me this afternoon to answer all these questions.

HOLTZCLAW

I appreciate your time.

WRIGHT

Today I have been talking with Eric V. Holtzclaw. Eric is the Founder and Chief Executive Officer of User Insight. Eric has an opportunity to interview and understand thousands of people annually and uses this knowledge in researching consumer behavior. He advises some of the world's leading brands to prioritize strategic investments in technology, advertising, and marketing for maximum return. Eric is also co-host of the weekly radio show, The "Better You" Project, which highlights the stories of those who start small companies.

Eric, thank you so much for being with us today on *Concrete Jungle: Survival Secrets for the Real World.*

About the Author

Eric V. Holtzclaw, Founder/CEO of User Insight, has spent more than twenty years creating opportunities through the practical application of emerging technologies and trends in business.

His professional experience includes: founding multiple successful startup companies, including one of the first profitable Internet enterprises, and implementation of more than thirty consumer-oriented and internal use products and services worldwide. Eric has the opportunity to interview and understand thousands of people annually, and uses this knowledge of consumer behavior to advise the world's leading brands to prioritize strategic investments in technology, advertising, and marketing for maximum return.

Eric V. Holtzclaw
User Insight
50 Glenlake Parkway, Suite 150
Atlanta, GA 30328
770-391-1099
www.userinsight.com

Chapter Seventeen
The New Law of the Jungle

An Interview With...

Teri McEachern and Shelley Wilson

David Wright (Wright)

Today I'm talking with Teri McEachern and Shelley Wilson. Collectively, McEachern and Wilson have more than fifty years of consulting to large, complex, rapidly-changing organizations. Their backgrounds in strategy, behavioral science, and transformational change have given them a deep appreciation for the seriousness of achieving business results and the hilarity of human activity. Quick witted and respectful, they bring candor and humor to leadership programs and executive team engagements. Learning can be both fun and focused while building essential leadership competencies along the way.

McEachern and Wilson have achieved certifications in a broad range of leadership and organizational development programs and professional designations, and have partnered in developing programs for nearly a decade.

Teri, Shelley, welcome to *Concrete Jungle.*

Teri McEachern (McEachern)

Thanks very much, David; happy to be here.

Shelley Wilson (Wilson)

Thank you.

Wright

You have named this chapter "The New Law of the Jungle," why did you decide on this title?

McEachern

The new law of the jungle is simple: *politics exist everywhere, ignoring them is something you do at your peril,* so running doesn't work, you need to stop, attune your Primal Five Instincts, know your three Survival Skills, then Super Leap without fear. Life is good in the concrete jungle if you simply know the rules. The jungle analogy we use throughout this interview is our attempt to have a bit of fun discussing a subject most people find very stressful.

Wilson

Besides, there are many similarities between life and corporate life; it was a convenient metaphor. Some days in the jungle it's magnificent—all the creatures working in unison, each with their own unique goals in a complicated structure, offering challenge and opportunity. Other days the torrential rain, powerful winds, and fight for survival can turn a graceful free fall into a straight shot, slamming through thick underbrush to the jungle floor.

Wright

As you both have experience in profit and nonprofit, public and private sector organizations, are politics the same everywhere?

McEachern

Not exactly, David. All organizations have politics and they do vary, each type of "jungle" has political conditions unique to its own culture. Typically the higher up the corporate ladder you go the more prevalent the politics become and thus the more savvy you need to become—if you want to thrive over the long haul.

Wilson

Politics are not just in organizations, they're everywhere. We see them in families, friendships, anywhere that people come together. It's just that in organizations, politics grow more vigorously, as most players seek very similar ends.

Wright

So how would you define politics?

MCEACHERN

Throughout the years, corporate politics have been defined in many ways. In 1999, Kacmar and Baron described organizational politics as, "actions by individuals which are directed toward the goal of furthering their own self interests without regard for the well-being of others or their organization." Farrell and Peterson in 1982 cite politically motivated behaviors as, "activities that are not required as part of one's formal role in the organization but that influence or attempt to influence the distribution of advantages and disadvantages within the organization."

To us, these definitions describe a part of the overall political picture and thereby discount the many positive outcomes that can be attained by navigating effectively in the political arena, both organizationally and personally.

WILSON

Teri and I relate more to the definition of politics offered in the work of Rick Brandon and Marty Seldman, both PhDs who define politics as, "informal, unofficial, and sometimes behind-the-scenes efforts to sell ideas, influence an organization, increase power, or achieve other targeted objectives." Their definition permits us to accept that not all political behavior is negative and that the outcomes are not always self-motivated.

MCEACHERN

For the purpose of our chapter, we define corporate politics, or the nature of the beast, quite simply as, *striving to achieve goals in a work environment through behaviors and actions*.

WILSON

This simple definition is broad, and thus allows for the goals to be self or organizationally motivated, and the behaviors and actions may be negative or positive, have or lack integrity. Again, corporate politics do not have to be negative, but they certainly can be.

WRIGHT

Yes, most people think participating in corporate politics is like selling out, or crossing over to the dark side.

MCEACHERN

That's so true. Politics, even the word leaves us compelled to shower. If someone were to ask you if you were politically savvy, would you admit it? If you did, does that mean you are dishonest, conniving, manipulative, backstabbing, or two-faced?

WILSON

Exactly, the thought of politics can instantly raise our blood pressure. We imagine the king of the jungle standing proudly on its mangled prey. Oh wait, that prey looks familiar, I think it's that guy from accounting. I guess I could help him out, but hmm . . . maybe I'd better just hide here behind the parrot's nest until things calm down—nothing I can do for him now. So we avoid, but we walk away with the feeling that we dodged a bullet, and another one could fly by at any minute. Over time it can leave us in a state of heightened anxiety, with less cognitive ability and good energy to do our jobs effectively.

WRIGHT

So avoiding this beast is a typical response?

MCEACHERN

Sadly yes it is, and it can also be deadly to your career. You can choose to ignore politics, pretend they don't exist and that you're not a player, or you can respect the game and hone your skills. We obviously advocate the latter. The sad thing is that many, many talented professionals run from their current organization frazzled, depressed, and screaming, "I can't take the politics anymore!" only to find that when they're in their new-found organization, despite the cool décor, it's teeming with another kind of political animal playing a whole new game.

WILSON

Precisely. All that work to resign, construct a new resume, and pound the pavement in an effort to find a sunnier jungle—one that has less underbrush, prettier birds, more bounty—and then *wham!* you discover that the political terrain is just as challenging as your last jungle, or perhaps even worse!

McEachern

Not to mention that some people leave corporate life altogether because of the politics.

Wilson

Absolutely. Masses of capable leaders quit altogether, happily reporting that there will be one less rat in the race. Some of these ex-rats are leaving very lucrative careers—jobs they loved and in which they excelled, but ultimately were worn down by the politics to the point of sheer exhaustion and burn out. This political phenomenon may also explain many employees who desire now to work from home, even if only for a day or two a week; it's like a mini vacation from the jungle. The truth is politics will find you, even if you make every effort to avoid them.

McEachern

When you partner this reality with the intensifying effects of the economic downturn, global competition, and the ever-increasing scarcity of opportunity and talent, you have all the makings of poison stew. Add a dash of generational mixing—Baby Boomers, X'ers, Y'ers—and you've got an advanced strain of jungle fever!

Wright

So how can you tell when you're at risk?

Wilson

Well that's the thing—you don't always know you're at risk. Sometimes you're swinging happily from branch to branch effectively meeting the challenges of the jungle and enjoying yourself and your jungle mates, and then one wrong turn and you're knee deep in quicksand. Picking up on jungle cues is critical—awareness is critical.

McEachern

Exactly. Self-awareness and awareness of your environment is so important. If you find your chipper demeanor lately has been overtaken by paranoia and you have become the worst version of yourself, you might want to pay attention.

When we start to lose control like this, not only do we start to fear the man-eating tiger known as our boss, the customer, or your vine-climbing colleague, we also get hijacked by our amygdala, which is a small almond-shaped section of the brain that triggers emotional response when our survival is threatened. By this point you may be working too much, calling in sick, or trying to find ways to get more time off. As time progresses you become insanely internally focused and organizationally centric, meaning you think you cannot get out, and that this jungle is the *only* jungle. Time progresses and your reality distorts to suit your mounting insecurity. No amount of caffeine is cutting it anymore, your energy levels are plummeting, and your vulnerability is increasing. If you look around, you may also notice that the pygmies are sharpening their spears to come in for the kill.

Wilson

If this wicked spiral continues to plummet at work, then your personal life will begin to crumble as well. Chances are you haven't slept for weeks or even months, your blood pressure is soaring, you've developed digestive problems, eye twitching, and perhaps even your childhood stutter has returned. Believe me, I have seen this happen to people. You're either talking too much and all about work, or you are so quiet that your vocal cords have melted into the back of your throat. You have a chronic cold, thinning hair, and a family that runs for cover the minute you get home. Your life as you knew it is over. Once you are at this point, your risk is great—your vulnerable state permeates a meaty scent throughout the jungle, inspiring the worst predators to plan for attack.

Wright

So how can corporate politics be a positive thing?

McEachern

If your goals, whether they're organizational or individual, and the actions, behaviors, and tactics you use to achieve them are congruent with your value system, then politics can be very positive. Being savvy in the concrete jungle is about knowing how to navigate through the swamp, remain positive, and even thrive, despite a few bites on the ankles every now and then.

Wilson

It can be very satisfying to set a goal for yourself and achieve it through influence, positive networking, hard work, and commitment, rather than using tactics outside your value system. Success over the long haul is measured ultimately by how you feel about yourself, what you bring to the table, and how others perceive you based on your actions and behavior. Remember, you can only control yourself, so try to use others' bad behavior as opportunities to practice and hone your own skills without getting knee deep in the mud with them.

Wright

So will you share with our readers some skills for becoming more politically savvy?

Wilson

Sure. As we touched on before, awareness is the first step. So here are the Primal Five Instincts regarding awareness that you can't let hibernate:

The Primal Five Instincts:

Know Yourself
Know Your Jungle
Know Your Jungle-Mates
Know Your Boss
Know the Borders of Your Camp

WRIGHT

So the Primal Five is really about awareness and assessing the current state, right?

WILSON

Yes, David, recognizing, of course, that all organizations are fluid and internal and external events can change the landscape. CEOs come and go, mergers happen, competition increases, demographics change, so you need to reassess often. The good news is that once you get used to assessing in this way it can begin to happen quite naturally. You pick up on changing cues, know what they could mean to you, your department, or your organization, and then you can adjust accordingly.

WRIGHT

Tell me more about the Primal Five.

MCEACHERN

Sure, number one is to know yourself. You need to ask yourself some key questions: What do you value? What is important to you? What is your work ethic? Are you a hard worker? Do you like to contribute? What are your marketable talents/skills? What are your strengths and your vulnerabilities? What are your emotional triggers? If you are not sure, ask somebody at work who you trust. You might be surprised at the answers and uncover some things you didn't know about yourself. Are you a learner or not? We know a lot of our participants who have stopped learning at some point in their career and this is a bit of a wakeup call for them. You need to map out your short-term and long-term goals. What is your motive to be in this particular jungle? Is it to get ahead, to pay the bills, socialize, punch time to retirement, learn, or become a CEO? You need to know what drives you.

WILSON

Some of the most successful people we've known have their own code written out that they carry with them, just on a small sheet of paper, to remind them of what their goals and values are, so as they make their way through the jungle they don't get lost. You need to ask yourself, am I competent at my job? Do I add value to this organization in this portion of the jungle? Then you need to know what evidence you have to support your belief. Is my competency evolving? Is my employability expanding? What do other people think of me? So knowing yourself is really a significant skill.

Many of us run blindly through our jungles and never stop to reflect on these important questions. Knowing yourself is a crucial step in setting your compass.

McEachern

Pimal Instinct number two: know your jungle. So let's dispel some of the myths about our jungles.

Myth number one is that all organizational or jungle decisions are based on fact and objectivity.

We would like to believe that, but it is simply not true.

Myth number two, promotions will always go to the most capable people. I'm sure we have all had experiences where this just doesn't happen and we're quite shocked and surprised by that.

Myth number three, copious amounts of overtime and dedication will be appreciated, recognized, and rewarded. Sadly, this is not the case in many jungles.

Wilson

Every organization or jungle is different in their sameness. Each has threats, albeit of a different nature, so you need to know what threats exist in your jungle. You need to learn how to view your organization in relation to competitors, how does it stack up and why. You should analyze how quickly your organization has shown itself to adapt to changing weather conditions and what is on the horizon that might be impacting soon. What do these changes mean to you and your department? What is the likelihood of the longevity of your jungle? Is it a good place to build a long standing shelter, or should you just pitch a tent and pass through quickly? What is the culture, what type of beasts are nurtured and recognized—the good, the bad, and the ugly or just the ugly?

McEachern

And this brings us to number three Primal Instinct: know your jungle mates. You need to know your colleagues and assess what your relationships are like at all levels within the organization, then ask what evidence you have to support your perception of the strengths or weaknesses of your relationships.

What is the generational makeup of your jungle and your jungle mates and how does it work? Are there barriers to communication? Who are the power players? Remember, there are many different types of power. The most influential people may not always be at the senior level—they may be experts in their field or motivators who can rally people to accomplish massive goals. You need to know the difference.

WILSON

Also, become aware of some of the common toxic archetypes we see in our work environments. For example, there are screaming hyenas. You know these guys. They're the hysterical alarmists. They have such urgency when they speak that you feel your pulse soaring, only to find that they are making much ado about nothing.

You'll also encounter a wild boar or two in your career. You know them: heads down, fangs up, coming through regardless. You have to move or you get run down. They are totally mission-driven and not necessarily that bright. Management needs to make sure they are on the right path, otherwise there is a wake of destruction behind them. You don't want to get a boar angry because if boars are distracted from their mission they can kill your career. If a boar is in a position above you, it can be extremely dangerous.

Oh, and watch out for the calculating cobras. These ego-driven snakes love the feeling of power over others. They are not afraid of the rush that comes with having control. They like it, they are winning at the game, and that's very important to them. They are unpredictable and erratic, provoked or not provoked.

Probably the worst of all—and we have all met one—is the stinging scorpion. They are part of every landscape and are really quite evil. They thrive on key relationships and corrupt along the way. They are most deadly, typically brilliant though, arrogant, and completely non-transparent, always packing an agenda.

McEachern

These are just some of the toxic beasts you will meet along the way; I'm sure you recognized a few.

Number four of the Primal Five is to know your boss. Let's avoid some hard knocks and clear up some myths right now. Myth number one: disagreeing with your boss won't get you fired. This is a cautionary note to everybody: yes it actually can get you fired. Myth number two, leaders know what they're doing. Not always, and not under all circumstances do leaders know what they're doing. Myth number three: when your boss asks the question, "Is everyone on board?" It is not really a question, it's a statement!

So knowing your boss is crucial. Ask yourself, what type of power does he or she have. How is it being displayed? Is your boss organization-centric or self-centered? What are your boss's values and how do you know? What has made him or her successful in this particular jungle? What annoys your boss? What is he or she best and worst at? Is there an opportunity for you to fill in the gap? Is your boss analytical, creative? What inspires your boss or lights him or her up? Does your boss typically nurture and develop people or burn them out? Does he or she exude self-confidence without excessive ego? People can be very attractive when they're like that. How best can you communicate with your boss—quick, creative to the point or detailed and formal? Once done, compare all of this to step one: knowing yourself, that first Primal Instinct, and decide if this is going to be a good partnership.

Wilson

The fifth Primal Instinct is to know the borders of your camp. A lot of times your borders are marked by function or responsibility, however, oftentimes we get our head down and we focus specifically in our own territory. This is fine as long as there is not a slash-and-burn happening next to you. The point is that no matter how well you function in your borders, you need to be aware of what's happening around you and what the leaders of those groups are doing so that you can continue to deliver what you need to, otherwise you won't have a broad enough understanding of the politics around you and you could get sideswiped.

WRIGHT

Sounds like you all have been talking to people in my company!

Once you have gone through the Primal Five Instincts, is that sufficient to ensure your survival?

MCEACHERN

No it's just a starting point. Once you have activated your Primal Five Instincts, you know your style, what's important to you, and your version of the concrete jungle. You must then develop survival strategies. You see, knowing is not enough—you must be able to move yourself through the jungle, keeping your career, your life, and your health intact. For this reason, we have developed three key survival strategies you can learn at any point in your career.

Three Survival Strategies for Success in the Concrete Jungle

Strategy 1 – Jungle Orienteering
Strategy 2 – Jungle Thriving
Strategy 3 – Jungle Fever Recovery

WILSON

These skills build on one another, taking you successfully through the basic necessities in navigating complex challenges, to learning how to thrive in any situation, and tips and tools on how to recover from political mistakes.

WRIGHT

Will you give us a sneak peak of some of the survival strategies?

MCEACHERN

Sure. In political terms we need to discover what is important to the organization, who has decision-making power, what defines success, and what is required to succeed in your jungle. You need to be able to align your job with the customer of the organization, as Drucker says, "The purpose of business is to create a customer." If you are a man-eating tiger you had better know something about your prey; if you don't know, you need to find out. Older lions are only willing to help those lions that are hungry for knowledge and take action to eat. Don't get this wrong, we all know lots of lazy lions that let others do the work and survive on their political skills. Those people know how the jungle works and magically appear at the right time and place and take credit for your work. Follow them but don't mimic them and get one step ahead. Remember, it's only a game to them; you need to watch out for these nasty kitties.

WILSON

Sometimes it's easy to figure out who has decision-making power, as it often aligns with his or her position in the pride. Sometimes it's much less obvious. Many jungle creatures have a range of protective adaptations from acute eyesight to elongated necks to seasonal coat changes. These can often give us clues about who's who in the jungle. Rarely is decision making transparent and you will never understand all the interdependencies that happen during decision making, but you must figure out who decides and then watch carefully how the rest of the lions are informed. If the pride moves in concert then the pride is aligned. If not, then be very clear about your next move or it could be your last.

MCEACHERN

Your success depends on what has gone before. What has made lions successful in the past is what behaviors they will use to hunt today. This is true except during times of rapid change when the prey has adapted to the jungle and are no longer afraid of an occasional roar. The political games really get going as lions fight for their turf and the right to feed. Eating is important, so be clear about what is on the menu and what it will take to feed for the day, where the next watering hole is, and where cover from the looming storm can be found. Exposure to harsh conditions will only weaken your reactions and resiliency.

WILSON

Our strategies are critical for new professionals entering the workplace. Lack of political savvy could mean the early death of a career if one doesn't have some essential skills; but don't expect to find the training manual for this subject in your jungle! You are typically on your own.

McEachern

Yes, teaching basic political skills in organizations is rare.

Wilson

We seem to digress to the dark and challenging side of politics, forgetting that these skills can be a positive thing.

McEachern

Politics can be very positive, it is like being on the edge of something new, something exciting; but you can't be afraid to make mistakes, resilience and attitude are critical to surviving and thriving in the jungle.

Wright

So how can you tell who to stay away from in the workplace? Are there certain traits in people you can look out for that you know will be toxic to you or your career?

McEachern

Absolutely. When the winds of change blow and bring the first smell of smoke, those jumping up and down on your back generally are not your friends. They are like slimy snakes slithering through the undergrowth waiting to strike. You can tell—you get butterflies in your stomach, you start sweating, your chest feels like an elephant is sitting on it. These people are toxic, run, don't walk away, never turn your back, and don't take your eyes off these folks.

Wilson

Jungle orienteering is not easy or simple but it is the first survival strategy. So let's talk a bit about strategy number two.

McEachern

Sure. Survival strategy number two is Jungle Thriving. Once you've managed to cover your basics, you are ready to start thriving in a jungle. You've moved beyond feeling disoriented and you've lost some of your natural innocence about how the jungle works. You are now ready to navigate your own course and help others. You can recognize subtle disturbances in the undergrowth, coming storms, and the rising tension between jungle mates.

WILSON

You'll know when you are in this state when you can recognize that scorpions sting because that's just what they do without getting all twisted up about it. The lesson here is simple: People will do what they do. Don't expect a higher level of performance or less politicking when things are tough. You can predict people's behavior, as past behavior will indicate future behavior. Zebras don't change their stripes, and scorpions still sting. You must become very good at sign reading and then navigating your way forward.

MCEACHERN

Thriving begins with questioning your perception and opening your mind and your heart to other possibilities. When you do this, the world seems full of opportunities and paths start to appear in the dense foliage making forward momentum much easier.

WILSON

Having allowed your eyes to adjust to the changing life conditions in the denser regions of the forest, you will find that you may have to give up control. This is funny because it's hard to control a pack of screaming hyenas at the best of times. Being politically astute means that you recognize that control is just an illusion. You can't really control the hyenas any more than you can control the rhino. The rhino will not be controlled no matter how much you pull and push. In fact, when provoked, his horn can be downright deadly. Influencing is much easier, since you have already attuned your Primal Five Instincts, your sense of balance remains intact, and the path and the signs become more obvious.

MCEACHERN

Imagine two groups of gazelles that need to form an alliance as they start the great migration. Networks of relationships have to be formed to signal the herd which way to go, where water is ahead, whether lions are prowling or lying in wait. Staying in sync with your new-found team members becomes critical, your influence can grow. Stay friendly, watch, and learn.

WILSON

Thriving also requires advanced emotional intelligence. You need to know when you are being hijacked, how to calm down, stay focused, and continue to move through the crisis or issue without panic or loss of intellect. So when you are suddenly being berated by the backbiting baboon, stop, take a breath, smile, and ask a clarifying question. Your tone is neutral, you have no preconceived answer in mind, and you wait and you listen. The backbiting baboon jumps up and down, pounds its chest, and barks out an answer. You thank it and ask another question, constantly moving the conversation forward.

MCEACHERN

Partnering during these encounters becomes a critical skill.

WILSON

Precisely. You may feel that you have no control, but you can always *influence*; this is a stance that can be adopted in any situation.

MCEACHERN

You must always be seeking to *align* yourself with people who have a similar value system to you. You need them during the good and the bad times and they can advance your signaling system throughout the jungle.

Of course, when you reach the edge of your traditional boundaries, care must be taken to step beyond your known territory. Being politically astute and influential means knowing when to push and when not to. It can mean the difference between surviving or running smack-dab into a wild boar.

WILSON

It's true—when you have strong relationships throughout the jungle you can survive, thrive, and even co-exist happily with the wild boar. In fact, you can appreciate the tenacity of wild boars and can influence them to push things through when the going gets tough. This is being politically astute, not political. It means using diplomacy skills to keep everyone moving forward together.

MCEACHERN

Exactly. These skills combine to give us a much broader view of our jungle and the interdependencies that exist within our jungle and with other jungles. This allows us to thrive in what had previously been the darker, more remote areas of the jungle without the paralyzing fear. Once you understand your value, have your ego and emotions in check, you have your table stakes in the jungle game.

WILSON

Remember, the higher up the food chain you go, the more challenging the game, the greater the risk, the more skilled the players, and the more determined the attitude.

MCEACHERN

Precisely.

WRIGHT

Okay, so what do you do when you are thriving in the jungle and you miss a warning sign, take a wrong turn, or just generally screw up?

MCEACHERN

Well, now, you're into survival strategy number three—Jungle Fever Recovery. Jungle fever can get you at any time. Never think that just because you've had your flu shot that the inoculation will last forever; that is not life in the jungle. Jungles are dynamic places and if it's not dynamic, then it's in decline and you don't want to hang out there anyway.

WILSON

Yes, when times are changing everyone's anxiety is running high. The wild boars and backbiting baboons seem to loom in the forest and attack everyone simultaneously. This is when political mistakes, miscalculations, and death will occur. But don't panic—recovery is possible, but there are some definite rules around recovery.

Rule number one, when you make a mistake, bite someone or harm one of your jungle mates, make it right quickly, move as fast as a cheetah and as gentle as a moth, this may not save you but it may save the relationships and almost all relationships are important during times of recovery.

McEachern

Rule number two, don't hate the jungle players—hate the game. Recovery is a matter of luck and skill—scorpions do what scorpions do and you do what you do, as long as your innate value system remains intact you'll be okay to go forward.

Wilson

Rule number three, if you get hurt, apply first aid immediately. Cuts in the jungle are dangerous. They can become infected, cause fevers, headaches, high blood pressure, depression, and a whole host of related illnesses. Know where help is and trust fellow professionals. You also want to move quickly toward your friends but don't expect them to always be there, they won't want to catch jungle fever, no offense but you could be contagious. Remember, jungle animals are easily spooked, especially when the Zulus are running and fever is in the air.

McEachern

Rule number four, you need to know when to look outside at another jungle or when to take the next vine to a different area of the jungle, timing is everything. Trace back to the Primal Five and validate what's important to you, be smart, calculate the risks to you and your family and take actions that align with your core value system. Don't wait for others to determine your fate. If the pot of water is boiling, the end is in sight.

Wilson

There are lots of great rules to learn, but you get the idea.

Wright

Absolutely. We have talked about the rules and the three survival strategies, what's next?

McEachern

Well, now we need to share how to Super Leap, from where you are in the concrete jungle to where you need to be. This requires mastering balance; it is actually a decision point; a moment in time when you make a decision to own your career, your life, and most importantly, David, your health.

Much has been written about these important moments. At what point do you stop swinging from branch to branch to take a minute and look out over the jungle and ask is this right for me? If the answer is a resounding yes, keep swinging. If there is a slow hesitation and a hollow echo of fear it's time to stop and ask, "When did I stop smiling? Was I dead when I got here or did they boil me slowly? How did I get so disconnected from what brought me joy and you realize for the first time how lost you've become. The jungle can be like that.

WILSON

So when you're sitting upon that branch looking out over the canopy you need to take a moment to think about your future.

MCEACHERN

Yes, and to Super Leap you need to accept that the jungle will survive. My job is not my life, it is not my family, it is not my health, the jungle doesn't define me. Super Leaping requires only one thing—an optimistic attitude, to Super Leap you must be an optimist.

If you think about it there are lots of political refugees in the concrete jungle—people who are wounded—they won't look anyone in the eye, they're on crutches wearing headbands from recent wars, suffering post-traumatic stress disorders. You will also find the inspired leaders, those committed to sustaining employment, and they all love the optimist.

WILSON

That's not to say that optimists are Pollyannas. They see the harsh realities, they know who they are, what's important, and where they want to go; they have influence, integrity, and are generally extremely confident.

MCEACHERN

Super Leaping is easier for them because they consciously contribute their talent, everyone loves the optimist and optimists value their relationships above all else. The new law is simple; smile, disarm your opponents, jump out of the way of the wild boar and never trust a calculating cobra. Politics are everywhere. You need to attune your instincts, learn your survival skills, live your life, and smile. Thanks David.

WRIGHT

Well this has been a great conversation. I certainly have learned a lot here today from both of you. I really do appreciate your taking so much time this morning to answer these questions. It's not only been delightful but informative and I'm sure our readers are going to get a lot out of this.

WILSON

That's great, David, thank you so much.

MCEACHERN

Thank you.

WRIGHT

Today I have been talking with Teri McEachern and Shelley Wilson. Collectively they have more than fifty years' consulting to large, complex, rapidly-changing organizations. They have achieved certifications in a broad range of leadership and organizational development programs and professional designations. They have partnered in developing programs for nearly a decade.

Shelley, Teri, thank you so much for being with us today on *Concrete Jungle.*

WILSON

It's been our pleasure.

About the Authors

Collectively, McEachern and Wilson have more than fifty years' consulting to large, complex, rapidly-changing organizations. Their backgrounds in strategy, behavioral science, and transformational change have given them a deep appreciation for the seriousness of achieving business results and the hilarity of human activity.

Quick witted and respectful, they bring candor and humor to leadership programs and executive team engagements. Learning can be both fun and focused while building essential leadership competencies along the way.

McEachern and Wilson have achieved certifications in a broad range of leadership and organizational development programs, professional designations, and have partnered in developing programs for nearly a decade.

Teri McEachern & Shelley Wilson
Cascadian Consulting Group Inc.
Toronto & Vancouver
Canada
604-331-0895 or
705-722-5920
tmceachern@me.com or
ispwilson@sympatico.ca
https://concretejungle.co

Chapter Eighteen

Leadership Secrets to Thrive in the Jungle

An Interview With…

Ted Gorski

DAVID WRIGHT (WRIGHT)

Ted Gorski is an Executive Coach and Founder of Get Your Edge, LLC. For more than twenty years, Ted has worked with emerging leaders and executives in organizations, from emerging leaders who are working to develop their leadership skills to CEOs looking to maintain their personal edge. He is a graduate of Corporate Coach University and holds two degrees from Bentley University. He is an author of the book titled *Leap Into Leadership: Becoming the Leader You are Destined to Be.*

Ted, welcome to *Concrete Jungle: Survival Secrets for the Real World.*

So let me ask you, what is one of the biggest challenges that face leaders?

TED GORSKI (GORSKI)

Ineffective communication is the Achilles heel of any leader. Effective communication is the ability to connect with individuals and to effectively impart a message. Individuals hearing your message should clearly understand their role. In a survey conducted by Leadership IQ, 67 percent of employees have shared that they learn more about their responsibilities from co-workers than from their managers/leaders. If an employee does not understand his or her responsibilities, goals and expectations, how does a leader define an employee's success? In a survey conducted by *Human Resource Executive* magazine dated September 2, 2011, 67 percent of companies are actively finding ways to increase communications with employees. In other words, these companies are finding ways to open and improve communication channels between leaders and employees.

Articulating is not sufficient. Messages are communicated not just through the words but also through tone of voice, speaker's energy, and body language. Individuals can interpret messages differently depending on their individual communication style. Do you know your communication style and how to adapt to the communication style of your listener?

WRIGHT

What do you think is one of the most underdeveloped skills that a leader possesses or doesn't possess?

GORSKI

Effective feedback ties very closely with effective communication. Effective feedback is the ability to clearly communicate how an individual is performing. If done properly, it can have an enormously positive and powerful effect. According to the 2011 Work and Education poll conducted by Gallup, 19 percent of employees are dissatisfied with the lack of recognition of work accomplishments. In an article written by Razor Suleman, CEO and Founder of Achievers, he states that "23 percent of employees are disengaged at work and are affecting business performance." In addition, these disengaged workers are negatively impacting your engaged workers. Unhappy workers become unproductive and disengaged workers. This can have negative effects to a company's bottom-line and thus a leader's effectiveness.

Here is the truth of the matter. From grade school, we are marked on what is wrong. As leaders, we continue this when viewing our employees. We search out what is not being done correctly. In other words, "catch" them doing something wrong. It is like paying the game "Gotcha." You know the game. Manager finds something wrong, yells "Gotcha!" and then proceeds to tell the individual what he or she is doing wrong in a harsh way. It can be compared with the teacher marking your paper in red ink. Not too encouraging. I prefer a different approach. Catch individuals doing something good and let them know you caught them immediately.

For example, I have an exercise called the "Good Foot Patrol." In the course of a day, walk around the office looking for "good things" being done and then acknowledge those individuals on the spot. The goal is to find as many as you can within a five minute timeframe. Of course, you can increase the time limit if you wish. The amazing part of the exercise is the reaction of the individual who is being recognized for doing something great. In fact, it makes that person's day. It pumps them up—maybe he or she is even more productive!

I coached a retail executive who owned three stores. He followed the typical style looking for things that were wrong. I assigned him the "Good Foot Patrol." In our next session, I asked him how the exercise went. He visited one of his stores and he saw a display that was absolutely magnificent. He then walked up to the counter and asked the store clerks, "Who put that display together?" As you can imagine, everyone scurried expecting negative feedback. Finally, a young lady stood up and said that she did it. He told her that the display was one of the most magnificent that he had ever seen.

I then asked him, "What did you see after you said that to her?" He jokingly said, "Well after she dropped to the ground and I had to administer CPR to her. . . . Actually, her performance that day went through the roof." I then suggested, "Imagine if you could affect that same performance in all your stores every day with every individual." I could see the wheels turning in his head. What did it cost him? Just a few minutes of his time a day. The feedback was specific and positive and got him better results faster. What could "Good Foot Patrols" do for your department? Your business?

WRIGHT

You often use a phrase that really interested me and that is being a precision leader. I know what it should mean to me, but what does that mean to you?

GORSKI

Leadership is about precision. I am fascinated by cliff divers. These divers must be precise in their actions. Any miscalculation can be the difference between life and death. They must consider all factors—wind, landscape, waves, water conditions, and jump height. When a diver jumps, he or she begins to gather velocity. Having the proper jump technique so that the water cushions the entry instead of impeding it is important. There is little room for error.

A cliff diver and a successful leader are similar in several ways. First, successful leaders have and communicate focus on the goal, the means, and the method. Second, both possess an awareness of their abilities. They know what they can and cannot do. They are aware of their limits and work to improve their skill. Third, both operate in precision. There is nothing wasted in their actions. Precise actions create successful outcomes. Nothing is left to chance.

WRIGHT

You say that leaders must go through an inside-out approach in their self-awareness. Would you tell our readers what you mean by that?

GORSKI

In my coaching business, I have experienced that the most effective leaders know their strengths, weaknesses, and motivations. They know themselves at a deep level. In order to lead others, effective leaders are self-motivated. For some leaders, many say that they are about results, getting ahead, and being the best. This is all well and good but effective leaders are much more aware. For example, what are your personal triggers? What are those words/phrases/situations that could cause you to get angered quickly? Making decisions when you are in an angered state is not as effective as when you are in a very relaxed, calm state. After all, your emotions drive your decisions that then drive your actions. It is important for leaders to be in a balanced state of mind when making decisions.

So the "inside" part of the "inside-out" approach means that leaders must lead themselves. Once they're able to do that, they can lead others, which is the "out" part. Much of my work with leaders is really getting them to know themselves before we even get into the concept of leading others. Self-awareness is the key.

WRIGHT

I read an interesting book several years ago by a leadership guru who said that 2 percent of the culture leads and 98 percent follow. He didn't say much about it except that he left the impression that the 2 percent were better than the other 98 percent, but you say that people would like to follow rather than be led, which puts a different spin on it. So what's the difference between the two?

GORSKI

There is a subtle difference between following and being led. "Being led" is a harsher term. It infers that you have to accept the fact that I am being led by you. It feels as though my actions are required, not a result of my wanting to act. For example, let's say that the organization chart indicates that I am your boss. If you view me as an ineffective leader, you might feel that you are required to be led by me. You may not go above and beyond and you might do enough to get by. This scenario is a proven recipe for ineffective results.

Individuals who want to follow a leader are making a conscious, personal choice. They respect the leader. They invest in the leader because they feel the leader is investing in them. This type of leader shows interest in the success of others. The leader cares for the personal development of others or the leader has a vision/purpose that is exciting. Individuals will go above and beyond for this leader; they go that extra mile, because they *want* to follow.

If I provide effective feedback, if I walk my talk and I care about you, then you will *want* to follow me. I would bet that leaders with a large group of followers achieve results far greater in the long run.

WRIGHT

Another interesting phrase that defines you in your business is engaging language. What is engaging language and how does it impact the effectiveness of a leader?

GORSKI

As coaches, we are trained to use engaging language. This type of language motivates, energizes, and empowers others. Effective leaders have the ability to use language that uplifts others. It is galvanizing. Think about it. When you think of the most effective leaders in the past century, who comes to mind? Some of the names I hear when I ask that question are John F. Kennedy, Martin Luther King, Jack Welch, and Ronald Reagan. When you examine these people closely, the one thing they a have in common is engaging language. So, what are some of the characteristics of engaging language?

First, it's positive. I am of the belief that positive thoughts bring about positive actions. Positive begets positive. Going back to what we said earlier about effective feedback and the "Good Foot Patrols," is that it is a about finding the positive.

For example, as I am giving you the overview of a new project, you might feel intimidated by the scope and skills needed for this project. As I compete my overview to you I say, "You are the person I selected and I *hope* you can do it." Now, when you hear the word *hope*, you might think, "Well, he has some confidence in me." On the other hand, instead of using the word *hope*, I use the word *know*—"You are the person I selected and I *know* you can do it." You still might feel intimidated but you will walk out of my office with much more confidence. After all, leadership is about confidence and instilling confidence.

Second, it is inspiring. It grabs them and fires them up. It makes them want to do great things. I would say that it touches the soul. When someone is inspired, he or she will make the extra effort. He or she is more vested in the outcome. He or she will want to do well and exceed expectations.

Third, it is solution-focused. Conversations become more focused on finding creative, positive solutions. It makes people action-oriented. It is about what needs to be done, what can be done, and that they can do it. There are three types of people: people who watch things happen, people who make things happen, and people who do not know what just happened.

But, guess what happens to most leaders. As stress elevates, they become more demanding, more negative. Their language becomes disengaging. It becomes problem-oriented instead of solution-oriented. It pushes people away. It adversely effects commitment. This is the recipe for disaster. So, even in the worst of times, publically remain positive, inspire others, and stay solution focused.

WRIGHT

I was interested in your terms, "realistically positive." Throughout my adult life, and I've been here a long time, I have always had this glass full, glass empty, it's either/or according to the way you think. Just recently I got a diagram from a friend of mine and it had a picture of a glass half filled with water. It had a bracket where the water was and it said water in the bracket where it was empty it said air, and under it, it said the glass is always full, so that really helped me a lot. I don't have to be either for or against, isn't that unique, after all these years? So my question is what do you mean when you say that leaders need to be realistically positive?

GORSKI

In today's environment, individuals have access to a lot of information and usually understand what is really going on with their company. Individuals are resilient. They can effectively handle good as well as bad news. In fact, these individuals usually have ideas that could help. I have seen leaders who feel they cannot share everything; especially the bad news. Leaders are taught to carry the burden, hold back the bad news, and remain positive. But, the reality is that individuals respect leaders who tell them "like it is." Holding back information and "sugar coating" the reality generally has a negative impact on the leader's integrity.

Just "be real." I coach my clients to be "realistically positive." "Be forthcoming about the challenges ahead and remain positive about achieving the desired results." Utilize positive language to "paint a picture" worth achieving and striving for. Engage individuals in the problem and tell them the realistic possible outcomes. Let them offer solutions and they will continue to follow you.

WRIGHT

Does a leader need to be charismatic to be an effective leader?

GORSKI

Do you need charisma to be an effective leader? This is the age-old question. In my view, charisma is overrated. I have coached many leaders who are not necessarily charismatic. These leaders are very successful in their own right. Don't get me wrong. They are perfectly nice people. They just do not have a commanding presence. Yet, they are well respected by their peers and employees. They are respected in their community.

We have been taught over the years that a leader has to be charismatic. We have images of JFK running in our minds. We are caught by the myth that you *need* to have "IT"—the IT you cannot put a finger on but you "know it when you see it." Charisma is great if you have it but it is *not* a necessity for effective leadership.

To me, there are many effective leadership styles. There are some things in common among all the styles. These include engaging language, focusing on the positive, knowing oneself, setting an example, being solution focused and, most of all, a people-first attitude, which will take you to heights unexpected.

WRIGHT

So what are three things leaders can do today to improve their leadership style. Perhaps our readers could emulate some things they could put into effect after they read this book?

GORSKI

First, become more self-aware. One of the self-assessment tools that I highly recommend for leaders to take is emotional intelligence (EI). It is a little known fact that high emotional intelligence (EI) is a better indicator of success than high intelligence quotients (IQ). Emotional Intelligence measures people's ability to manage and control their emotions. After all, emotions are the foundation that drives one's decisions and actions. EI assessments go beneath the surface to understand how our emotions impact our decisions.

Think of an iceberg in the ocean. Above the water is the top of the iceberg—the leader's behaviors. This is what others can see. But underneath the water is the bottom of the iceberg and the majority of the mass. This is what others cannot see. These are the things that are impacting the leader's actions and what causes their behaviors to be displayed. According to a survey posted on Careerbuilder.com, 71 percent of hiring managers say they value emotional intelligence more than IQ in an employee.

Tying into self-awareness is understanding one's triggers. This includes identifying and realizing how their triggers affect their effectiveness. The key is not only identifying a leader's triggers but addressing how to deal with them to make better decisions. Once you know your triggers, it is important for a leader to get "back in balance." In other words, a controlled state is vital so that they can address the challenge.

Second, use engaging language. Engaging language motivates, "fires people up," and energizes others. Listen to your language. How are you communicating to others? Are you drawing people in or pushing them away? Are you positive in your approach? Analyze your language. As I mentioned earlier, the difference between I " 'hope' " you can do it versus I "know" you can do it is quite subtle but it has a huge impact on results. It is a difference between successful and not successful.

Third, provide effective feedback. Walk around the office with the mind-set of rewarding greatness by simply saying, "Great job." Be specific on what made it "great." For example, "Bob, great job on addressing that customer issue. You came across empathetic and you went above and beyond." The more specific and timely you are with the feedback, more likely that the individual will duplicate the behavior. Remember the retail president with the "Good Foot Patrol" earlier? Why not experience it yourself?

Improving these three areas can have a positive impact on your effectiveness as a leader.

WRIGHT

In your executive coaching experience, would you give our readers a success story they can see where you helped someone else as a leader to be more effective?

GORSKI

I was called to coach a manager who was having difficulties being assertive. She would go into senior executive meetings and withdraw. The department managers would notice and "steam-roll" her. It was severely affecting her performance, confidence, and self-esteem. These behaviors carried over into her team as well. Her assertive and aggressive team members would "walk all over her." A knowledgeable leader was becoming a "fraction of her former self."

The first thing I did was to help her become more self-aware. An emotional intelligence assessment was conducted. The assessment identified issues that were impacting her assertiveness abilities. She worked on some exercises that shifted her mind-set. Slowly but surely we isolated and addressed the triggers that caused her to shutdown. Strategies were developed to help her better handle those situations. Additional techniques were developed to help her maintain her assertiveness abilities without going overboard.

Soon thereafter, a very stressful situation occurred in her department that in the past would have caused her to withdraw. Instead, she relied on the techniques that were developed. She was able to address the issue in an assertive yet positive, effective way. This surprised her boss, a vice president, and the head of Human Resources. A second situation occurred quickly after the first and she was able to handle it flawlessly. Today she continues to come across assertively, has more respect of her peers and more self respect. Yes, she is getting much better results as well for her department.

About the Author

Ted Gorski is a Leadership Coach and Founder of Get Your Edge, LLC. He coaches high performers on becoming precision leaders. He is the past two term Presidents of the International Coach Federation of New England. He is certified in conducting DISC, Emotional Intelligence Assessments, and NLP (Neuro-Linguistic Programming). He is the former host of the *Business Advantage* radio show heard on WKXL in Concord, New Hampshire. Get Your Edge was a finalist of the *New Hampshire* Business Review's 2011 Best of Business Awards.

Ted Gorski, Executive Coach
Get Your Edge, LLC
PO Box 10367
Bedford, NH 03110
603-472-3821
ted@GetYourEdge.com
www.GetYourEdge.com

Chapter Nineteen

Achieving While Maintaining Life Values

An Interview With...

Reverend Timothy Jones

David Wright (Wright)

Today I'm talking with Reverend Timothy Jones who, before he was a life counselor, motivational coach, and author, worked with governmental bodies, captains of industry, and top trial lawyers in Canada as their investigator for more than twenty-five years. With exposure to career criminals, millionaire fraudsters, and self-serving politicians, he found mentorship in some surprising places along the way.

Tim brings the street savvy of a quarter of a century in civil intelligence to this book, blended with the experience of a grief counselor and consulting hypnotist working from one of the largest psychotherapy clinics in his community.

Reverend Jones, welcome to Concrete Jungle.

Rev. Timothy Jones (Jones)

Thank you very much. Please call me Tim.

Wright

Okay. Thank you.

Tim, you went from a police officer to civil intelligence to ordained ministry and life counselor in a little less than forty years. Most people would think that seems like a bit of a journey, and some might think you've been at opposite ends of the pole. How did it all start?

JONES

By an act of teenage rebellion. My mother wanted me to be a doctor and my father wanted me to be a lawyer but upon approaching the end of college, it struck me that I had neither the patience nor the desire to spend another seven years sitting in a classroom. I wanted out of school, so I applied to and was accepted by the Toronto Police.

At that time, in the "70s, there was a growing awareness that due to manpower restrictions, police were limited in how long they could spend investigating complicated white-collar crime versus the more visible criminal offenses. Corporations began exploring different ways to mitigate their damages and turned to their lawyers for help.

Lawyers, being the inventive folks they are, started hiring specialist investigators away from police departments around the world and paying them much more than a police department could. The draw is that it's tremendously satisfying for an investigator to follow a file to completion rather than being diverted elsewhere, as can happen in busy police departments.

I was recruited by some former Scotland Yard people in Canada to work with them in civil intelligence. They wanted someone with a law enforcement background who was not yet "police-institutionalized" who could be trained to work with them in sensitive areas. During the next quarter of a century I had the opportunity of working with government bodies, boards, and committees, captains of industry and in politics.

WRIGHT

In politics? That sounds interesting. Will you talk about that a little?

JONES

Politics proper is indeed a fascinating world, especially from the inside, but it's not for the fainthearted. It can be a dirty, mean game where political parties eat their own. Although seen as the epicenter of power, you have to understand that politics itself is really all a mirage. It's easy for the unwary or the arrogant, whether elected members or staff, to go off the path when they begin to take themselves too seriously.

Some forget that in politics, you're only there for as long as you're elected by the folks back home. Similarly, in business, you're only there for as long as you're useful. In the large picture, everyone but everyone is replaceable, although a surprising number of people don't think that and take their situations for granted.

Although Americans have made regular use of professionally trained investigators in politics for years, in Canada, the media reported that I was one of the first criminal investigators retained by a political party in Opposition to more closely examine the actions of government ministers.

WRIGHT

Wouldn't that upset the government?

JONES

Yes. It makes them very nervous. A fact of life, though, is that when a political party fails to gain enough seats during an election to form the government and come second, they become the Opposition and their mandate changes to being the devil's advocate. Their job is to examine the policy activities of the government of the day and "keep them honest," as the saying goes.

Traditionally, most political parties in Opposition relied on sending the ubiquitous "brown envelope" to reporters to bring something contentious to their attention. The thinking was that reporters would investigate, "break" the story, and then the Opposition could self-righteously hammer away at the government in the legislature quoting published sources.

Newspapers, though, have their own priorities and don't always respond on a timely basis, so for the first time, they—the political party in Opposition—determined they would retain their own "proprietary" investigator from outside the political system.

WRIGHT

What sort of matters did you investigate?

JONES

It all quite quickly focused on conflict of interest allegations and ministerial credibility. During the eighteen months or so I was involved directly, there were several embarrassing ministerial resignations and demotions, all arising from conflict of interest allegations made in the legislature.

WRIGHT

Doesn't the governing party vet their prospective cabinet members before appointing them to a portfolio to avoid those sorts of scenarios from arising?

JONES

In a cursory way. Lawyers for the governing party interview prospective ministers as best they can but there's a time factor after the election that restricts their thoroughness. Too, depending on who gets elected, the leader of the party has to choose his or her cabinet with regional, cultural, and gender representation in mind, and the leader has to consider favors owed for previous support.

It also depends on the veracity of the candidate's responses. Some less politically experienced candidates just don't see the potential pitfalls and others, in their ambition, aren't completely forthcoming. Others become more arrogant as they go on and become their own worst enemies.

WRIGHT

In your experience in politics and in business, Tim, how have you seen people lose track of where they're going in the concrete jungle?

JONES

Let's define the jungle we're talking about.

Most of us think of the "concrete jungle" as a place "downtown" where business rules about how to act are clear. However, like a jungle, the more exposure you have to it, the more complicated it can become. So just when you think it's this or that, you find out it isn't. It is whatever it is at the time and people react in different ways in order to find a comfort level in that flux.

How people decide to react to that changing environment in a large part determines their timbre in life.

For example, when first elected, new Members of Parliament come into the process dedicated to representing their constituents" concerns.

Then, during a period of time, in order to help their constituents and boost their own careers, they might find themselves drawn into modifying their political standards and perhaps even their personal values by their party leader's policy directions.

How? Along the way, they might find themselves supporting motions and initiatives they may not have agreed to when first campaigning, aligning themselves with special interest, minority, or fringe groups with whose policies they don't agree, and turning a blind eye to cronyism—all for appointments to prestigious committees, for increased media exposure, for an opportunity to ask questions in the House at peak times, or perhaps just to be accepted by "the club."

That parallels the business paradigm. Fresh out of school with little experience in the school of hard knocks, people start with the idea of doing their best and along the way, merge into the "better car, bigger house" philosophy. They learn the art of compromise and negotiation, which is a normal part of the push and pull of business and politics; however, that can lead to trouble when they let their ego, pride, or greed override their ethics along the way.

You don't have to look any further than the recent housing situation in the United States after which the bi-partisan Levin-Coburn Report found, "the crisis was not a natural disaster, but the result of high-risk, complex financial products, undisclosed conflicts of interest, and the failure of regulators, the credit rating agencies, and the market itself to rein in the excesses of Wall Street."

How many brokers, nationwide, just didn't understand the equations they were given to work with but implemented the subprime approach anyway? Wouldn't you think it's just common sense that if your client can't afford a property, the only people to lose when you juggle the numbers so you can sell it to them is the buyer?

On the other hand, we're our own worst enemies. During an interview with *CNN* in April of 2012, Deepak Chopra pointed to the dismaying effects of our virtual society and the pretend world of social networks, and like entities. He commented that because life has become more perception than reality, we've fallen into the habit of buying things we don't want with money we don't have to impress people we don't even know.

In our virtual world, the interpretation of reality has become distorted. Take Web pages, for example. Anyone can have an attractive and sophisticated Web presence, even though there may be little or nothing sustaining it. Those factually unverified Web presences can become a fantasy of how people want to be perceived and after a while, they come to believe their own press.

WRIGHT

I imagine you've seen a little bit of that in your fraud work. Have you found a common denominator in individuals you've investigated?

JONES

Sadly, yes. Over a quarter of a century, I've had the opportunity to investigate almost every conceivable variation of fraud involving a mix of some surprisingly prominent people along with some very nasty people. Believe it or not, aside from crimes of passion or just plain stupidity, in a society geared toward material acquisition, it has always been surprising to me how often sober second thought takes second place to ego and just plain greed.

When we complete an inquiry, we know exactly who did what, when, why, where, and how, but still ponder, "I wonder why they did that?" And you know, it can sometimes start in very innocent ways if you're not mentored responsibly.

Let me give you an example from my own life. Once, while following a target early in my career, as it was still early in the file, I was hanging back a bit to retain some distance and anonymity and I lost the target for about five minutes in the maze of streets around his residence. I did a circle check of the neighborhood and found his car at a nearby friend's house.

In my report I didn't write that I'd lost sight of the target. My supervisor at the time, though, a decorated former Scotland Yard detective very experienced with gangs, spotted that immediately in my report and said, "You lost him here, didn't you?" I said yes, but pointed out that it was only a matter of minutes before I found him again.

He sat back, gave me "that" look and asked, "How long does it takes to murder someone?"

Standing there "um-ing" and "ah-ing," wondering what in the world he knew that I didn't, he said, "In the few minutes you did not say you lost sight of him, which you'd probably be tempted to testify to in court when asked because you wouldn't want to lose credibility by going against your own sworn report, he could have shot or killed someone and in the absence of witnesses, you, my lad, would be his alibi."

He continued, saying, "Then I'd have to fire you. You'll probably be charged and if convicted of lying under oath, you'd be lucky to get a job as a coffee boy for the rest of your life. You'd be better off in jail where at least you'd have three 'hots and a cot.'"

That was a life lesson for me. If clients aren't made aware of the good, the bad, and the ugly, they could potentially go forward misinformed, which could end up being not only hugely damaging for them, but also for my professional reputation.

In life, perception is reality, and once your integrity is believed to have been compromised, it takes a long, long time to dig your way back out again, if at all. We try to impress this on people in training by illustrating that the media will rarely, if ever, print a retraction with the same vigor with which they first enthusiastically splashed the allegations across their front pages.

The demands of business and the race to keep up with the Joneses can lead people to lose track of where their word is taking them, and once articulated, they've started a chain of events they must now support with other words and actions—digging a bigger hole, in other words.

WRIGHT

On the other side of that, have you noted a common theme in the clients who have sought your expertise?

JONES

Definitely. Successful people recognize they can't be all things to all people and they don't fall into the trap of thinking that asking for help is beneath them, a practice that ego and inflexibility doesn't always allow for in the inexperienced or the self-important. If you cling to the one way you were originally trained and are unwilling to ask for advice or help, it can lead to frustration and feelings of isolation when co-workers, or family for that matter, cease asking for your advice.

That, in turn, can lead to choosing to adopt the "safe" fallback position of bullish adherence to bureaucratic rules-following, which is just a cop-out when faced with an indefensible position. In most cases, a simple application of common sense at the beginning would have avoided the whole situation.

That philosophy is echoed by the boss or parent who answers the question of, "Why?" with, "Because I said so!"

Benjamin Franklin wrote that the definition of insanity is "doing the same thing over and over and expecting different results" (*Memoirs of Benjamin Franklin, Letter to his Father,* 13 April 1738). Successful people in both business and life are open to new ways of approaching tasks and eschew the phrase, "Because that's the way we've always done it."

No one knows everything. This is no longer a generalist world. There is so much knowledge out there that nowadays the smart way to compete in the long-term is to develop specialist skills to complement your particular occupation's accepted givens. That's what seasoned CEOs look for in their advisory teams.

Mentorship, too, plays a great part in success. By sharing insight and knowledge of the industry, a successful mentor demonstrates and upholds the values and ethics of the profession he or she represents. To mentor is to be mentored. You can't help but learn from your student, and reverse mentorship is a richly rewarding life experience.

WRIGHT

So when you look back on your experiences, what do you think makes a great mentor, and are there characteristics that good mentors seem to have in common?

JONES

What, really, is a mentor? Is it a teacher, an advisor, or a supervisor? Is it someone who leads their life in the way in which you yourself would like to lead yours? Or is it someone who has acquired what you, too, would like to acquire?

History shows that a person's inherent values tend to determine the type of mentor to which they're drawn and the newspapers are filled daily with stories of executives receiving salaries, bonuses, and retirement packages far beyond anything 99 percent of people will ever see, even though the company lost money through their corporate guidance!

Even a child can do the math on that one, so no wonder emergent generations, who are entertained with smartphones and tablets instead of people before they even start school, can have confused values. Speaking of that, I wonder how many people still consider Bernie Madoff a mentor.

WRIGHT

Point taken. One does wonder sometimes what changes people along the way.

JONES

That's a key skill in the concrete jungle—the ability to keep life values in balance when sweating the small stuff. People like Bill Gates and Warren Buffet recognized that no matter how many they could afford, they can only drive one car at a time and only eat one steak at a time.

They also realized, looking around themselves, that there are just too many out there who can't afford either, and founded The Giving Pledge where the affluent oblige to give away at least half their wealth to charity, either during their lifetime or upon their death.

The philosophy of "he who dies with the most toys wins" is obsolete. You can't take it with you and we all have a responsibility to each other, whether we've met or not. The reality is that those who leave the most behind are the ones to whom those around them meant more than material gain. That doesn't mean one shouldn't strive in life, that's what humans do, but again, no matter what someone accumulates, or not, their lasting values are how they affected, inspired, and motivated others.

So for me, a mentor is not necessarily a particular person, but someone who reacts to a situation in a way that prompts me to model my thinking after that reaction or approach when faced with a similar situation.

WRIGHT

So you believe that mentoring is an experience and not necessarily a specific person's life?

JONES

Isn't that what a mentor does? A mentor motivates you to learn progressively while integrating enabling experiences into your life. As that brilliant philosopher, Anonymous, said, "Give a man a fish, you feed him for a day. Teach a man to fish and you feed him for a lifetime."

There's a practice rooted in Zen called a "beginner's mind." It is developing a mind-set innocent of preconceptions, expectations, judgments, and prejudices. The "beginner's mind" is a skill empathetic therapists develop in order to better understand their clients" vision of their world.

For example, if you develop the attitude that you've heard it all before, you've closed your mind and are comparing what you're hearing to what you, in your own experience in your own life, already believe. You are prejudicially either agreeing or disagreeing in your mind about what is being said or done, which in the long run closes your mind.

There's a very simple way to start opening your mind, though. When people say to you, "Hi, how are you doing today, David?" and you answer as if you're carrying the weight of the world on your shoulders with something like, "Ohhh, okay, I guess," then you will self-fulfill your belief that you are indeed carrying the weight of the world on your shoulders. However, if you say, "Great, thanks! How are you?" and reply that way regardless of your flat tire this morning, it will become a habitual response and, as perception is reality in psychology also, you will actually feel great.

You get what you give and sometimes, when confused or dismayed by life in the concrete jungle, it's just that simple.

WRIGHT

It's a tool rather than truth or fiction.

JONES

In death as in life. As a minister, I've been privileged to be invited bedside with the dying and can tell you that when the fatally ill come to accept their impending demise on this Earth, they express a common desire to amend what they see as their mistakes so they can cross the next threshold with a sense of having done the right thing—whether they were religious or not in the fullness of their lives.

Although human, it's too bad most of us go through life so self-absorbed that it takes a personally hurtful experience like losing a loved one or reflections in our last days to make us stop and think about why we're here and what we're doing.

WRIGHT

It's interesting you'd say that, Tim. Did those types of experiences have anything to do with your decision to retire from intelligence work and change your professional direction in life?

JONES

The world changed for me in 2000 when my very healthy stepson died suddenly and accidentally at the age of twenty-four.

My first wife and I were unable to have children, which eventually led to our parting, and my stepson and his sister came into my life when they were nine and eleven respectively. As they already had a father living elsewhere, I could never take them for granted and treated them as equals from the very beginning.

In return, they changed my life. They made me wonder about working eighty to a hundred hours a week for the almighty buck, and their innocence and trust in me made me want to be a better person. Although I pretended to grumble about the 5:00 am drives to the hockey rink, I missed so many of their events during our fourteen years together due to my work that I questioned my direction in life and its relevance.

Then, upon my stepson's death, I went through the grief experiences exactly as Elizabeth Kübler-Ross described them. Once the shock and denial passed, I begged, implored, and pleaded that if He truly was the Almighty, to reverse things and take me instead. There was no answer, and at one point I became so horribly and deeply angry that I denounced God using every foul name I could muster. I challenged Him to show Himself and when He didn't, I threatened Him, and dared Him, all to no avail.

The silence was deafening and despite attending group grief counseling, the heaviness became a deep, dark abyss with no end. The family relationship fractured and became severed and feeling cheated and deserted, I wondered around in the emotional wilderness for a year or so, pretending everything was okay to the outside world and continuing to work—after a fashion.

Finally, at one point, lying in bed on yet another sleepless night, too emotionally and physically drained to rail any more against God for the injustice of a youth dying, I somehow became aware of a certain stillness, of a quietness, somewhere in my mind, in what I later came to identify as that inner part of myself people call the soul. I listened for a while and found some comfort in the quietness of it, but upon rising every day, the heaviness came back. Once found though, I was drawn to that quietness again and again and once there, would allow myself some peace but would then feel guilty and quickly push it away. Pretty soon though, as it was becoming my only sanity, I sought out that stillness, and finally stopped fighting it and gave myself over to it completely for survival's sake.

At one point, I remember sensing something else within and in hope, said, "If that's you, God, I need help." The way forward from there became clear. I never questioned it and it led me to study through two earned degrees in ministry and to dedicate myself to helping others in the same position.

Since then, the fear of dying has lost its hold on me. I believe in God's reasons for our living and dying, and once I've done what I'm here to do, I'll look forward to going home to my family again.

Funny thing, though. I'll catch people who've known me for years looking at me when they think I'm not looking, wondering, I suppose, what has changed. Those who have experienced it could tell them that grief can be a tremendously transformative change for the good, which can lead to some of the most inspirational, meaningful times of our life.

I say "can lead" in the sense that you can choose to lose yourself in yesterday, or you can go forward inspired by yesterday.

WRIGHT

I can certainly see how those experiences would make you a more empathetic grief counselor. I understand you're also a Board Certified Consulting Hypnotist, Tim. We've read a lot about how professional athletes and corporate leaders improve their performance and outlook with self-hypnosis. How did you get involved in that?

JONES

Contrary to what we see in the movies, I learned "the truth" about hypnosis at sixteen when a psychiatrist at the world renowned Sunnybrook Health Sciences Centre in Toronto taught my father self-hypnosis to help control his blood pressure following a near-fatal brain aneurism.

My father was a former WWII RAF officer shot down over France who evaded capture with the help of the French Resistance. He became a no-nonsense career journalist who wasn't given to psychological "gimmickry." However, although doctors originally only gave my father five years or so of productive life following his stroke, at the time of his death nearly fifteen years later, he was an national speaker and writer in civic affairs.

There is no doubt in my mind that daily self-hypnosis provided my father with nearly two decades of productive, healthy life that he would not have otherwise enjoyed.

With that in mind, I enrolled in a comprehensive self-hypnosis course in my thirties to help enhance my focus and physical endurance during long and arduous surveillances, some of which could go on for days at a time. I found it instrumental in helping boost my natural abilities to increase memory retention, logical reasoning, and concentration during complicated fraud files. I also found it tremendously helpful to accurately retrieve and define witness memories.

WRIGHT

You were saying you've up-trained for more than a thousand hours in the science. Did you do that to use hypnosis in your counseling practice?

JONES

Absolutely. The standard counseling or psychotherapeutic expectation on average is a weekly session for three months or more. I asked myself if there wasn't a quicker way to help people and, based on my own experiences, started integrating motivational hypnosis into sessions. Clients then started reporting amelioration within four to six once-a-week sessions. Nowadays, aside from "booster" sessions, I rarely see any one client for more than six to eight sessions.

WRIGHT

So how does self-hypnosis actually compare to the other counseling techniques like psychotherapy or psychoanalysis?

JONES

Hypnosis has been used successfully in the medical world for centuries and nowadays is very prevalent as a complementary health and wellness remedy. A distinct profession, its comparative usefulness was evidenced in 1970 in a landmark study by UCLA clinical psychologist Dr. Alfred A. Barrios, PhD, as published in the magazine *Psychotherapy: Theory, Research and Practice* (Volume 7, Issue #1).

Dr. Barrios found that six sessions of hypnosis resulted in a 93 percent success rate, while twenty-two sessions of Cognitive Behavioral Therapy (CBT) talk-therapy only enjoyed a 72 percent success rate, while six hundred sessions of Psychoanalysis found a 38 percent success rate.

Motivational Hypnosis has consistently been found to be six to ten times faster, deeper, and longer-lasting than talk-therapy alone. As a matter of fact, all humans enter the hypnotic state naturally many times a day—every time we become absorbed in a good book or movie, when we listen to a good speaker, and every time we focus or concentrate deeply.

We know, too, that all hypnosis is actually self-hypnosis. For example, just before falling asleep, have you ever given yourself the last thought of, "I will wake up at 6:00 am tomorrow," then found you woke up minutes before your alarm went off? While in the natural hypnagogic theta brainwave state, which directly precedes the delta level sleep states, you gave your subconscious a post-hypnotic suggestion. That's how easy it is, and that's how easily you control it. Consulting hypnotists show you how to widen and deepen that state to help overcome self-defeating habits and lifestyle behaviors you've chosen to change, like smoking, over-eating, or effective public speaking.

As a matter of fact, Olympic and professional athletes regularly integrate self-hypnosis into their training routines via positive imagery in a meditative state.

WRIGHT

It's used in medicine and dentistry too, isn't it?

JONES

Around the world, yes. We know that up to 75 percent of North Americans are anxious about going to the dentist. We also know that more than 20 percent of those people are so anxious that they wait until their dental issue becomes painful before making an appointment. Unfortunately, once the issue presents itself with discomfort or pain, intrusive treatment may be required, which may well exacerbate their anxiety.

Motivational hypnosis is an excellent tool to help overcome the sensitizing anxiety and quite literally, the dental patient can mentally drift off to a "safe place" like a soothing beach or a calm forest clearing for the duration of the appointment. They can also easily learn how to direct their mind to experience an injection as just a gentle pressure, and be calmed instead of alarmed by the sound and feel of dental instruments.

For those allergic to chemical analgesia or anesthetics, deep-state hypnoanesthesia is used in surgery and childbirth and the science is successfully employed in the form of positive outcome imagery in hypno-oncology.

Motivational self-hypnosis, though, is not just for the talented, the intelligent, or the specially trained—it's for the ordinary, everyday person with ordinary, everyday concerns like self-confidence, sport enhancement and, as we've already mentioned, for helping overcome self-defeating personality traits or acquired habits like smoking, overeating, nail biting, or anxiety before exams or public speaking, just to mention a few.

WRIGHT

As a minister, Tim, do you find some people shy away from you, thinking that you might be more religious than they expect a counselor to be?

JONES

Actually no, not at all, and I'm not religious, per se. Understand that faith is different than slavish religiosity and I'm no "holy roller." I shudder inwardly when I see television images of "faith leaders" promising an eternity of fire and damnation unless you give them money so they can continue their "work."

On a personal level, I just never saw the equity in insisting that my prophet is more real than yours when faith groups have historically agreed that all rivers run to one ocean, so my training as a Protestant minister led me to focus on interdenominational chaplaincy. With my street background, it's very comfortable to follow the same approach as military chaplains in that I may not proselytize ("collect souls") to those in minimized conditions, but am dedicated to be a presence of support in times of need.

Recognize, too, that contrary to popular belief, more than 50 percent of all clergy concentrate on counseling, teaching, writing, research, and chaplaincy rather than congregationalism. As a matter of fact, during the past decade, most new clergy entering ministry are in their mid forties or fifties and have acquired substantial life experience before committing themselves to service to others.

Interestingly, while discussing the relative merits of denominationalism, a very wise and battle-scarred Catholic priest, also heavily involved in psychotherapy, once philosophized to me that throughout history, regardless of language, race, color, or creed, a mother's smile of love is universally understood by all. And that metaphor, he said, is how we come by the gravitas of faith, not by the act of religiously dressing up every Sunday, if you'll allow me to phrase it that way.

Clients usually come to me through word-of-mouth and, if anything, they've commented that due to my background, training, and direction in life, they feel I can be trusted. There is a huge amount of confidence out there for clergy as counselors, despite the controversies surrounding some churches' policies.

WRIGHT

Well Tim, we're trying to encourage our readers to live better or be more fulfilled by reading the experiences of our writers. Is there anyone or anything in your life and career that has made a difference for you and helped you survive life in the concrete jungle?

JONES

The overarching philosophy held by enlightened people drawn from lessons learned in this life is to treat others in the way they themselves would like to be treated were positions reversed.

We've all at one time or another heard someone, perhaps even ourselves, when commenting on someone's life situation, say, "That'll never happen to me!" or "I'll never be in that position!" Really? Never? Never is the biggest word in the dictionary and it's inextricably bound to Murphy's Law.

Bob Proctor hit the nail on the head when he said, "You are the only problem you'll ever have, and you are the only solution." Once you embrace that belief and stop blaming others for life disappointments, you'll find that growth is a personal decision, and once started, positive change is inevitable.

It's not necessary, though, to suffer the slings and arrows of outrageous fortune or experience deep bereavement to "get it." Increased self-awareness doesn't hit all of a sudden like a bolt of lightning.

It develops by living life and learning life skills along the way to build a solid foundation that allows you to turn challenges and confusion into focus, opportunities, growth, and confidence.

It develops by empowering yourself through humility and good mentorship to build self-esteem, self-worth, mental discipline, and an inner power and goes hand-in-hand with personal growth.

It develops by opening to a higher power, allowing you to find more meaning and purpose in life so you can connect more deeply with yourself and your intuition.

Oh, there is just one other little thing—no matter how smart you think you are, marry someone smarter than you, like I did. Poet, lawyer, and priest John Donne expressed that "no man is an island" and I might not be doing what I'm doing in life with the same level of perceptiveness if it wasn't for my wife. As a matter of fact, my grace over dinner every night is, "Thank you, God. Thank you, Nancy."

WRIGHT

I can certainly agree with that, Tim. Well, this has been a very interesting conversation. You've talked about some unusual things and I know our readers will appreciate the time you've taken to answer all these questions.

JONES

Great talking to you, David. Thank you.

WRIGHT

Today I have been talking with Reverend Timothy Jones, a motivational speaker, life counselor, and writer who blends a quarter century in civil intelligence with his experiences as a grief counselor and consulting hypnotist.

Tim, thank you so much for being with us today on Concrete Jungle.

JONES

You are very welcome.

About the Author

Tim Jones' focus is on helping people take back control of their lives by reframing how they react to life issues.

Serving in ordained ministry with an active focus on chaplaincy in funerary and grief management, he's a seasoned counselor and a Board Certified Consulting Hypnotist, Certified Instructor and Fellow with the world's oldest and largest professional and training association, the National Guild of Hypnotists (NGH).

Tim's comprehensive background in both traditional and Ericksonian motivational hypnosis techniques, NeuroLinguistic Programming (NLP), and Cognitive Behavioral Counseling (CBC) enables him to help a broader range of people address a wider range of issues of personal concern.

His professional expertise, life experience, and supportive approach assist clients to quickly realize their desired personal changes.

Timothy Jones (Rev.)
BMin, MHt, CI, BCH FNGH
9 - 6975 MTC Circle, #521
Mississauga, ON. CA L5N 2V7
416-829-4161
Rev.Timothy.Jones@gmail.com
RevTimothyJones.ca

Chapter Twenty

The Key to Success in the Concrete Jungle: Be Nice!

An Interview With...

Joshua and Dana Beil

DAVID WRIGHT (WRIGHT)

For the closing chapter of this collection, I'm talking with a dynamic brother-sister team who are part of a global consulting practice, with clients in more than thirty countries. They specialize in working exclusively with hotels and resorts and are experts in creating revenue for their clients' properties. They could be in the snows of Vail one week, and on the sands in Cancun the next. From flagship properties to city-wide clusters, with so many cultures, languages, and unique practices to deal with, they have developed a surprisingly simple approach to success in this increasingly complicated world. It's simple, but it's not easy.

It's my pleasure to welcome Joshua and Dana Beil to *Concrete Jungle: Survival Secrets for the Real World.*

JOSH AND DANA BEIL (JOSH/DANA)

It's our pleasure to be here, thanks for the invitation.

WRIGHT

Josh and Dana, during the past five years, your firm Drake Beil & Associates has growing rapidly amid one of the most challenging macro-economic conditions in a century. Your organization's Service Excellence Upgrade Program is now installed in more than 230 hotels and resorts in thirty countries. What rules of business have you been following to achieve this success and how do you hope to maintain it?

JOSH

Thanks. In this new concrete jungle, the old adage "you catch more bees with honey than vinegar" has never been more appropriate. Our corporate philosophy, and a significant reason for our current and continued success, can be boiled down to this single rule: be nice. It is the essence of "the golden rule" (do unto others), and something we practice both internally and with clients.

WRIGHT

That sounds too easy. It must be more complex than this, isn't it?

JOSH

It certainly is, especially in the face of rudeness or potential confrontation. So, your "niceness" must be genuine or people will feel it. This includes maintaining your facial expressions, tone of voice, and demeanor. Demonstrating sincerity and integrity can be hard, but we've found most people are not prepared for extreme courtesy.

This is the over-arching principle. Ultimately, if you respond nicely in all situations, co-workers and clients will have nothing to hold against you in the future, which is a critical tool for surviving in the concrete jungle.

WRIGHT

Fair enough. Will you expand on how this corporate philosophy came about?

JOSH

Sure. I will give you the key reasons *why* it is critical to "be nice" and Dana will give you some concrete examples of *how* to implement this rule.

WRIGHT

Sounds great.

JOSH

First, nearly everything in life is a normal curve. Just as some people are tall, others are short, and there's an average height and weight. In every business, you are going to have the outstanding performers and poor performers, with the majority in the middle. Said another way, half the people in any given room are on the left side of the bell curve, or below "average," and make mistakes regularly. That said, even outstanding talent make mistakes from time to time.

The lesson for the concrete jungle is to understand that mistakes happen and to respond with kindness. The person who made the mistake probably already feels bad about it. Saying anything negative or rubbing it in can only hurt you and make an enemy in the future, whereas if you are nice about it, you will probably make a friend and an ally.

Next, there are different types of learning styles. Some people prefer to see things and are visual learners. Others prefer to hear or talk about things and are auditory learners. Yet others prefer to touch and feel things and are tactile learners. While everyone has a combination of these three, research shows that we tend to have a dominant learning style. Dana and I were fortunate in that our father, Drake Beil, has a doctorate in learning theory, so we were getting lessons on this at the dinner table before we even really understood or appreciated it.

So the way you process information and learn something may not be how the person you are trying to explain something to, or sell your product or service to, learns. This creates a fairly fundamental disconnect between two people and it can often lead to organizational misalignment or worse—confrontation or a blown pitch. Essentially, you may come off as cold or distant or simply "not nice" to someone else if you are too aggressive with your learning style. Even worse, you may not even realize it.

Why this matters in the concrete jungle is that people have a higher degree of trust of information that comes in through their dominant channel. It takes some practice, but you can rapidly identify how people you interact with learn best. Once you figure this out, you can tailor your messages to their personal learning style. If you can help someone to learn something new the way they learn best, it's pretty easy to have an influence, not to mention a friend.

Diving a little deeper into something I mentioned earlier, niceness and sincerity go hand-in-hand. You can't be truly nice while being insincere. What's more, if you ever got the feeling that someone was lying to you, you were probably right! I believe this "spidey sense" is an intuitive defense mechanism that has been evolving for thousands of years.

In the concrete jungle, insincerity, which usually takes the form of lying or cheating, will catch up with you. Additionally and importantly, the concrete jungle is also the connected jungle. In a world of Facebook and LinkedIn, your professional community keeps getting larger and your reputation stays with you digitally. The best way to develop your personal brand is to be nice.

Wright

So how does one maintain sincerity and niceness if you are on the receiving end of rudeness and insincerity? That seems pretty difficult!

Josh

Absolutely. Our gut reaction is typically to "fight fire with fire," and to escalate a confrontation. The best advice I can give in this situation is to know how to control your facial expressions and body language, as somewhat more than 50 percent of in-person communication is non-verbal. Going back to the fire metaphor, the best way to fight fire is to smother it with niceness.

Wright

Business can often get political, and politics can involve half-truths and deception. How does being nice factor into this reality?

Josh

It's a great question, as politics comes with every organization and industry. The reality is that people often do things for political gain, and this can sometimes trump doing a job well. Moreover, I've found people would often rather be wrong and do it their way than follow your good advice.

Brains, looks, and talent will only get you so far—you cannot ignore the political hierarchy of your own organization or of your clients'. In terms of being nice, you can almost always get to the superior of the person giving you trouble. However, once you have gone over someone's head, your relationship with that person is more than likely to be compromised even further in the future. That is why you should always try to work problems out directly, and privately, with people if there is conflict. Avoid escalation unless absolutely necessary.

WRIGHT

Good advice. These days, escalations happen by way of e-mail quite often. How well does niceness work in cyber-space?

JOSH

This can get very tricky (and sticky). Most of us have probably been involved in an e-mail conflict that spiraled out of control, and this goes back to something I mentioned earlier: more than 50 percent of communication is non-verbal. If you take all facial expressions and body language out of the communication equation, as with e-mail, miscommunication becomes much more likely. Moreover, once sent, an e-mail cannot be "taken back" and furthermore, the negative impact of "e-mails-gone-wrong" can be compounded if and when other people's names are included in the "copy to" section or forwarded the thread. Being nice is the easiest way to avoid these potential digital pitfalls.

WRIGHT

It sounds like being nice helps to avoid conflicts from starting or getting worse.

JOSH

Yes, and things can almost always get worse—in both life and business! It's a pretty pessimistic perspective, I realize, but I suppose it's my version of Murphy's Law. I try to remember that millions of people don't have adequate food or shelter when my Internet is down or I don't have a good cell signal.

WRIGHT

Moving from "why" to "how," Dana, before you give us some practical guidance, will you give us some background on how this guidance came about?

DANA

Absolutely, my pleasure. As we were finding our way through corporate professional world, we found that the path isn't exactly laid out for you. There certainly isn't a munchkin with a map guiding you to "follow the yellow brick road." You are left to fend for yourself for the most part. We found ourselves in so many bizarre situations along the way, each one was a lesson we never forgot.

WRIGHT

So how did you come across the best ways to deal with these "bizarre situations?"

DANA

Well, honestly, you have to be ready for absolutely anything, and actions speak louder than words. It's not as easy to "be nice" as one might think. Sometimes you have to swallow your pride, smile, and give someone else credit, and a lot of times interact with people who don't necessarily want you around. In a nutshell, you have to know *how* to "be nice."

WRIGHT

How have you found it possible to maintain your philosophy and be nice?

DANA

I'd be happy to elaborate for you. First, you have to be gracious in both victory and defeat. As much as we would like to be the victor in every situation and win every argument, chances are overwhelming that we are going to lose as often if not more than we are going to win in the concrete jungle.

This doesn't necessarily mean that you were wrong, in your opinion. It might just mean that you were outranked, or other agendas dictated an outcome that you had no control of. Simply put, politics won. In these instances, you can't allow people to see you get upset if you lose the argument, and more importantly, you have to keep your "game face" (and smile graciously) when you do. In fact, take it a step further and see if there is anything you can do to help your opponent make his or her decision work to the best of your abilities, and let the person know you are more than happy to help with whatever you can. In essence, "kill with kindness."

With that said, people hate a sore loser, but an arrogant winner is worse. If it so happens that you have been successful and won your argument, you absolutely *cannot* rub it in. You don't want the people you have to work with mad at you or disliking you because then you have created an even more difficult environment for yourself. As they say, you might have won the battle, but the war is far from over. Even if you have won your case, stay humble and remember to take into account the opinions of everyone around you. You may be right, but keep in mind, they probably still think they are too, and chances are they are probably resenting you for it. You want to remind them that you want to do everything in your power to work *with* them to make sure that everyone is satisfied with the outcome.

In a concrete jungle, it's hard enough to command respect and build strong relationships. It's harder still to remain humble. If you are successful, it is your inclination to take credit for that success, but what you have to remember is that you wouldn't have been successful without the help of a good number of other people. Even if they didn't do that much to help, even if they were against the idea from the start, be nice and share in the credit.

Chances are they probably feel somewhat sheepish that they were wrong in the first place, or more likely, somewhat angry that you were right. However, they are probably going to have to continue to work with you, and you want to maintain as little friction as possible.

When you are thanking them for their effort in making it work, it *has to be sincere,* or else you are going to come off as arrogant; then they have something else to hold against you. Being successful with a good idea is good, but the real question is: can you do it again? You know those speeches actors give when they win an Oscar? "I would like to thank the Academy and my fellow cast members. I couldn't have won this award without them." Well, you need to thank the rest of the "cast," whether you like it or not, it's just the nice (not to mention the right) thing to do.

This actually leads beautifully into my next point, which is: be flexible! The schedules that we are faced with in this concrete jungle are merciless, especially in the industry that Drake Beil and Associates works with—the hotel and resort industry. The people we work with are essentially running a small city within a building, and dealing with a million different things all at the same time—and they have to accommodate us as well. We *must* be able to be extremely flexible, and deal with last minute scheduling and location changes and we have to do all of this without showing any level of aggravation or irritation. In fact, it should be our pleasure to work around their schedule, and go anywhere they need us to because we are the vendor!

There is a ton of competition out there, and chances are that there are people lined up behind you to take your place if, for some reason, you don't work out! You are always replaceable, and nothing is forever in the concrete jungle.

I believe Tim Gunn said it best: "Make it work." If they need to meet at a different time, fine. If you don't have as many people show up to the meeting as you expect, fine. Work your absolute hardest to make the best of whatever situation you are in, and always keep that smile on your face. Don't sweat the small stuff. Make it work for them!

WRIGHT

Great advice so far. What else can one do to be nice in the concrete jungle?

DANA

If there is anything I have learned while working in the concrete jungle it is that food is cross cultural, and you can win the hearts of everyone you work with if you just do one simple thing—bring food! Think of it as visiting someone else's home for the first time. What do you normally do when you are a guest visiting someone's house? You bring a gift! We find that food normally works best. Snacks that provide a sugar rush are even better! First of all, no one expects it and it is always a nice surprise. Not to mention that they like you better instantly if you can provide a little "pick-me-up" during a long day, especially if your meeting is in the middle of the day, and people are starting to hit that 3:00 pm/4:00 pm wall that is so common. The food will wake them up and make sure that they actually have the ability to listen to you and comprehend what you are telling them instead of the obligatory nodding and smiling just to appease you.

I would find out ahead of time what is a popular snack in the area that people like. For example, in New York, cupcakes are *the* ultimate snack. They provide instant happiness, and, all of a sudden you are staring at a sea of smiles. A favorite snack will not only win their hearts and attention, but surprisingly it will help them remember you in a positive light and you'll probably gain a few more friends! You want to stand out among the rest of the hundreds of vendors they meet with every day, food will help you do that.

While food can be a wonderful way to create a moment of niceness, long-term niceness is all about your professional follow-up. For example, you might have just spent hours with a client company, and you might have had a great meeting where its leaders nodded and smiled and agreed with all of your ideas. During the meeting they showed passion, energy, and enthusiasm! All this was great. But the moment you leave that building, consider the following: Out of sight, out of mind. You have to take the time to follow up with your clients!

Again, you have to remember that they are dealing with a million other things and probably won't take the time out of their day to follow up with you, simply because they barely have any down time. Do not take this as an insult, but as an opportunity to reach out and reconnect. Make sure that they have everything they need from you and that you haven't left any questions unanswered. Without any follow-up from you, it is your own fault if things aren't going according to plan.

Also, you must always make yourself accessible and available to answer questions at any given time, and make sure to get back to them in a timely manner. For example, return their call at the end of the same business day when they tried to contact you. If you don't, then you are considered unreliable and unhelpful.

WRIGHT

Great stuff. What final guidance do you have?

DANA

My parting thought is that in order to be nice, it is critical to create empathy. Get to know your clients on both a personal and professional level. It's pretty easy to figure out immediately the people who are going to be real business partners for the future versus the ones who are just there in the interim. The real ones take the time to answer your e-mails (even if it is a day or week later), and call you back. They are the ones who don't throw you under the bus. They tell you the truth about the reality of the situation, even when the reality isn't necessarily what you want to hear.

These are the people you want to get to know a little better. Take the time to learn about them—their family, where they went to school, and what their goals are for the future. This does a couple of things: it expresses to them the idea that you aren't just there for business and that you care about their well-being on a deeper level. It also establishes a friendship for the future—one that might continue even when that person has moved on to bigger and better things.

Don't be surprised when you get a phone call with a request asking to work with you again. Remember that "word-of-mouth" is *everything!* Selling yourself is a difficult job, but if you have others doing it for you because they care, then that is worth its weight in gold for your future. And all it takes is being nice.

About the Author

Joshua Beil is Vice President of Technology at Drake Beil & Associates, a leading hospitality consulting group specializing in Service Excellence Upgrade Programs with hotel and resort clients in thirty countries. In his role, Josh manages the development of the company's online Web applications, with a focus on scaling through automation. He also acts as a senior associate at hotel property launches and renewals. Previously, Josh was the Director of Social Media & Technology at a Level 3 Communications (NASDAQ: LVLT) where he provided strategic and tactical sales support. Before that, Josh was CEO and cofounder of Skywave Broadband, Inc, the largest commercial WiFi service provider in Hawaii. He was named one of Pacific Business News' "Forty Under 40 for 2006," and in 2005, he was named a High Tech Leader by the Pacific Technology Foundation. Josh has also previously served as the Senior Analyst for Exodus Communications as well as the internationally known market research firm, IDC. He holds a Certificate in E-Business from UCSC Extension, and he graduated with honors from the University of California at Santa Cruz with a major in Psychology.

Dana Beil is a Senior Consultant for Drake Beil and Associates. She is based in New York City. Dana specializes in Training and Development. She is an expert in creating revenue—"Yield"—for hotels and resorts worldwide, and in multiple disciplines: Rooms, Spa, Retail Sales, and F&B. With a degree from Emerson College, she has been a regional trainer and consultant for major cosmetics lines, and launched Service Excellence Upgrade Programs with more than sixty clients in properties in Atlanta, Chicago, Dallas, Denver, Miami, New Orleans, New York, Orlando, Philadelphia, San Francisco, Canada, the Caribbean, and Mexico.

Drake Beil and Associates

josh@drakebeil.com
dana@drakebeil.com
www.drakebeil.com